The Bronze Quill

The Society of Women Writers WA

A catalogue record for this book is available from the National Library of Australia

ISBN-13: 978-1-922343-96-3

Linellen Press
265 Boomerang Road
Oldbury, Western Australia
www.linellenpress.com.au

Dedication

This book of award-winning writing
by members of The Society of Women Writers WA
is dedicated to our beloved Patron Ruth Reid
who turned an amazing 100 years old
in this, our 40th Anniversary year.

Contents

Acknowledgments

For this book to reach its completion, we thank all members who contributed to the collection of prize-winning writing of the Bronze Quill competition.

We also thank the book designers, proofreaders and editing group for their time and dedication in seeing this collection come to fruition.

Foreword

This anthology is a collection of winning entries from current members of The Society of Women Writers WA over many years of the competition's existence.

So what is the Bronze Quill?

The Bronze Quill is the beautiful perpetual trophy awarded to the winner of each year's State-wide competition for The Society of Women Writers WA members only. It pits the talents of storytelling, wordsmithing, researching and imaginations up against each other, all entrants striving for the honour to display the Bronze Quill with their name on it.

The competition moves annually through the disciplines of Short Story writing, Poetry and Creative Non-Fiction writing, the judges, all well-known artists in their fields, having the challenging task of wheedling down to a handful of entries to find the winner.

Usually, a Winner, Runner-Up, one or two Highly Commended entries and Commended entries are awarded.

Regardless of the number of awards presented on any year, those who receive even a mention can be justly proud they have achieved great heights in their writing.

This book celebrates their achievements.

Jan Altmann

The Elephant in the Art Gallery

Commended Article 2012

'I've lived in Zimbabwe', said my friend, 'I know what elephants do', and I can tell you that they do it in large amounts. 'What I don't know is why it has to be displayed in the Tate Modern in a work of art'. As someone who doesn't actually 'do' Art but with an interest in critical theory, I am often confronted with comments and questions like this. Why is a dead shark, or a dead sheep, considered to be an art object? Why did a room with the lights going on and off win the 2001 Turner prize? Why did a gallery cleaner attract media attention for clearing away some crumpled newspapers and used coffee cups? Is a diamond-encrusted skull a work of art, or just a conspicuous display of wealth? And why did a live Asian elephant painted pink with gold patterning and standing in a make-believe living room, create a stir in Los Angeles in 2006?

I don't really have answers to such questions, but the questions themselves are challenging and they aren't going to go away. My first inclination is to defend the artist, but frequently I find myself sympathising with the questioner. Is there really a point to be made in displaying a garbage bag containing nothing but air, as was done in the Sydney Biennale in 1998? This really would seem to be a case of the Emperor's New Clothes.

There is no point in pretending that there is philosophical significance or aesthetic value to something just because it is in an art gallery. There is, however, also nothing to be gained by dismissing something as 'not art' just because its like has not been seen in a gallery before. What has been seen before are works depicting recognisable objects, people, landscapes or stories. There was, of course, usually something more behind these objects, landscapes or stories, which could be either pursued or disregarded. For those who wanted to explore the significance of the story or the importance of the person in the portrait the means of doing so were available. Those who chose not to do so could still enjoy looking at a recognisable image and appreciate the skill of the artist.

Big questions (elephant-sized ones) and small questions could both be asked of the same artwork. A Constable landscape could consist of just a cottage, a stream and some leafy trees against a blue sky with some fluffy clouds. But, it could also be a transcendent experience in which the upward spreading of the trees lifts the viewer outwards and upwards into the sky and the heavens beyond. The difference between then and now is that back then the small and the recognisable lead on to something bigger. There were 'road signs' to follow and we could have it both ways.

Modern Art removed the road signs. Science managed to convince us that there was not just one story, and that space and time did not stay still long enough to be experienced or observed at one time or in one image. Artists and writers decided that if the world had changed so drastically then they had better get on board and try to examine and explain things according to these new perspectives. Critics tried to clarify the situation, and that is probably where the problems really began. They told us that the little picture didn't matter, that we didn't need it. They claimed that the world had changed and that representation was irrelevant, even declaring that a recognizable image on its own had no value, and that it was time to escape from the 'tyranny of the object'. When representation was relevant, then photography could do it better. This didn't mean that art had nothing to do with reality. It just meant that it was not concerned with reproducing that reality as it actually appeared or seemed to appear. Who looks at the world standing in one position and facing in one direction for a specified period of time?

The problem was that the missing step between the small picture and the large one had to be supplied by the artist in a catalogue or on a 'didactic panel' hanging beside the work. Take Carl Andre's Equivalent VIII (1966) – that set of firebricks set out on the floor of the Tate, and purchased by that establishment in 1972. Andre made several of these, each consisting of the same, or an equivalent, number of bricks but in different formations. He described them as 'encouraging viewers to imagine walking through different depths of water'. The whole idea was so confronting that one arrangement was defaced with paint. This response was not from someone who didn't know what they were looking at (that was obvious). The problem was that it was in an art gallery, and also that bricks didn't relate directly to water or earth, or any of the other elements. There may be a sensation of 'wading' in bricks and then stepping into water so that we pass from a solid 'reality' into a less solid, or more imaginative one, but there are no sign posts within the work to say so.

Damien Hirst's dead shark suspended in a tank may inspire questions about life and death, and produce a realization that even powerful and frightening life forms like sharks eventually die. It is, after all, entitled The Physical Impossibility of Death in the Mind of Someone Living. The problem is that the mind of the 'someone living' has to make this leap with little help from the artist. His lamb suspended in formaldehyde is called Away from his flock. This is meant to raise questions about why and how animals (and humans) live in communities, but again the pathway from the one to the other is hardly obvious. Hirst's diamond encrusted skull is called For the Love of God. Perhaps it is in the 'memento mori' tradition. It doesn't matter how rich we are we all end up as skulls. One critic described it as a 'most gorgeous visceral experience', but then added that it would appeal mainly to 'diamond junkies'. It could be a confronting experience, or it could be a crass display of wealth, and a clever marketing trick. When it was sold for £120 million it turned out that the buyer was a company headed by none other than Hirst himself. It is only this manipulation of the market that makes it different from 'primitive' masks inlaid with turquoise and mother of pearl made by tribal artists.

In the same way, it is possible that Martin Creed's Lights going on and off is a reference to the creation of the world as told in the Book of Genesis. It is also a way of drawing attention to the phenomenon of sight and insight as human faculties and the fact that there is no vision without light. It is also possible that it is just his way of being clever with electronic wiring and the light switches.

As for the work displaying what elephants do, it is called No Woman, No Cry and it won the Turner prize in 1998. It shows a woman weeping over the racially motivated murder of a young African man. The judges praised its 'originality and energy' and its dynamic use of colour. They also admired 'its multilayered references to contemporary urban culture and awareness of the history of art'. The elephant dung is worked into the canvas and refers to the artist's African heritage. It certainly is a moving expression of grief and loss, but it is no Mona Lisa. The critics hailed the work as returning to 'real' painting after several years of prizes going to conceptual works like the Lights going on and off. The dung was coated with resin and described as jewel-like.

Now, stones and jewels have symbolic values, as does the excrement itself. My book of symbols says that excrement contains the power of the being that produced it. In Alchemy it is the nigredo, the dark distillation which is the first step on the way to the philosopher's stone. In analytical psychology, the term became a metaphor for the 'dark night of the soul, when an individual confronts the shadows within'. All this is 'big picture' or 'grand narrative' or elephant-sized stuff, but it takes a bit of digging around to get to it. It may speak of colonialism and exploitation, but it may also speak about people paying lots of money (and awarding prizes) for waste matter which would be better spread on the rose garden.

The pink elephant didn't leave droppings. It appeared whole and alive, completely covered with pink paint and elegant gold patterning. It was displayed in a shop window fitted out as a living room, complete with a television and a couple of people sitting on a sofa, with the title Home Sweet Home. The elephant was meant to symbolise all the world's problems being ignored by the television viewing couple - a valid comment. The perpetrator of this event was Banksy, the elusive British street artist – the one who made the film entitled Exit through the gift shop, which really says it all. Anyone who visits a major gallery will be aware of the gift shop enticing us to spend lots of money on the way in or out.

A cynical view suggests that much of what is seen in both public and commercial galleries has more to do with marketing clever ideas than with art. Robert Hughes is scathing about such displays and events. He was quite certain that the market should not decide what is art, and what is not. A dead shark is just that, and someone paying hundreds of thousands of pounds for it does not make it art. In a way, however, the market does decide, but only up to a point. There is still a choice as to whether there is an elephant in the art gallery or just an emperor with no clothes on.

Art is about expressing, sharing and giving meaning to human experience. What creates and mediates this sharing is a big question worth thinking about. So next time you visit an art gallery, don't accept everything you see as 'art'. Beware of naked emperors, but don't ignore the elephants either.

Jan Altmann

Genderqueer

Highly Commended Article 2015

'Do you really think that I could ride a horse, and lead six thousand men into battle if I wore petticoats?' demanded Joan of Arc of her Inquisitors in 1431. She recanted some of her 'heresies' and was cleared of others, but continued to wear male clothing and to cut her hair. For this she was condemned to the flames. Such behaviour was seen as a horrible and blasphemous crime. Deuteronomy 22:5 said so: "The woman shall not wear that which pertaineth unto a man, neither shall a man put on a woman's garment: for all that do so are abominations unto the Lord thy God."

Even in the twentieth century, when women began wearing pantaloons so that they could ride bicycles without getting their skirts tangled up in the wheels, a group of American preachers railed against such a practice. To imitate the opposite sex in this way, they thundered, was objectionable. It is, confusing, immodest and wholly unsuitable for good, Christian women.

We no longer burn people for cross-dressing. We don't even find them horrible and blasphemous, but we do find them a bit confusing. We like to put things, including people and the way they dress, into boxes. It helps to identify them, not just according to sex, but also ethnicity, wealth, and social status. We know which box we belong in, or think we do, and we are not always comfortable with anyone who doesn't fit into a box that we also know about.

No doubt for both men and women dress can be an expression of sexual orientation, but women seem to have more logical reasons for adopting male garb than the other way around. A certain James Barry completed a degree in medicine at Edinburg University, and in 1813 became a successful and innovative army surgeon. 'He' rose to the rank of Inspector General in charge of military hospitals. The odd thing about Dr Barry was that 'he' had been born Margaret Ann Bulkley. Margaret dressed as a man for all of her adult life mainly because in the early nineteenth century women were not permitted to attend university let alone become doctors, and certainly not army officers.

George Sand dressed as a man as a statement not of sexuality but of equality, and for her personal safety. She was married with children, and had affairs with men. She wore pants, frock-coat and top hat simply so that she could walk through the streets of Paris's Latin Quarter without being raped or taken for a prostitute.

Generally speaking nowadays, women who wear pants have an easier time of it than men who wear frocks. Ellen DeGeneres has very short hair and often dresses in male attire such as jacket, pants, shirt and tie. She is openly gay and is married to a woman. Her style of dress has been described as 'tom-boy chic,' not 'queer' or 'butch' as in 'butch and femme'. Is it the case that, unlike Joan, women can now wear men's clothes, even military uniforms, without comment, but if men wear dresses they are transvestites, cross-dressers or just plain queer?

Historically, the female role has been one of submission and passivity. This too was required on religious grounds. One man who felt himself attracted to cross-dressing felt that as a

Christian he could not do so because it was not what God had ordained. What God had ordained was for men to be spiritual leaders within their families and communities and female attire just did not fit with such a role.

Why then would some men choose to adopt female dress if it meant becoming subservient? Throughout history men have adopted what we would call effeminate garb without causing offence or losing status. Louis XIV, France's Sun King, had the longest reign in European history (1643-1715). He obviously enjoyed having his portrait painted in flowing, ermine capes, long wigs, silk stockings and high heeled shoes. Louis was seen not as wearing feminine clothes, or making statements about gender, but as displaying his wealth and asserting his power and position as an absolute monarch. He was though, rather proud of his legs, and probably a bit metrosexual.

Joan, Margaret and Louis had logical reasons for cross-dressing – reasons which are no longer as relevant as they once were. Men and women still dress according to their personal taste and professional situations, but it is no longer necessary to go to these extremes. Cross-dressing nowadays occurs for complex, various and sometimes confusing reasons.

Fiction writers, script writers and psychoanalysts have been looking into these reasons for centuries. Freud called it sexual 'inversion.' In literature both male and female characters cross-dress for convenience and for comic effects. Shakespeare's Viola became Cesario in order to serve Duke Orsino. Of course she falls in love with him, and the lady he pursues falls for Viola dressed as Cesario. Byron's Don Juan was sold as a slave to a sultana. He was dressed as a woman because the sultana cannot be seen to take lovers. The sultan can, however, and sends 'Juana' off to his harem. More recent fiction writers and script writers have also been looking into the question. Mrs Doubtfire is about how a father, after a bitter divorce, dresses as a female housekeeper in order to spend time with his children. In the French film *The New Girlfriend* (2014) a young husband and father dresses in his dead wife's clothes. He loved his wife and still desires women sexually, but enjoys dressing as a woman. Female accessories like shoes, stockings and make-up are attractive to him. He finds the female role to be liberating. Such a scenario calls into question the traditional roles of masculine and feminine, and presents a situation that could change the whole nature of sexual identity. Of course things become complicated when the dead wife's female friend becomes involved.

Calling into the question the nature of sexual identity is a concern of Grayson Perry, a forty-something-year-old married man who won the Turner Prize for Art in 2003. For the presentation he appeared as 'Claire,' in a blond wig, a brightly coloured dress with short, gathered skirt and puffed sleeves, along with flat shoes and frilly socks – very cute on a five year old girl! Later Perry delivered the Reith lectures in which he addressed the question, 'Why DO men wear frocks'? He sees the 'descent' into a feminine role as a "flight from masculinity" because men are the most pressured gender, and because traditional masculine pursuits such as hunting and warfare can be negative. He suggests that wearing frocks is a way of escaping from the complexities of being a man in the twenty-first century.

Perry also suggests that identity is a process not a given. He thinks that there may be 'fault lines' between genders. We can be Chinese-Australian, black and gay, why not male and female? The New Girlfriend also looks at just these questions.

The 2014 Eurovision Song Contest was won by Thomas Neuwirth. Tom goes by the name Conchita Wurst, and for 'her' winning performance Conchita wore a long glittering evening gown, long dark hair, exquisite make-up, and a beard. 'She' has been described variously as a 'drag queen,' a 'bearded lady' or just plain 'genderqueer.'

It may well be that sexual feelings and attitudes towards sexuality are expressed through clothing. But I think Perry and Conchita are drawing attention to much more than sexuality or clothing. They are challenging the whole idea of putting gender, however it may be expressed, into boxes.

Can we live without boxes? Probably not. When we meet someone we see them as young or old, black or white, male or female, without really being aware of it, and preferably without making judgements. It is quite natural to notice if someone is young or old, short or tall, or even if they have a different ethnicity from our own. It reduces complexity. Sometimes we need to make quick and firm decisions about how we communicate with people. Uncertainty can make this difficult. We can't ignore the categories that we know, but how do you communicate with an elegant young woman with a beard or a forty year old man who dresses like a little girl? There are no boxes here.

Joan broke all the female stereotypes of her time. Women were supposed to serve and obey, and it was probably for these reasons that she was later sold to the English. Cross-dressing is no longer heretical, abhorrent, or even against the law, but people like David Bowie, Julian Cleary and Ellen DeGeneres still challenge our conventional ways of thinking about dress, and I'm sure they enjoy confusing us.

Dress has always been used to make statements about social class and social identity. It has been used to both conceal and to express gender identity, but the whole idea of using it to question the very nature of that identity is something new and challenging.

I really don't mind if someone is straight, gay or somewhere in between, but I still notice if a young man has bright, red fingernails or a young woman has unusually short hair. Is there an inbuilt need to see things in terms of difference in the first place? Why does cross dressing arouse our attention, and why is it more acceptable in a Shakespeare play than in a supermarket?

Grayson Perry and Conchita Wurst are deliberately challenging categories as they are applied to gender. Perry is particularly interested in the meaning of human identity in and of itself, and what part gender plays in this. So far, types and stereotypes relating to gender do not allow anything that does not comply with social norms or the world as we understand it. Perhaps these norms and the categories which carry them do need to be challenged. Perhaps being outside the box should be empowering not confusing. We need people who are disruptive, who push boundaries, even break out of their boxes. They dream, they see things differently, they challenge injustice, they ask awkward questions. They invent things, and perhaps even discover new planets.

Cross-dressing is a space which creates intervention and disruption to our conventional ways of thinking. It challenges not just the categories of male and female, but the whole idea of category itself. We need challenges, but we also need to allow boys to be boys and girls to be girls when they want to be. We need boxes, but let's try to keep them for shoes, take-away food, and last year's tax receipts.

Let's try to allow people to enjoy being male or female, or combinations thereof, without putting them into boxes, and also to allow those who find fulfilment outside the boxes to enjoy whatever they choose. Genderqueer, gender-bending, cross- dressing, metrosexual: my computer did not put red, wriggly lines underneath any of these, so they must be real words pertaining to real things or ideas. Even if we are not sure what they mean at least they are recognised, and that would indicate a degree of acceptance whatever they are.

Jan Altmann

Are We Enlightened?

Highly Commended Article 2018

Who are we? What do we know, and how do we know that we know it? How do we know if it's true or not? What does it mean to be true? Is anything true anymore? Such questions probably make you feel a bit like Sergeant Shultz: "I know nothing." And when Artificial Intelligence, big data, and even 'fake news' are thrown into the mix I certainly experience that 'know nothing' feeling. Why do we even bother asking such questions?

We ask them because philosophers in ancient times through to The Enlightenment (especially The Enlightenment) told us that we should – brilliant men like Descartes, Hobbes, Locke, Rousseau and Kant. Yep, they were all men. Cultured, well-educated, well informed and erudite they certainly were, but they lived in the seventeenth and eighteenth centuries. Talk about 'Dead, White Males!'

Yet for several years now well-meaning academics and journalists of our own time have been lamenting the fact that we have forgotten what they taught us. They have been asking a new set of questions, like, 'Are we losing our reason?' 'What has happened to all those values that made western, liberal democratic societies so great and so successful?' Values like individual rights, justice, equality, freedom, and the rule of law. The ability to involve ourselves in critical thinking, scientific debate, logical argument, they also think is in doubt. It seems to some of them that we have exchanged enlightenment for mere information and opinion, so freely available through social media and digital technology.

'The past,' as we say, 'is a foreign country. They did things differently there.' Individual rights, justice and freedom certainly meant very different things back in the good old seventeenth century. They believed in religious freedom, but in England, according to the Toleration Act 1689, this extended only to those who had taken the oath of allegiance to the crown, and who were not Jews, Catholics or atheists. Dissenters were required to register their meeting locations and were forbidden from meeting even in private homes. There were no problems with multiculturalism, political correctness or identity politics. They simply didn't exist. We even had to invent the words for them.

So, what did The Enlightenment teach us, is it still relevant or do we need to change a few of its teachings, and how would we do this? Fortunately these great thinkers also gave us the means to deal with these questions, even though they would not have known it. They gave us the concept of 'progress.' This has afforded us the ability to adapt their thinking so that we can use it rather than lose it.

The front cover of my copy of *The Leviathan*, published by Thomas Hobbes in 1651 presents an illustration of a very large king towering over the landscape, and wearing a shirt made up of dozens of tiny people. This is to demonstrate that the way to stable government was for the people to surrender all their rights to the monarch. Hobbes states outright that 'Subjects owe to Sovereigns simple obedience in all things', so long as these are not opposed to the laws of God. He supported this idea with the philosophy of the Social Contract, which was hardly a contract in the usual sense, and certainly not democratic.

Let's not forget, though, that Hobbes had just lived through a civil war and the execution of a monarch. War, anarchy and chaos were real threats. His solution of centralised and absolute power, however, does not have much appeal today.

Samuel Pepys was another member of the Enlightenment. He was the son of a humble tailor, but overcame disadvantage and class distinction to become Secretary of the Admiralty, a Member of Parliament and president of The Royal Society. He became surveyor-general of the naval office, where his meticulous record keeping did much to expose corruption – honourable deeds and achievements to be sure.

His famous Diary begins in January, 1660 and this reveals his personal life to be a bit less honourable. He could have dinner with his wife and then go to a cabaret with Mrs Bagwell, or 'sport' with Mrs Fitsimmons. He makes it quite clear that such sport included 'taking his pleasure' with whichever lady was in his company at the time. And if the dinner which had been provided by his wife didn't happen to please him he was quite at liberty, indeed sometimes 'obliged,' to beat her. I suppose the stick used was 'no thicker than his thumb,' which was the general guideline in those times. Such a day would, usually, have ended with 'supper, prayers and bed.'

John Locke is rightly considered one of the most forward thinkers of The Enlightenment. But some of his views are pretty unappealing to us today. In 1669 he co-authored the Constitutions of Carolina, which endorses aristocracy, slavery and serfdom.

In his *Two Treatises of Government* published in 1689 he at least offers some concessions to women, pointing out that they should not be treated as possessions. They could even have control of their children, so long as the father was not present. He argues generally for a more civilized society based on natural rights and contract theory.

He obviously learnt a lot in twenty years – or maybe not.

Locke was a major investor in the English slave trade. Individual ownership of slaves was not practised in England as it was in America. But his much quoted assertion that "Slavery is so vile and miserable an estate of man, and so directly opposite to the generous temper and courage of our nation; that it is hardly to be conceived, that an Englishman, much less a gentleman, should plead for it" (Second Treatise on Government, Ch.4) sounds a little hollow. Slavery was made illegal in England in 1772; it was outlawed for the whole of the Empire in 1807, but not actually abolished until 1833. Englishmen – enlightened ones including Locke – thought it was a 'lamentable but necessary evil.' Dr Johnson (also much enlightened) did at least issue a challenge when he asked 'How is it that we hear the loudest yelps for liberty from the drivers of Negroes?' But getting rid of slavery was just too much of an inconvenience.

Racial inferiority was deeply ingrained in Western society, especially in America.

There was a deeply held conviction that black people were less intelligent than white. In the 1800s, long after The Enlightenment, many scientists and anthropologists argued that black people were closer to apes than humans. In 1859 Charles Darwin's theory of evolution was seen as supporting such a view.

Jean-Jacques Rousseau thought democracy was a good idea, but like the abolition of slavery he also thought it was not very practicable. He proposed a 'The Social Contract' (1762) in which power should be shared equally between the Sovereign, the Parliament and the people, but commented that such an arrangement could easily descend into despotism or anarchy. It embraced a view of human equality previously unheard of, but there was no place for women, or even men who did not own land. Women were, for Rousseau, weaker and less rational than men, and must depend on them. The the natural order of things, thought Rousseau, was that women should obey men.

His main work that deals with women is a novel called *Emile*. Here he makes it quite clear that women are incapable of rational thought or reason. Their role in life is to be wives and mothers, and their educational needs should be considered in accordance with this. In his *Confessions*, written later in his life, he does credit several specific women with gaining him entrance into the intellectual circles of society, but he remained happily misogynistic. Women were subject to their fathers and husbands, and that was the end of it.

Mary Wollstonecraft challenged Rousseau in her *Vindication* and other writings, questioning his idea that women's only purpose is the pleasure of men. She writes with great irony of his 'confessional' story of affection for an uneducated and ignorant servant girl. Mary claims that Rousseau used this poor girl's shortcomings to devalue the intellectual capacities of women generally.

Such an attitude does explain why such 'enlightened' men sent their sons to university, but believed that their daughters needed only to be provided with a suitable husband. In fact most fathers probably agreed with Immanuel Kant that 'laborious learning or painful pondering' would destroy their merits and weaken their charms. 'A woman with her head full of Greek, or who talks about mechanics like the Marquise de Chatelet,' he wrote, 'might as well grow a beard.'

Despite these sorts of prejudices principles such belief in scientific evidence, individual human rights and freedom of speech slowly took hold. England's Bill of Rights (1689) established the right to of 'freedom of speech in Parliament' which is still in effect today. The Declaration of the Rights of Man and of the Citizen, adopted during the French Revolution in 1789, affirmed freedom of speech as an inalienable right, even if a woman (Olympe de Gouges) was guillotined for claiming that it should extend to women. The Universal Declaration of Human Rights, adopted in 1948, asserts that everyone has the right to hold opinions and to express them. Every citizen may, accordingly, speak, write, and print with freedom, but shall be responsible for such abuses of this freedom as shall be defined by law.

It is their belief in progress, however, that offers a possible solution to maintaining, and at the same time updating, the values of the Enlightenment. With progress, they thought, human society could achieve 'truth, virtue and happiness.' Moral and spiritual progress would surely follow. We have progressed, as they taught us to do, but need to keep going.

We must not lose our belief in the ideas of Liberal Democracy, Tolerance and Individual freedom, but use them. We need to refocus and reevaluate them, making them more inclusive, not less. Equality, diversity and tolerance must be used to engage with cultures and ideas other than our own. Free speech needs to include listening as well as speaking. Democracy needs to be practiced in in a way that gives expression to diversity but not dictatorship or mob rule.

We need to understand that The Enlightenment was produced in a particular place and at a particular time in history. We do not need to reject what it taught us, but to adopt the spirit of those times, and to readjust the values that it left us.

Above all, let us keep asking questions – new ones as well as the old. We belong not just to one time, but to the past, the present and the future. In this way we may gain a new sense of who we are as thinkers and as social beings. We may answer some of those irritating questions and even progress towards even more enlightenment. And just perhaps we may discover that aristocratic, educated white males are not the only ones to be enlightened.

Jan Altmann

Linda Blackshaw

Seth

Commended Short Story 2007

He carefully folded the bright blue shiny paper around the large box. As he put the last piece of tape on the box, he tapped it for luck.

Hope he likes them, but what do I know about presents? According to Milly, I always get it wrong. Daniel carried the box out to the car. He sat for a few moments before heading off. For the first time in his life, Daniel McIntyre drove below the speed limit. His uncertainty about the gift lay in his stomach like a clump of cold porridge.

As he turned into the avenue, he could see balloons and streamers hanging off the letterbox. They bobbed and banged together, just like the nerves in Daniel's body. Sitting in the car for a minute, his flight button paused; Maybe I should come back later. It would not have taken much to make him flee the scene, but his pride got him out of the car and up the driveway. Nearing the house, he could hear childish yells and giggles coming from the back of the house.

Hell, I'm early. He shrugged and rang the bell, anyway. Milly will find something wrong no matter what I d.

"Daniel."

"Tim." He shook the offered hand. Daniel kept his face blank as he looked at his son's stepfather. The man who had him all the time, not once a fortnight, two weeks in summer and alternate Christmases. As he followed Tim out into the garden, Daniel heard Milly say, "Gather round, children, and we'll play pass the parcel." Sunlight played on Seth's chestnut hair, highlighting the different shades of red. Seth had Daniel's hair, straight and thick. His son's glistened as his head bobbed enthusiastically, keeping time with the music. The parcel stopped at a lilac fairy whose wings stood proudly at attention.

Before the music could start up again, Seth spotted Daniel. "DADDY." He leapt to his feet, but before he could leave the circle, his mother called, "Sethy, sit down," She glared at Daniel. "You can see your father after the party."

"It's all right, Seth. I'll grab a drink and watch the party from over there." I always get it wrong. I just can't win. I think Milly would be glad if I just vanished. She'd like to forget that Seth's my son, too. Why she must call him 'Sethy' I just don't know. Daniel watched Seth, a faint smile on his face. He wanted to wrap his son up in his arms and vanish, to keep him forever. Milly had even wanted to change Seth's name to Tim's. "Be better," she'd said. Better for who? Seth's my son, not Tim's. Daniel remembered that she had tried to register him at school as Barstow, but Seth told Daniel. I soon put a stop to that.

The party continued and soon the cake came out. After everyone had sung Happy Birthday, Seth brought a piece over to Daniel." Dad, can I …"

"Seth, you can talk to your father after. Come along your friends are waiting."

"Go and play with your friends, Seth. I'll not leave until I've seen all your presents."

"Honest, Dad."

"Scout's Honour" Daniel held his hand up, pretending to be a scout. With a laugh, Seth ran back to the party.

Finally, the last child left clutching the bag of lollies and the balloon that each one had been given. The lilac fairy trooped out, her wings drooped, and her little wand was bent.

"Daddy, come and see what I got. Can I open your present-now?"

"Course you can, Seth. What else did you get?"

"Mum got me clothes. Nan, a book, and Gramps gave me money. I got cars and paints, and Tim got me an electronic thing. It's educational."

Daniel sighed; maybe my gift's not so hot. He handed the large box over to Seth. Milly glared when she saw the size of the box. "I thought we agreed, no expensive presents. You've spent too much."

"No, I haven't, Milly."

Seth carefully peeled off the paper. When he lifted the lid off the box, his eyes rounded in surprise. Inside were several parcels of varying sizes. His mouth formed silent numbers as he counted them. "8," he squealed with delight.

"Yes, Seth, one for each year. Here, open that one first. No, the red one."

Seth opened the first gift. "B … but, Daddy, these are …."

"Now yours, 12 tin soldiers, 6 blue and 6 red."

"But …"

"They were Grandpa George's then Gramp's then mine and now they are yours. Maybe someday you can pass them on too."

When Seth opened the boxes, he'd added 6 matchbox cars, a build-it-yourself cardboard garage, a submarine you filled with baking soda to make it dive, a book of things to do for boys and a head which grew hair when watered, to the tin soldiers. He came to the last two parcels. Both were flat, but one was larger than the other, and that is the one Seth opened first.

"A kite. Look, Mum, it's a dragon kite. Daddy, you made this, didn't you? This is what you were hiding in the studio last week."

"Yes, and no. I was hiding the other one as well."

Seth opened the last package. It was a small painting of four heads. All the heads were topped with varying shades of red hair.

"I painted a picture of my Grandpa, your Grandpa – me and …"

"ME!" yelled Seth. "Look, Mum; look, Tim. It's all the McIntyre men."

"So, it is Seth. Please take your presents to your room. Your mother and I need to talk to your father."

"But."

"Do what Tim tells you, Seth. NO arguing. Just do what you're told. Your father will come and see you before he leaves." Milly pressed her lips together and frowned at her son.

"It's okay, Seth. Once I've spoken to Mummy and Tim, I'll come and see you."

"Promise."

"Promise."

"Let's go into the lounge. Like a drink, Daniel?" Tim showed Daniel through the door.

"Better not, Tim. I'm driving. What's this about, Milly?"

Milly wet her lips, paused, then rushed on, "Tim's got a new job in Singapore and we can all go. It's a good opportunity, Daniel. Don't be difficult. You can have Seth for a month in the summer and, of course, you can visit us anytime you like."

"NO."

"We've spoken to the lawyer, and he says the court will approve the change in visitation." Tim spoke flatly, in a voice that brooked no argument.

"Visitation, such a cold word, Tim. We're talking about my

son here. What does Seth think of this?"

"We haven't told him yet. I thought it would be easier if you agreed and we told him together."

"You expected me to agree. Where on earth did that idea come from? I know you'd rather I didn't exist, Milly, but I am Seth's father. Why the hell should I let you take him away so I can't see him for months on end?"

Milly glared at Daniel. "You'd be able to e-mail and, of course, phone anytime."

"E-mail doesn't make up for hugs, Milly. I can't let you take him. Not without a fight."

Tim interrupted, "We're leaving next month."

"Not with Seth. He's staying here."

"He has a passport. You let us take him to Disney W ..."

Daniel interrupted. "That was different. It was only a holiday."

"It's only for 2 years. Don't be difficult, Daniel," Milly pleaded.

"Difficult. Difficult. You have no idea how difficult I'm going to be, Milly. I'll have Seth's passport cancelled. ""Milly's Seth's mother. The court will," Tim butted in.

"I know who Milly is, Tim, but you seem to forget I am Seth's father. You can't take him."

"Be reasonable, Daniel."

"You be reasonable. You can see him for a month in summer and e-mail and phone whenever you like. Why don't you just pop over anytime you like." Daniel clenched his fist and hoped Tim would say something more?

No, I can't hit him. They'd use that against me later.

"I'm not leaving Daddy."

The three adults turned and saw Seth standing in the doorway.

"Seth, it's not up to you. The court will decide." Milly went towards her son.

"NO!" Seth yelled, then whirled around and ran out the house.

"Seth, come here," his mother called out to him, but Seth did not stop or look back. Daniel ran after his son, but as he got out the door, he heard a squeal of brakes and a thud.

"God, Seth." Daniel saw a white Volkswagen. On the ground in front of it lay Seth. Seth's leg lay at an awkward angle and there was blood on his forehead. He was unconscious. Daniel kneeled beside him and shouted back towards the house, "Call an ambulance!"

"It wasn't my fault. He just ran out in front of me." There was a hint of tears in the woman's voice.

"I know whose fault it was, and it wasn't yours."

Linda Blackshaw

Maria Bonar

What she needs is a good read

Winning Article 2015

The digital revolution has led to a steep rise in erotic fiction written by women, for women. Erotic literature has a long history, dating back to the ancient Greek poet Sappho of Lesbos, who wrote erotic poetry to her lover. In the early 20th century, DH Lawrence's *Lady Chatterley's Lover*, Henry Miller's *Tropic of Cancer* and *Tropic of Capricorn*, and Pauline Réage's *The Story of O* were banned, along with many other books deemed to be obscene. Erotic literature largely remained underground; reading it was a clandestine activity.

Historically, library collections of erotica have not only been segregated from other books, but their titles have been omitted from official catalogues. The British Library, which has the biggest institutionally held collection of erotica (apart from the Vatican), finally published a bibliography in 1981 of the 'Private Case'. This catalogues 1,914 erotic books in the collection which was established in 1857 and contains works by notable figures including the Marquis de Sade. Prior to this, the only major library to have freely listed its erotica collection in a general catalogue was the Bibliothèque Nationale de France.

Several years ago, I bought a copy of *The Complete Illustrated*

Poems, Songs & Ballads of Robert Burns, only to discover online recently *The Merry Muses of Caledonia,* his forty page collection of bawdy poems and lyrics, none of which appear in my book. I've been short changed!

The sexual revolution of the sixties fostered an increase of erotic books by female authors such as Erica Jong's *Fear of Flying* and Anaïs Nin's *Delta of Venus* in the 1970s. Anne Rice's *Sleeping Beauty Trilogy* exploring BDSM* practices was published in the 1980s (under the pseudonym AN Roquelaure). Several publishers of erotic fiction were founded during this period, including Cleis Press, Red Sage, Circlet Press, Blue Moon Books and Down There Press.

Sex therapist and educator, Joani Blank of Down There Press published a series of educational books about sexuality and erotic pleasure. In 1977, she also established 'Good Vibrations' a sex-positive, woman-friendly adult store in San Francisco, selling sex toys and other erotic products.

Virgin Books launched its Black Lace imprint in 1993, specialising in erotic romance by women, for women, selling four million books world-wide before publishing ceased in 2009 due to a slight downturn in the market and because by then, so much erotic material was available free on the internet.

The introduction of eBooks and e-readers caused a marked shift from print to digital material. Unable to find a publisher for her sexually explicit romance novels, Tina Engler founded Ellora's Cave in 2000, one of the first eBook publishers, initially publishing romantic erotic fiction exclusively in eBook format, later moving to printed works. Engler dubbed this genre 'Romantica' and registered it as a company trademark. Ellora's Cave sold millions of eBooks around the world, to date publishing 10,000 titles by over 800 authors. Their best selling subgenre is BDSM* erotic romance. One of the advantages of eBooks is that they are much cheaper to produce and distribute, both nationally and internationally, than printed books. As profit margins were higher, Ellora's Cave paid authors 37% royalties compared to the traditional publisher's rate of approximately 7%. Many Ellora's Cave authors moved to full-time writing and made a good living from it, which can be notoriously difficult to do. The higher royalties rate became the industry standard.

Money talks and sex sells. With eBook erotic fiction sales soaring while brick and mortar bookstores were closing down, other publishers eagerly joined the digital market with erotic romance imprints, including Kensington's Aphrodisia, Avon's Red, Harlequin's Spice, Mills and Boon's Blaze and NAL's Heat.

Women who would never admit they liked reading erotica, or who were too embarrassed to buy an erotic novel with a raunchy cover from a bookstore - like the one featured on the right - or to be caught reading such a book, could now find and browse eBook titles online and download them discreetly and cheaply. With the increase in fantasy and paranormal erotic fiction, there was a smorgasbord to choose from. The internet and e-readers provided a virtual plain brown paper wrapper. Women could now covertly read the most sizzling, sexually explicit stories anywhere, for example, while travelling on public transport. Victoria was not the only one with a secret...

The Kindle was introduced in 2007. In the last quarter of 2010, Amazon announced that in the US their eBook sales had surpassed sales of paperback books for the first time.

Anonymity, availability and affordability fuelled the growth in eBook erotic fiction for women. The typical readers appear to be middle-class women under forty, although some erotica authors note there is a growing male audience too, judging by their fan mail. This generation of women has grown up with television shows such as *Sex and the City* which follows the lives of four women with ever-changing sex lives who confide in each other and talk openly about their sexual adventures. They are less conservative than the previous generation.

The internet also led to an explosion of amateur erotica, including 'fan fiction' - stories about characters from an original work of fiction such as a television series or a movie written by fans of the work, rather than the original writer. E L James' *Fifty Shades of Grey Trilogy* released in 2011, began as fan fiction on an internet forum with its origins in Stephenie Meyer's vampire series *Twilight.* The online forum gave James' work instant exposure and it became a viral hit, with more than 250,000 copies downloaded before it was published as a conventional book.

Despite overwhelmingly negative criticism, by June 2015 the *Fifty Shades of Grey* juggernaut had sold over 125 million copies worldwide and set the record in the UK as the fastest-selling paperback of all time. It topped best-seller lists around the world and has been translated into 52 languages. James' latest novel, *Grey: Fifty Shades of Grey as told by Christian*, sold 1.1 million copies in just four days, after it was launched on 18 June 2015.

One of the factors credited with making the Fifty Shades Series so successful, was the monochrome grey book covers on paperbacks. They were packaged like mainstream novels, unlike the embarrassingly flamboyant covers on most erotic fiction, which bring condescension for the genre and expose the buyer or reader to snide remarks. Speaking of the condescension erotic romance attracts, Australian author Kate Belle notes that other genres, like trashy action thrillers or crime novels don't receive the same level of scorn.

The Fifty Shades Trilogy became erotic fiction for everywoman, taking the genre from the top shelf in the far corner of the bookstore and placing it front and centre - not only in the bookstore, but in the supermarket. It was available from Costco, Sainsbury's and Tesco in the UK. At the peak of its popularity, pyramids of Fifty Shades paperbacks were stacked up at the entrance of my local Target store, selling at $7 each. Following its success, publishers again eagerly launched erotic imprints; HarperCollins' Mischief Books, eXtasy's Erotica, and Ebury relaunched the Black Lace imprint, adding to its Rouge range of spicy romance.

Dymock's 'Steamy Fiction' shelves

Libraries are now stocking a range of erotic fiction that would have raised eyebrows not so very long ago.

Despite the scorn heaped on her for wooden, repetitive and juvenile sounding prose and her inaccurate representation of BDSM*, EL James appears to have whipped up the perfect cocktail for her readers:

Fifty Shades Cocktail

> Dip the rim of the glass in sugar and vanilla.
> Pour in a measure of the traditional Mills and Boon romance.

Add

- One shot - Anastasia Steele, the naïve young virgin
- One shot - Christian Grey, the handsome squillionaire

Blend with

- Numerous shots of ersatz BDSM*
- One mask
- Handcuffs
- Two silver balls

Garnish with cherries and serve spanked, not shaken. Live happily ever after.

James' readers are not deterred by her prose. For them, the novels clearly hit the 'sweet spot'. Her phenomenal sales in the mass market are an author's wet dream. In addition to the books, Amazon lists a range of '50 Shades of Grey accessories' including charm bracelets, iPhone covers, condoms, pencil cases, wallets and a 'Contract & Tie Kit'.

In her essay on the pleasures of writing and reading erotica, Anne Rice says the sadomasochism fantasy in her books is presented as a glorified game, "a place to go to enjoy the fantasy of being overpowered by a man or woman and delightfully compelled to surrender and feel keening pleasure, without the slightest serious harm".

This is precisely what happens to Ana in Fifty Shades. Christian overpowers her with his use of BDSM* and delightfully 'compels' her into surrendering and feeling keening pleasure (over and over again), as a result of his imaginative and well-practised sexual arts. This fantasy evidently resonates with many women.

Lacey Alexander, author of *What She Needs,* hopes her deliciously decadent and downright sinful books will take the reader on the ultimate erotic adventure and encourage her to embrace her sexual fantasies.

What she needs is a good read.

**BDSM - an overlapping abbreviation of bondage and discipline (B&D), dominance and submission (D&S), and sadism and masochism (S&M).*

Maria Bonar

Last Dance

Commended Poem 2017

I danced with you grudgingly
that first time.
You, with your slicked-down hair,
shirt smelling faintly
of horses and sheep.
Me, lip curled, nose in the air.

Changed days! I'm ashamed that
the first time we danced,
I treated you with such meanness.
When you rescued me
from the bushfire,
passion flared between us.

On the wings of the morning
you came for me
riding your chestnut mare.
I swung up behind you
we rode through the smoke,
sparks shooting high in the air.

Gum trees exploded in
mad bombs of fire.
Crackling flames chased us high up the ridge.
Wind gusted like thunder
as we cleared the crest
and Peg galloped down to the bridge.

On the wings of the morning
you came for me
riding your chestnut mare.
You called me sweetheart
and pledged me your love,
with a diamond solitaire.

At Blackboy Hill
we whirled our last dance.
"Be over by Christmas," they said.
Neither you nor Peg
returned from France.
Sadly, we never did wed.

On the wings of the morning
I think of you
riding your chestnut mare.
Mad bombs explode
as you ride through the smoke
at Villers-Bretonneux.

Maria Bonar

Lynne Cairns

Muresk

Runner-Up Poem 2017

I pull the curtains back
Sleep facing the sky
Hoping in vain for stars.

Morning brings the consolation
Of swooping, swirling
Cockatoos
White on white, against the clouded sky

Screeching, they drop
To applique the treetops
With white ephemeral flowers

Or fall to earth
To startle shadowy sheep
That drift among
The stubble's blunt-cut fringes

Lynne Cairns

Sue Clennell

When rabbits were sixpence

Runner-Up Short Story 1992

"Wet pants, wet pants!"

May climbs the Virginia Creeper to the roof, ignoring her clinging knickers and the jibes of the boy below.

It's the spiders in the dunny. She tries to hold her wee too long because there are spiders in the dunny.

The men have finished working. It's something to watch, to see men working in 1930.

The huge steamroller that shook the whole of the next street has gone. The huge steamroller that needs an extra man on the back to balance it. May wouldn't even brave the pavement while it was ironing out what the men shovelled before it.

Down below the boys are playing on the road, kicking a football of bundled newspapers and string.

Daniel is the best football maker. His footballs last the longest.

From the smugness of her perch May watches her tormentor jump on the iron back step of the moving baker's cart.

The baker is bad-tempered and Daniel has to keep a wary eye for that moment when the driver may curl his whip back and flick him with the tip of it. The crack can break the skin open.

"Willie whipee' hind," yells one of Daniel's arch-rivals, and Daniel judges and jumps as the driver jerks around.

Mother is calling from the kitchen window for Daniel to collect any horse dung. He might not bother, except it is a chance to race the other boys in the street to it.

Daniel sometimes sits on the roof too, and hoots his opinions on how long the neighbours spend in their lavatories. Or else he and May run along the slates from one end of the terraced houses to the other.

This afternoon May is waiting for her father to come home, to see what he will bring.

Father is a gentleman. This is what people in the street say about them. Everyone knows it.

Her parents are the richest people in the street. They have an ice chest, an axe and an umbrella.

With the axe father can chop wood for money. Too little money, says mother. He is kind-hearted.

All the neighbours borrow the umbrella. It is something to be proud of.

They are like three magic things in a story, three magic wishes the neighbours would like to have – an ice chest, an axe and an umbrella.

May picks a leaf from the vine and digs holes into its fleshiness with her thumbnail. Here are the eyes, this is the mouth. She widens the eyes so that she and the leaf are looking down on the boys. They look at the slate waves going down to the rubbish dump and rubber factory.

When people don't have money to pay for the chopped wood, or to pay father for helping to shift their furniture, they give him a bag of fruit or soap. It's best not to ask where such things come from, says mother.

The house is shouting again, this time with Helen's voice.

Why can't I go and … to be a secretary?"

"I keep telling you we can't afford to keep you while … And then you'd get less than in the factory!"

"Well let me learn dressmaking. They'd take me as … won't have to pay anything."

"The money would only cover your fares and food. There'd be … coming in. Don't be so selfish girl … of the family to consider. You're staying at the factory."

"Why can't Dad get a proper job?"

"Your father wasn't trained … only knows how to be a soldier. This is not the sort of life he had in England."

"I don't see why I should support … And he knocks back a job because he says the other man had a family to support … well, what are we?"

May doesn't like the Helen talking house. She is frightened of the sister who hates the factory, hates home.

Helen is rough. She talks of fights in the factory, fights with scissors, women pulling each other's hair close to the machines.

"Well I'm going out tonight … is to it!"

Helen doesn't do as she is told.

When Father Williams brought the shoes for Daniel he talked to mother about Helen.

"She is one of the lost generation, Mrs Richards, wasted talent."

Helen is lost.

A man is coming into their front gate with a string of baby rabbits. "Kittens," he calls them, "Sixpence each or two for ninepence."

May notices he goes out with the same amount. Mother hates stripping the fur off them, and anyway, today is Friday, it will be Pea soup and chocolate pudding, her favourite tea. The worst tea is Sunday, when the watercress man comes.

"Gross sandwiches," says Daniel.

And now father comes through the gate, he doesn't look up at her, doesn't know she is there.

May drops her leaf and clambers down.

In the kitchen the flies caught on the cardboard strips hanging from the ceiling buzz and swing as father accidentally knocks them.

"May, wash your hands for tea. Perfume, Arthur, you can't eat perfume. What good is it?"

The soup is ladled out thick and green and, "May I think you could give your doll to Olive now. You're getting too big for dolls, you'll be going to school soon."

May's face reflects the red lino on the table.

"But she's my dolly, Santa gave her to me."

"She was just a loan dear, until your sister grew up."

"The roof-top prowler doesn't need a dolly," teased father.

"You haven't been on the roof again May?"

She is in the bath now in her little sister's water. The water is grey with soap. When May moves her legs out she can see the water between them, and when she closes her legs she can't. Open, close, open, close, swish, swish.

Up high there is a small window. The window is crinkled so the night can't get in. It is open so the peppercorn tree can.

May jams her shoulders and neck against the end of the bath. Her parents' voices drift with the steam in the outhouse.

"I haven't got any more … I told you what I got for delivering that 44-gallon drum … 2/6 for the whole day!"

"Danny said you were playing cards at … with a roll of money."

"Danny's a liar … roll of money in these times?"

May lets her body float upwards. Up, down, up, down. Over on her stomach, plop. The air is cold on her back.

She puts her mouth right down into the water. The water

covers her chin and laps the top of her bottom lip.

Helen comes in to help her wash.

"Get a move on, Danny wants a bath before the water gets cold."

From the kitchen comes the sound of flesh and a clatter. The stove, thinks May.

Mother has been pushed against the stove. Then more flesh. May opens her mouth to scream but Helen presses the flannel against her face.

We don't want the neighbours knowing our business, stupid," she hissed. "God, how I hate this place. I'm leaving as soon as I get a man to marry me. Get out of the bath!"

May runs along the passage freshly clad. Bladder bursting she wets herself again as she climbs into bed.

It is dark, and there are spiders outside every door.

Sue Clennell

Upon gaining sexual maturity

Commended Poem 1999

1.
My father says don't stay single, Sue.
Single women are strange.
My father says books by women writers
are no good.
It's very hard finding books for your father
says my mother,
it's very hard finding books
about pirates.

The Reader's Digest says men
give love to get sex
and women give sex to get love.
That is true says my father,
know that and you will stay married.
My mother once threw a teapot
at my father,
it hit the ceiling.
Maybe she shouldn't have thrown it.

I saw my father cry when a plank
fell on my head and he didn't know
if I was going to die.
Fourteen is a dreadful age to see
your father cry,
but I didn't know my father
was a new age guy,
I didn't know he was a new age guy
in the fifties.

ll.

I didn't read the instruction book
that came with my ex,
so I guess it's my fault.
Funny how he was such a prude
and the things he got up to,
and I wasn't such a prude
and the things I didn't get up to.

Well they say if you tell dirty jokes
it's because you can't do anything
and I wonder if it's because
I tell dirty jokes.
Sex myths interest me
bald men are supposed to be sexy,
I've often wondered about the hardware man,
he goes to church

are church men sexy?
Very, says my mother
church men are the worst, as in the most.
At school a girlfriend told me
to turn a man on you rub behind his ears.
You turn a man on if you touch him anywhere
says my mother as in give a man a match
and he'll start a raging bushfire.
I guess I should have read the instruction book
that came with him.

Sue Clennell

Sue Colyer

Parade of Snakes

Highly Commended Poem 2017

Snakes came singly to the pink stone slab
On a hot summer's day, and I at the garden gate to rest there.

From the embankment slope to the terrace above,
I came to the gate, to wait, to stand and wait,
As Lawrence waited, for snakes to parade before me.

The snakes appeared, each one alone,
From the shelter of the gloom of shade
Trailing their coloured scales to the sun warmed stone.
Black, brown, pink, green, lustrous.
Lifting their heads to observe their observer,
momentarily warmed,
Silently.

They lay before me at my gate
And I, like an intruder, a voyeur, must wait.

Each in turn lifted its head, with cautious stare,
And flicked its two-forked tongue to sense the air. A warning?
Then coiled, and turned back to the shelter of the shade.
A passing parade, a shimmery rainbow slipping by.
Though some are endangered, they survive,
Ubiquitous and harmless, in the forest's emerald greenness.

I smiled at this procession
of ophidian colour and optical conversation.
How honoured I was that they came to my warm oasis de paix,
And depart calm, unharmed and safe
In the shelter of this rustic haven.

No voice said: Kill them. Only humility, to feel so connected.
No violent act. What wonder to have had a chat!
To talk with Lawrence, to vision his snake
both admired and feared.

I was not afraid, nor were the snakes.
We were both at home, sharing our mutual hospitality,
A moment in time and space,
Resting in the warmth of the garden sanctuary.

Sue Colyer

Acknowledgment: D. H Lawrence's poem Snake *[1923]*

Pat Curtis

This Car Free Life

Winning Article 2006

I'd like to start a club for non-drivers, but I have a problem. How would the members get to the meetings?

People look down on me as a non-driver, and resent giving me lifts. They cannot understand how a middle-class woman with a university degree doesn't drive when even people on social security regard a car as a necessity. One woman said, "I'd go crazy if I didn't drive!" I was too polite to tell her that she was crazy for frenetically chasing around from place to place like a headless chook.

I do own a driving license. I renewed it just in case, but now I've reached my late sixties, it's unlikely I'll take to the roads. It is useful though when I need some form of identification. I passed my test in my forties, after a number of attempts. The location was a remote suburb. The time: three o'clock one weekday afternoon when seniors were having a 'kip', and many women drivers were watching 'soap operas' before collecting their offspring from school. I hardly encountered any other vehicles.

My first task as a driver was to fetch a sandwich for my husband during our lunch break at work. I drove about five hundred yards to the local deli and parked in a solitary space. My mission accomplished I returned to find a 'four-wheel drive' had parked alongside my car. When I attempted to reverse a resounding bang echoed as I hit the 'roo bar' of the monster alongside me. Out of nowhere a crowd of onlookers appeared. Instinctively I drove away too embarrassed to show my face. My husband who was waiting on the verge said as I opened the car door, "That was an expensive sandwich!"

I was now too scared to drive alone, but friends and relatives were terrified to accompany me. My husband who is not a male chauvinist but a realist remarked, while fastening his safety belt, "I have only this belt between me and eternity!' It was a relief when my son nabbed the car to travel to'Uni'. It gave me a good excuse not to drive.

I have rationalised and come to terms with my car free status. I admit it would be great to get to places quickly rather than a simple journey becoming an expedition, but there are compensations. At least by not driving I'm guilt-free by not adding to the road toll or polluting the atmosphere. The cost of running a car is astronomical, and the money saved allows for luxuries like foreign travel. I don't suffer from road rage or the frustration of traffic jams. Instead, I catch up on my reading, and talk to interesting characters on trains and buses which provides material for creative writing. Walking keeps me fit and wards off osteoporosis. I'm still considering the club for non-drivers; I've worked out we'll meet in a central place in town with easy access to public transport. Above all, I'm enjoying my 'Car Free' life.

Pat Curtis

Geraldine Day

Proposal Slips

Winning Poem 2005

He worked in his father's boatyard
taught me how to balance on water
proposed during the rising of the tide
for fortune and fertility.
We planned a pastel spring wedding
but the florist was a busty bitch
with attitude who gave him
a private viewing of what was in bloom.

On the rebound I snaffled
a bank manager and plain gold ring.
After the honeymoon I failed
to reach his daily expectations.
His whores phoned but his fists talked
and I calculated the risk
on my investment was too high.

His best friend took me skinny dipping
to soothe my wounds, professed his love
before duty resurfaced. He called
on a secure line, sealed letters
with colour coded kisses
his arms always out of reach.

The widower's children floundered
in their responsibility to him,
packing lunches, selecting ties
and my heart ballooned to suffocation.
He demanded I love him more
but I couldn't.

On a pebble strewn beach
I was discovered by a Frenchman
who spoke softly, made me laugh.
He grew carnations, hummed opera
drank milk from the kitchen jug
measured women by the length of their legs
his proposal retracted for a slinkier model.

The drummer wore the pink sweater I knitted
raced me barefoot through forest glades
offered a bouquet of autumn leaves.
He showed me glimpses of who I was
shattered my glass horizon
so I flew to the other side of the world.
He proposed by mail two weeks later
but I'd already tasted the sun.

The carpenter had a warm Gloucester brogue
liked my legs and attitude
gave me space, nailed me to the floor
his smile singing loud songs.
He didn't wear ties, knew no whores
had arms wide enough to fill
my heart with roses.

Geraldine Day

Familyscape

Highly Commended Poem 2014

In sepia oval, Gramps dark suit
puckers against a starched white shirt.
His hands, young then, softly curl
the firm grip on wood turning tools
not yet soured with arthritis.
Straight backed, valid, his gaze
unafraid to question.
I wish I had known him then.

Top left outlines Dad's cycling jaunts
to continental beer gardens
before war stopped that nonsense.
He salvaged London beneath a dangerous sky
dodged buzz bombs, red rimmed eyes
searching for silence.
Come the dawn he rescued the dead.

And there, top centre,
the farm cottage, roses thorning
round the stable door. The windows
have been replaced, no diamond shaped secrets
and hidden stairs now, gone the weekly tin bath
nights in front of the fire.

Circled, top right, the Sunday morning family,
gloves and prayer books, freshly laundered pigtails.
Not far, the church, no excuse not to go.
Words beat a stained glass drum.
"Thou shalt not sin", a conger eel
of movement between the pews.

Bottom left, Christmas is rectangular
with brittle corners. The tree highlights
the fizz and bluster of family
a table heavy with the smell of cooking
gap-toothed cousins leaping the splay of presents
for bargain crackers and hidden threepenny bits.
Black and white conversations had mellowed
and loopholes of colour surfaced from the ancestral tunnel.

Geraldine Day

Word Sleuth

Commended Poem 2014

I have waited for words draped
against the Sydney Opera House
nestled in a secret garden
at The Rocks savouring the summer
wine slither of linguine and, yes, I have felt
their sharp blue-iced edges on Franz Joseph.

I inhaled them amongst damp pungent colours
of Vermont, on subway clatter in New York
an image found in Times Square, lost
in wild remnants of a hurricane.

I glimpsed a sestina in the slow
motion of an ancient gorge
the weathered glass of a crocodile's eye
the dawn shadows of Purnululu.

I searched, stumbled, smelt words
in the coffee crush of a Montmartre market
cobbled alleys and olive groves
tasted them in a handful of sunset.

Maybe I'll ride a thermal to Santorini
follow signposts on a footloose journey
into the arms of a dark eyed lover.
Then, surely, a poem will find me
shape its own language of mosaic
verbs across a breathless sky.

Geraldine Day

Balance

Highly Commended Poem 2017

Today, driving together to visit our shared family
for updates of footie mishaps, T-ball wins
and count new baby teeth,
I hear your breath in the quiet of the car.
Ahead, a bruised rainbow bands the fizz of morning
the storm passed. Yours beginning.
Your foot brakes as I slow for traffic lights and we smile
know your driving days are over,
know your pain will never shift gear.

Do I tell you of my trip? How the Tuscan hills captured me
and I toasted them with blue champagne.
Rome tired me with its no-holds barred traffic
but how could I not love the piazzas, statues,
the language of tortellini.
And Paris, Paris, layered in spring, flaunted love
along the nightgarden banks of the Seine.
Do I tell you all this? But no, it would be churlish
so I keep it to myself.

Our love splintered, days widened, words shortened
and you leapt through a pause in conversation.
The overdrive of family unwrapped strewn
feelings of anger, exposed a gateway of balance.

I notice how hard you focus on the road,
pointing out turns and speed limits,
hands doing their own version of new-age jive.
Do you miss the dancing?
Still feel the rhythm of coloured notes?

Your throat rattles, breath motes dip and fade.
Memory scrabbles for names, what the doctor said yesterday
but you remember you have no photo of our grand-daughter
words spilling, breathless, guilty.   Chasing yourself.
Finding a stranger.

Geraldine Day

The Visit

Runner-Up Poem 2020

He is much slower now.
One fast year and his shirt
buttons resist the fumble of fingers
speech slurs in the corner of his mouth.
Appointments, tablets, therapy
but his feet still take their own path.

She takes the stairs less and less
her hip backstitching the pain to her spine
stacks her day on the bottom tread.
Patterns of pressure curdle in her voice
refuses to imagine a lonely bed.

I shower when instructed, eat breakfast alone
welcome the recycled rattle of milk bottles
the thwack of the daily letter-drop. Outside
a pastel sun dithers behind a skin of cloud
searches for an escape route.

Next door's cat jumps the fence, ignores me,
inspects daises, pansies, a fallen leaf
settles under a rhododendron bush
spies on the dip and glide of butterflies.

Four weeks later, home, jet-lagged, a silent fridge
I rummage for a midnight meal, a can opener
baked beans and Ryvita, hot tea and shelf milk.
No friendly clink of a milkman's visit
but the bathroom's free.

Geraldine Day

June Earle

One Perfect Day

Commended Short Story 2001

Pushing the remaining cornflakes around the bowl, I listened as the rain beat down on the roof. The chimes on the verandah, tossed about in the wind, sounded like a brass band. A twig hit the window, stuck, then slid, pushed by rivulets of water. The kitchen looked like a battlefield. Cups and plates stacked on bench tops defied the laws of gravity while discarded cereal boxes, open jam jars, crumbs galore and scrunched up napkins littered the table. The smell of toast clung to the air with their voices – I could still see them – David and John, grown men squabbling over the strawberry jam. Some things never change. Lightning flashed, lit up the kitchen like a ballroom. In the distant thunder rumbled time to kindle the lounge fire.

"Nanna."

Blue eyes stared at me from a marmite-smeared face. Only five, and already the image of David. One hand held an unfinished crust, the other clutched Toby, once his father's teddy bear.

"Come here, let's clean you up a bit." I gathered him onto my knee and wiped his face.

"Nanna, Toby wants to go to the beach."

I kissed the tip of his nose, "Darling, it is not beach weather – it's cold and wet, the wind is howling." A peal of thunder rattled across the sky. Nicholas looked at the ceiling, jumped off my lap and ran to the French doors.

"Where did the big growl go, Nanna?"

"It's up there somewhere, playing chasey with the clouds."

I filled the sink with hot soapy water and began clear the table. I hated mess. While it was lovely to have the family home, I seemed to be forever; cooking, cleaning, washing, and picking up after them. Last month it had been a wedding, then a birthday. Still, I must not grizzle – that's what mums are for, to come home to – and I would not have it any other way. With the last cup and saucer put away, I stood back to admire my kitchen. "Yes, that would do until the next onslaught."

Hailstones dumped on the roof. I had better see what Nicholas was up to.

Outside the world was grey with patches of green thrashing in the gale. The red shed walls and garden blurred in the rain. Well, tomorrow would be soon enough to survey the damage. My little man needed cheering up.

Nicholas was another David – he loved the outdoors, hated being confined. Poor Nicholas, first the chickenpox, now winter had set in. Seated cuddling Toby, he stared out the window, his little shoulders drooped. Still clad in pajamas, his blond hair needed a brush and one slipper was missing from a foot. He came to me, looked up. "Nanna, will it stop raining? Can we go to the beach?"

His words reminded me of another child looking up at her grandmother, asking the impossible – but grandma had made it happen.

"Nothing is impossible in the land of imagination," she had said. And again, I smelt the fragrance of lavender and heard her cheery laugh. "Yes, if she could do it for her granddaughter, then I shall do it for my grandson," I told Nicholas. He looked puzzled; I tousled his hair.

"Nicholas, with a dash of my magic, you and I are going to the beach."

He jumped up and down, clapping his hands. "We're going to the beach; we're going to the beach." The sound of his feet and clapping hands mingled with the roll of thunder and clatter of rain on the roof.

"We can't go to the real beach because it's far too wet and cold. We will make a pretend beach in the lounge."

"Yippee." Toby soared into the air, pleased with our plan; we skipped around the room.

Soon I had a fire blazing in the grate. Nicholas helped roll up the mats, placing them in a line along the hallway. We shifted pictures, precious ornaments and pushed furniture to one end of the room.

"Okay, Nicholas, what do we need for our beach?"

"Water. Can I swim, Nanna? Please, Nanna?"

"Well, we have to have make-believe water, and I'll take you for a ride in your father's old rubber dinghy. You run upstairs, put on your bathers, sunhat, and tee shirt. I'll be in the garage looking for things to make our beach."

The blue tarpaulin would make great water. Two buckets of white beach sand stood in the corner. "I'm sure the budgie won't mind if I use his sand," I muttered. I could not risk sand spilling onto the carpet. The boys' old wading pool would be just the ticket to prevent that. The straw broom and mop made ideal oars – imagination, that's all you need. After a few trips, our beach started taking shape. Nicholas sat in the sand, filling his red bucket and chatting to Toby.

It hadn't been easy getting the dinghy down from the rafters. It took several prods with a garden rake until it tipped. It bounced off the car bonnet and cannoned into the shelves; stacked contents tumbled. They needed sorting anyway – a job for tomorrow. Somewhere in the garage were several shoeboxes of shells from my craft days. I had intended to cover mirror frames and tissue holders. After some rearranging, I found them – you never know when things will come in handy. For a bit of extra authenticity, I grabbed the crabbing nets.

The storm passed. A faint jingle came from the knotted wind chimes, the rain now constant and heavy. I closed the curtains and turned on the lights. Instant sunshine! Well, almost.

"What do you think of our little beach?"

Nicholas's irresistible smile tugged at my heart. He jumped up and down; gave an excited yell.

"Nanna, can we have a tiger?"

"A tiger on the beach?"

"Yes, tigers swim. I saw them on television."

Well, I could not dispute that. Where does one get a tiger? Thinking cap on. I moved to the study and removed the enormous tiger picture from the wall. My old dolly, reclining amongst the cushions on the sofa, should make a perfect siren of the sea. I removed her bonnet and dress. Her long dark locks fell over her shoulders and back. Perfect. What I needed now was one of my husband's socks pulled up over her legs, and my pearl necklace. A rock. I needed a rock. The galvanized tub on the verandah! This was fun; I missed the closeness, the sharing that goes when children grow into adults. That's why God gave us grandchildren.

When I returned to our beach, Nicholas had placed my footstool in the dinghy. He sat on his yellow plastic chair with Toby on his lap.

"You can sit here, Nanna." He patted the stool behind him. Leaning the tiger portrait against the lounge chair did not give me the effect I wanted. I braved the outdoors, dragged in two potted palms from my drenched porch, left puddles in the hall, which I tried to ignore. Between the leafy fronds, the tiger looked at our beach, ready for a swim.

"Is he going to eat us, Nanna?"

"No, we're safe with this one. Now I'll put the beach umbrella up, and we can have our lunch under there."

"I want cheese and tomato sandwiches, one brown bread and one white one, and I'll have raspberry cordial in my Donald Duck mug. Please, Nanna." He continued to bury Toby in the sand. Nanna needed a cup of tea.

"Nanna, Toby wants a pickled onion."

"We mustn't forget Toby –a pickled onion for ted is on the list. I'll put beach music on and we'll have a sail in the dinghy."

"It's not a dinghy."

"It's not? Let me guess, it's a submarine."

"Don't be silly, Nanna – it's a pirate ship."

"Right, we'll sail away in a pirate ship. I'll get my hat." I left the room to find last summer's hat.

"Nanna! Nanna!"

Running back to the lounge, I feared the worst. He stood in his pirate ship with a concerned look on his face.

"What is it? What's wrong?"

"Mum always puts sun cream on me – she'll be mad if I get burnt."

"Sun cream … right." Another trip up to the outer limits.

"Nanna."

Halted once again halfway up the stairs, I called to him. "What now?"

"I haven't got a beach towel. I want the one with the dolphins on it, please."

"Your dolphin towel and the striped one for me – how could I forget towels?" The staircase seemed steeper. This imagination business was exhausting.

We sailed to Africa. Toby hid beneath the towel when the

lions came. Captain Nicholas saved the day, turned the ship about. Together we heaved on the sails, left Africa far behind and sailed to India for lunch. On the way, we tackled sharks and gigantic waves, caught crabs in calm waters. Nicholas waved to a beautiful mermaid who coaxed him with tales of buried treasure. Later, we sat beneath the beach umbrella, listening to the waves and caw of fat seagulls on my relaxation tape.

Nicholas snuggled into me. "This has been the bestest day of my life, Nanna."

I pulled him close and cradled his head in my lap.

"I love you, Nanna." The long lashes fluttered and closed. I kissed my fingers and pressed them to his rosy cheek.

June Earle

Southern Exposure

Highly Commended Article 2006

West Cape Howe National Park,
where sea cliff climbers hang out over the ocean
and hang-gliders rival birds of the air.

Western Australia's most southerly point is the granite fortress of West Cape Howe. High above turbulent seas, daring cliff climbers urged on by squawking gulls, scale walls of glistening grey. Below, swells rise in slow motion, gain lightning momentum and smash into rocks, reducing extraordinary waves to froth and spray. On prevailing summer easterlies, hang-gliders soar with birds; para-sailors bob under canopies of coloured silk above an ocean of the deepest cobalt blue.

West Cape Howe comprises 3,517 hectares of National Parkland. Rich in wildlife, birds, and wildflowers, exceptional cliffs plunge into wide sandy bays of the twenty-three kilometres of dramatic granite and limestone coastline. Here remote has nothing to do with television townies come to experience adventure and a guaranteed adrenaline rush.

George Endacott, a retired English vet with extensive wilderness driving experience, runs 'Little River Four Wheel Drive Tours' to West Cape Howe out of Denmark. A naturalist speech sprinkled with Aussie slang, he is tail-made for the tourist.

The day tour begins early. The karri, having shed their bark in late summer, show long trunks of orange and grey; masses of green leaves drip with dew. We break from the forest, lose the bitumen and skid on phantom tracks, nose into clutching fronds of fragrant peppermint bushes. Suburbia disappears from the mind as eyes adjust to the diverse, unfamiliar landscape.

Our vehicle bounces along lengths of black rubber conveyor belting, thwacks timber palettes snaking through thickets of heath and banksia. Progress is slow, rewarded with time to take it in. Land gives way to sky as we tilt. Sand squeals from determined wheels as George coaxes the Landrover into gear and braces his hands on the steering wheel. It walks down a steep rocky grade.

"CRIPES, HOLY COW, can we do that again?" George laughs. It's a common reaction.

An hour in a Landrover is equal to a week's workout at the gym. If you're not blessed with long legs alighting from a Landrover is tricky. A half slide/half fall approach is best, followed by a helping hand on the rear to shove you back. A stretch and walk along Shelley beach dotted with jigsaw jetties and makeshift fishing huts is most welcomed.

During morning tea, we spy sea eagles diving for fish. George points to places of interest; Lowlands beach Golden Gate beach (popular with surfers) and Cosy Corner, where boat building once thrived and sealers and whalers stalked the sea.

The four-wheel-drive approaches a large stumpy root holding its ground. George does an 'upsy daisy'; runs the wheels over one side to give the vehicle the greatest clearance. We enter a patch of bonsai shrubs dwarfed by nature's hedge-cutters – sharp salted winds. Vegetation, clumps of bleached grass sprout between lichen-patched boulders. In the valley, alive and mysterious twisted trunks buckled by the elements transports us to a unique world.

George reels off plant names (scientific and common). A suspicious wallaby watches us with interest. Rabbits sun themselves in sculptured rock gardens of heath geranium where red petals smile, tempting bees. It poises the air like a half-open bud.

At Dunsky Point, chairs and table appear. Lunch is a salad affair: a choice of cheeses, bread rolls and meat washed down with a good cup of tea, coffee, or water. We yarn, soak in the atmosphere. A skink joins us, takes a leaf of lettuce and scurries away. George relates the tale of the dead cow that did not stay buried; curious Kangaroos hang around to hear the end of the tale. Disturbed by the laughter, they bound into a copse of Albany woolly bush.

Via Torbay and the old Denmark Road, the Landrover heads for home, farewelled by a myriad of crowded birdsong in Karri oak and tea tree. Startled straw-necks ibis churn the surface of a pond and batter the air, striving for height. We spot the first sign of civilization: a fence. Our tour winds up with wine tasting at Tingle-Wood Wines in the Southern Dales of Denmark.

Goodbye? Perish the thought! West Cape Howe will call us back for the splendours of spring and migration of whales; or to watch the daring seek thrills above the waves.

June Earle

Margaret Ferrell

Snowspheres

Commended Short Story 1992

'There's a certain slant of light,
Winter afternoons – '

The woman stands in the dark at the hotel window, watching snowflakes float lazily to the road already white. London traffic is quieter, as if muffled by some gigantic continental quilt. She remembers the brilliance of Sydney left behind; like comparing colour photos with black and white.

Sadness reclaims her. But perhaps this is why I'm here again, she thinks. Winter is necessary. I have to go through the darkness to get to the light. But I can reconstruct my life. As a child, I made my own world – a long time ago.

She gazes through the glass into the lamp-lit scene beneath, into another world.

***

With two hands encompassing the cool weight of the glass orb, Jane crossed the room to the window to hold the sphere nearer to the pale light filtering in from outdoors. Then she dropped on to the carpet, placing the snowsphere where she could see into it. She studied the houses inside; a cluster of them with roofs of red and brown.

Up on the hill stood a church with a tall spire and stained-glass windows of red, blue and green. Pine trees grew near the church on the hillside. The village green had a stream running through it and there was a tiny park with a clump of holly bushes. The village shop and post office stood at the end of a winding lane, near a weeping willow tree. All the people were inside their homes. But Jane knew what she had to do now. She always saved up this pleasure.

***

She lifted the heavy glass sphere, trying not to make any sudden movement. Grandmother once remarked that, for a seven-year-old, Jane had good control. Then she shook the snowsphere hard, her eyes never leaving the scene.

Thick flakes of snow suddenly filled the sky, drifting down on to the village, falling, falling and whirling through the air. Soon, snow lay deep over the village.

Jane watched and smiled as the air cleared to show a white landscape. She had made winter begin.

***

Jane wondered about the people in the village. Only occasionally had she seen any of them. They stayed indoors most of the time. Just now and then, by a particular movement of the sphere, she was able to see an inhabitant.

Once, as the flakes danced, she had seen an old man. He was bent and frail, and reminded her of her grandfather. She had just been able to make him out in the myriad of white as she gazed, mesmerised, into the fragile world she held in her hands. The landscape was perfect in whiteness touched by the sun. She saw the old man hold back the curtain to see the sun sparkling on snow.

She cradled the sphere now. She moved her hands up and down, up and down, finishing by holding the glass ball level with her eyes.

Snowflakes fell gently, like duck-down looking for a place to settle. She could see through the flakes to the house closest to the church. The door had opened. The old man beckoned.

'For the listener who listens in the snow,
And, nothing himself, beholds
Nothing that is not there and the nothing that is.'

***

The snowsphere had been in Jane's hands so long that it felt warm. That feeling made her think of the day she met the boy who lived in the house nearest to the post office. He had told her he was nine. The sun shone, coming out from behind clouds, surprisingly warm. It was as if Autumn held a cloak of scarlet, gold and brown to ward off Winter's grey a little longer.

She had walked down the lane where hedgerows, thick with berries, sprawled on either side. The air had been still that afternoon, heavy with the damp smell of fallen leaves. Through gaps in the hedge she could see cows, contentment curved around their forms as they rested in the shade.

The road wound past the old barn, where a weeping willow barred the corner leading to the brown-roofed house. It was then that the cascade of leaves was lifted aside by the boy. She thought of him always as the brown boy because of his hair, eyes, acorn-coloured skin.

It was instant friendship. They talked, and he led her to his home, a whitewashed cottage. The door stood open. His mother held out her hand to Jane, guiding her past the grandfather clock at the foot of the spiral staircase.

When she left the cottage, the weather had changed. A few flakes of snow fluttered in the air like hesitant birds. As they touched the ground, they vanished into uncertainty.

Jane looked into the sphere. She made a small movement, and a few flakes fell, melting as they touched the ground.

***

Later, left untouched, the snowsphere had turned cold. Jane watched for the signs of life she recognised within its self-reflecting world. The village stayed quiet. Nothing moved.

She lifted the snowsphere in two hands and, holding it in front of her, she did a little dance around the room, alternating her dance steps with a hop and a jump. Then she whirled herself around, imagining herself a ballerina.

Now she held the snowsphere close. She dropped on to a footstool. Balancing the base of the snowsphere on her thumbs, her fingers supporting the sides, she pressed it against her forehead so that she was gazing into the glass world.

Snow fell in large, slow flakes. Snowflakes began to weave a thick pattern of laciness. A tide of whiteness flowed over the village. All the light was in the snow, moving like soundless surf.

Jane continued to look into the globe, waiting, feeling the silence so alive. Who's coming? she wondered.

Slowly, slowly, the snowstorm lessened. Colours streamed across her vision – pink, green, orange, blue, red, purple: a rainbow broken loose, more like the Aurora Borealis ribboning the sky. She could see between the flakes now, to the village. The snow had almost stopped as a shaft of sunlight fell on the village church. Jane stared. Now she could see the reason for the colours.

The stained-glass windows were lit from inside. The church door stood open and the village people, clad in bright winter woollens, were making their way into the building.

Jane followed them, down the aisle, towards the crib. There was the brown boy, and the old man. They held out their hands in welcome. The chill of the air had turned to freshness. The tide of snow light had streamed into the church bringing new life, tangible, something perfect that she wanted to hold. She closed her eyes, trying to capture the moment.

Jane opened her eyes and looked into the world in front of her. She smiled as she saw it just as she wished it to be.

***

A long time afterwards, Jane looked into the snowsphere. She saw a thin covering of snow. A robin hopped from the cover of a holly bush, its red breast a spot of colour in the whiteness of the grass. But the snow was more fragile now because the robin's imprints had broken the surface. In the old man's garden, clusters of snowdrops showed all of their height, no longer struggling to keep their heads above snow.

Her hands were warm on the orb of glass. A section of snow slid off one of the red roofs. Melting snow dripped from the lych-gate below the church, and a patch of green appeared in the brown boy's garden where the sun had touched the snow.

Winter was being nudged out of the way. Jane continued to watch until the white landscape turned to green.

***

The woman's thoughts return to the hotel room. She moves to turn up the heating and switches on a lamp. She turns away from the scene through the glass.

Rob used to arrange everything, including her publicity tours. Six months ago, friends said: 'Time will heal. You'll get over it.' Then they'd driven off through the crematorium gates into the humid heat of Sydney.

And I haven't been able to write; not a word, since that day, she recalled. I've been in the grip of winter.

A muted Big Ben strikes midnight, reminding her she's been lost, somewhere else for hours. Then she becomes aware of the perfume of hyacinths. She turns to trace the fragrance.

There, on the dressing-table, are six blooms. She finds herself smiling. The telephone is close at hand. It's morning tea-time in Sydney, a good time to catch Sue.

'Sue, it's Mum. Yes, it's snowing here – magic because there's no traffic in this street and the snow hasn't been spoiled yet. Yes, I'm all right. I'm beginning to feel again. I'm daring to hope. And I'm going to visit my publisher tomorrow. I'll walk there through the snow. And yesterday I saw daffodils in the park opposite, ready to burst open.'

Margaret Ferrell

The quotes are from the writings of:
Emily Dickinson (Poem 258)
Wallace Stevens (/The Snow Man)

(An adaptation of this story was published in The Silver Collection 2007 SWWWA

Sonnet

Commended Poetry 1996

When I reflect on how our love has grown
To make me feel both tenderness and fear –
Fear you will yearn the cherishing you've known
When time removes me; I must make you hear.
A flowering plant is there only to please
For some short time; it fades, we know, and falls
To leave a space; deprived, one always sees
The colour missing, empty scene; it palls.
But, still contained, deep in the earth grow roots
Which seem to die only when out of view.
As scent of water draws forth budding shoots,
So memories refreshed bring peace to you.
Beyond the space of future, and of past,
Don't ache for me, I know our love will last.

Margaret Ferrell

Published in *Perceptions:* Poems by Margaret Ferrell 2000.

Other People

Commended Short Story 1998

Elfreda smiled. 'Welcome to our home. We are very pleased to see you both.'

Why is she so tense? thought Marion. To their left hung a Flemish tapestry. Its colours glowed above a chest where a pewter tankard spilled over with the blue of leschenaultia. Beyond lay a sitting-room with flowers, paintings, a sculpture of a young boy and carved furniture. A wall covered in books held German texts, English classics and Australian history.

'Are they not beautiful? We have these to improve our English,' said Elfreda. Gregor brought wine. 'We have kept this bottle for ten years. It is our pleasure that you share it with us this evening.'

Elfreda carried a tray of canapés to the inlaid coffee table. The two couples, seated on elegant period furniture, faced each other. Marion marvelled that the colours of wine, caviar, cream cheese and cucumber complemented the gleaming darkness of the table.

A pedestal candelabra close to Elfreda highlighted the paleness of her skin, shone on the silver in her hair, making Marion think of a Dresden figurine.

When she admired the china, Elfreda said, 'I must show you my Rosenthal.' She brought out a deceptively simple white bowl rimmed in gold.

As she returned it to the cabinet, Caspar ran into the room.

'Here are your dolls, my darleeng,' and she led the Pekinese to the soft toys propped up against a walnut cabinet.

***

Next morning, Marion and James talked. 'They're different, you can say that about them.'

'I'd call them strange,' said Marion.

James wore his pondering look. She waited, knowing he'd take up the conversation in his own time.

'Remember when I told you about that patient of mine, the one who had blocked out her memories of the war? She refused to talk about her experiences. Well, Elfreda reminds me of her.'

'Gregor told you they'd been in South Africa for years.'

'Mm, he did say that, but there was more he wanted to tell me, I'm sure.'

'Listen, that's the phone.' James heard a gasp, then silence. 'But why?' he heard her say.

***

'Gregor's gone.'

'What do you mean, gone?'

'He's disappeared. Gregor just said – it was time.' Marion hurried on, 'I know, I know. It all sounds so cryptic. I just had to listen to Elfreda. I've said I'll go round.' James pursed his lips. 'Doesn't she have any other friends?'

'Apparently not, and there's something else. Gregor's taken Caspar with him.'

'Well, now I do see the problem. That spoiled little pooch. Which one is Elfreda really grieving for?'

'You're being unfair, James. See you later.'

Their street lay five minutes away. Marion needed that time

to think about Elfreda and Gregor.

Both so thin, strained, they never stopped talking, at least Elfreda didn't. Gregor's silences had been palpable. And the photograph of children on the side table, grandchildren perhaps? Then the phone call during the evening. Gregor answered in monosyllables, proffering nothing. When he returned to his chair they looked uneasy. I'm probably imagining things, Marion thought. Maybe there's a simple explanation.

Elfreda didn't respond to the doorbell immediately. When she appeared, her eyes were shadowed grey circles. 'Thank you for coming,' she whispered. At the same time, Marion saw Elfreda's hand trembling as she fumbled with the door knob.

'What am I going to do? I can't drive far on my own. Gregor takes me everywhere. He didn't think ... he knew it would come ... but we hadn't planned yet for ...' Marion's thoughts raced. Elfreda's concern was not, then, for Gregor so much as for herself.

'Elfreda, let's sit down and you can tell me what's wrong, and what I can do to help.' Marion gently guided her to the settee and sat opposite.

'They called last night. Bertold wants Gregor there. Gregor has to stay with them for a while.'

'What do you mean, Elfreda? Where is Gregor going to stay?'

Elfreda looked up from studying her fingers. She shook her head.

'Has Gregor gone to help a friend? I thought you said he had disappeared.'

'I said he *will* disappear. It is my English. I do not always make you to understand.'

'I don't understand, Elfreda.'

'Then I will explain. I have to tell someone. I don't make

friends easily. Perhaps I can tell you. But when I do, you may want to see me not again.'

'Tell me, and let me decide that,' said Marion.

'You see the lovely things we have here. I showed them to you when you came with James. I like to touch them, to take care of them. I love fine pieces. They make up for ... other things.

'After the war, in Germany, we lost everything. I was still a child. My mother and I lived with box furniture. But we were lucky. I grew up with a mother. Some didn't.

'When I was twenty, I met Gregor. He is ten years older. He wouldn't tell me what had happened to him in the war. He said it was too painful ... said we must change our name so that he could start again. I agreed.'

Marion noticed Elfreda's eyes had become moist. 'Shall I make some coffee, or tea? Would you like that?'

'You are so kind. Thank you.'

By the time Marion had coffee ready, Elfreda was composed again.

'Our lives were good. Gregor trained in electronics. We had a son, later a daughter. She did not live long ... some strange infection ... all a long time ago. But I still remember the day we buried our baby. We helped each other, Gregor and I. We still had Hans.

'Everything changed the day Bertold came to visit Gregor. By then we were living in Munich. They were together for three hours. When Bertold left, Gregor said we must leave Munich, move from Germany. I was – what do you say – stunned?' Marion nodded.

'Why, why, I kept asking? Gregor had to tell me then ... Bertold and Gregor were in the war together. They both had official positions at one of the camps; organisational work, Gregor called it.

Where was this camp? I asked. Since he told me, life has never been the same. I had lived for years without knowing that my husband had been one of the youngest in charge at Buchenwald.'

Elfreda's voice faltered. Marion listened in horror mixed with pity. How did they live with this knowledge?

'Where does Bertold come into this?'

Elfreda looked up. 'He is the one who warns Gregor when it is time to move on. That day in Munich, he planned for us to go to South Africa. We stayed there eight years, but Hans did not choose to come with us. He was studying at University. We could not force him.

'Those who search for war criminals never give up. Word came that we must leave South Africa. We arrived here, and now after ten years, it is time to move again. I hope Gregor will be safe. He has made arrangements for me.'

'He will send for you?' asked Marion.

'No, not this time, no, we must be apart.'

'Why, and why has he taken Caspar?'

lfreda's eyes filled. 'Gregor knows I cannot much longer look after Caspar. Two months I have.'

'Two months for what?'

'The doctor told us it cannot be longer.'

Marion stretched out her hand to grasp Elfreda's. 'But why is Gregor leaving you at such a time? Surely it is better to be together.'

'No, we have talked in the last year when the signs were bad for Gregor. He lives with his guilt every day. Trial and prison; I do not want it to end like that for him. My time is soon. The plans are made.'

Suddenly she stared at Marion. 'You people in Australia ... you don't know about it. Our son, Hans, is part of the neo-Nazi movement. It makes everything worse for Gregor ... the involvement ... Bertold knows what is going on. But now, you are involved too, are you not?'

Marion felt chilled as if icy fingers held her. What was she to do with this new knowledge?

'I'll come back, help you with shopping or anything else you need.'

As she walked home, she could only think of the many *objets d'art* that surrounded Elfreda. Bizarre, she mused, that in the midst of such a tragic story, my thoughts should centre on these. We don't really know other people and their lives. Of what use are possessions? Something to focus on, I suppose.

***

'Well, you've taken your time!' said James, as Marion walked in. 'I expect you've been hearing all about Caspar's exploits. Why has Gregor run off?'

Marion didn't answer. After a long silence, she said, 'James, you and I have decisions to make.'

Margaret Ferrell

Tommy and the Rainbow

Commended Short Story 2001

(A story to be read to young children)

Tommy darted out to the kindergarten gate where Mum waited, and tossed his ball high in the air. Then he saw the rainbow, a magic thing of red, orange, yellow, green, blue, indigo and violet.

Rainbows made him think of Joseph's coat of many colours in the book Miss Peters read to them. Rainbows made him think of his best marble and the curtains in Auntie Kate's bedroom. Rainbows are special, he thought.

'I know all the colours in the rainbow,' he told his Mum. 'Miss Peters sings the song to us and I can sing it too. Miss Peters says it's an old song, but I like it.'

'What's the song called, Tommy?' asked Mum.

'I can sing a rainbow, sing a rainbow, sing a rainbow too,' sang Tommy.

Tommy wanted to ride on the rainbow. Every time he saw one he thought, I wonder what's at the end of it? He knew if he did get a ride on the rainbow he'd have to be quick; they disappeared so fast.

In bed early that night, the curtains left open so he could see the sky, Tommy thought about the rainbow. The daylight wasn't yet gone. It had been a day of sunshine and showers and now, there was the rainbow again, a longer one this time.

Tommy stared and stared, wishing it not to go away before

he got a ride. As he watched, the rainbow became brighter and brighter and … who was this on the window-sill?

A tiny man stood there, no bigger than Tommy's thumb, with a pointed head and a coat that changed colour all the time. Tommy gazed at him.

The little man's eyes twinkled and he cocked his head to one side. Tommy's eyes were growing bigger every moment. 'Who are you?' he asked.

'I'm Indigo, the Rainbow Man. I paint the rainbows in the sky. You wanted a ride on the rainbow, Tommy.

'Come, come, come with me,
On the rainbow we will ride,
Come, come, no time to waste,
Rainbows melt away in space.'

The tiny man held out his hand and while Tommy was wondering how they were going to manage such a big step on to the rainbow, Indigo said, 'Close your eyes, tightly, Tommy.'

Tommy did as he was told.

Then Indigo said, 'You can look now.'

Tommy opened his eyes to find something like a river of gold stretching in front of his window and reaching out, right out to the rainbow.

'Fasten on the magic skates, Tommy,' said Indigo. He rubbed his hands together and there appeared a shining, sparkling pair of skates which Tommy fastened on in a flash.

'Right, Tommy, let's go, 'whispered Indigo. 'We have no time to waste.'

On to the golden path sped Tommy, Indigo leading the way. In no time at all, they had reached the rainbow. Tommy found, to his surprise, that high, rainbow-coloured gates barred the way. But Indigo rubbed his hands together once more and said,

'Open, rainbow gates, open wide,
Tommy's come to have a ride.'

The gates opened wide and through went Tommy.

'Now,' said Indigo, 'take off the magic skates and leave them here for your journey home.'

Then Tommy noticed that a white horse, more beautiful than any he had ever seen, had suddenly appeared. But by now Tommy was no longer surprised by anything Indigo could do. Indigo rubbed his hands together and whispered so softly that Tommy almost didn't hear it –

'Violet, indigo, red, yellow, blue,
Show Tommy what you can do.
Green and orange,
Blue, yellow, red,
Ride the rainbow
On golden thread.'

Before he could say anything, Tommy found himself on the white horse holding the reins of golden thread with Indigo perched on his shoulder.

They were off, and it felt like floating instead of riding. Up and away they went, into a fantastic and gorgeous land. There were blue and violet trees and flowers of every colour, waterfalls of green and pink and orange.

Tommy could make the white horse slow down by pulling on the golden reins. He pulled now and the white horse seemed to know that Tommy wanted to enter the strange forest just ahead of them. Into the rainbow forest they rode and the white horse stopped.

Indigo said softly, 'Oh dear, I thought we'd be safe today but the Giant Nimbus lives here and has heard us. Hold on tightly, Tommy. He's going to chase us.'

Now they were going like the wind, faster, faster, faster through the rainbow forest, past trees and plants and flowers of every colour. Behind them, they could hear Nimbus roaring and thundering.

'If the Giant Sol is around, he'll help us,' cried Indigo.

'I wish he would,' gasped Tommy. Nimbus was gaining on them. They could hear his heavy footsteps getting nearer and nearer, and the colours of the rainbow were paler now.

But just when Tommy thought Nimbus was sure to catch them, Indigo cried,

'It's Sol, he's coming. I can feel his warmth, and look, Tommy, the colours of the rainbow are brighter again.'

They could hear Nimbus growling and grumbling in the distance because he knew he was beaten.

The white horse was reaching the end of the rainbow now. 'This is where I live with all my helpers,' said Indigo. 'It's almost time for this rainbow to disappear and I have to get my colours ready for the next one.'

Tommy gazed in amazement as he looked into a golden cave. There were pots and pots of every colour. 'I wish I could help you,' sighed Tommy.

'You can,' said Indigo. 'Here's a brush. I'll show you what to do. We'll paint the next rainbow.'

So Tommy dipped in his brush. He painted and dipped, he splashed and dipped and smoothed the colours until Indigo said, 'Time to go, Tommy, if you're to get back safely before this rainbow disappears. And remember, don't tell what you've seen. It's our secret.'

The white horse took Tommy back to where he'd left the magic skates and he fastened them once more. Down the gleaming golden path he swished in the time it takes to blink an eye. But then he found himself dropping, dropping, dropping down from the sky.

'Don't let me fall, Indigo, don't let me fall,' cried Tommy. He heard a voice say,

'Are you awake, Tommy? You've had a long sleep and it's time to get up. This is a kindy day.'

It was Mum's voice, not Indigo's. Tommy looked to the window. Indigo had disappeared. He had been there, though. They'd been on the rainbow together. Tommy thought about where he'd been and what he'd seen. What a great adventure I've had, he thought.

He opened his mouth to start telling Mum all about it and then he remembered. It was a secret. Nobody must know. Then maybe, just maybe, indigo would come back for him another night.

Margaret Ferrell

Pat Fletcher

Nightfall

Winning Short Story 1989

'There are bats in China,' he said, surveying me through the prongs of his fork.

I was watching the changing spectrum of colours in his whisky tumbler as the stormy weather of the late afternoon cleared. A shaft of sunlight, piercing the fine mist of a shower's end, caught in the planes of the crystal. Standing on its onyx coaster, the glass seemed suspended, like a pulsing star in an inky sky. It was the one brilliant object in the darkening room, except, I thought as I looked at him, for the glint in his watery blue eyes.

Twenty years before, when I first met him, he was a dominant presence in any room. Tall and powerful, confident, often overbearing, he commanded attention in those days. People clustered around him to hang on his words, to hear his stories. But, in time, as his mind started to wander, so did their attention, and his eager audience found other wits to entertain them.

Diverting he still was, and I wondered what had triggered his remark. The key lay in the cue word, or in his expression. Sometimes I won these little games, but mostly he triumphed by confusing me with a red herring, like a child asking a riddle to which there is no answer.

He watched me, but in the gloom I couldn't tell whether the look was coaxing or mischievous. The wrong reply could equally produce a hurt silence, an angry retort, or a shout of glee.

I was usually permitted a few minutes to reply to his unexpected comments, and as I pondered I let my gaze wander around the vast room.

Antique showcases lined the walls and vied for space with a conglomeration of furniture. He had ivory carvings, some given, some commissioned, together with wooden artefacts and bizarre objects, like bones and teeth and things I preferred not to look at. There were stones from all over the world, and coins, worthless souvenirs alongside a pink jade china-tea set, and a tiny elephant cut from an emerald. From the walls hung trophies and clocks, and, at the far end, a full-length portrait of his late wife guarded the treasures.

Once they were lovingly cleaned and polished. Now they gathered dust because no one cared anymore.

He was old, and tired, and he felt himself abandoned.

He had summoned me, as he sometimes did, to sit with him while he ate his evening meal. I'm not sure why I submitted to his demands. I had my own chores and interests next door. Perhaps I felt sorry for him. No, his imperious manner had brought him the loneliness he deserved. I respected him for accepting his lot without complaint. I was intrigued at the intellect that took him to millionaire status and back thrice in a lifetime. I admired the spirit that had explored this earth from pole to pole, its heights and depths.

The shell of a man that sat at the head of the long mahogany table was once a giant, and there were more tales to tell than he had time for.

The once sapphire eyes peered at me expectantly.

I made the cautious move, repeating the word without

emphasis. 'Bats,' I said.

A shadow of disappointment crossed his face, but then he jerked his head forward eagerly.

'Millions of them,' he said. He had checked me and it was my turn again.

His name was Hudson Knight, a noble name for a remarkable person. He claimed to be the illegitimate son of an English aristocrat, and there was no one left to deny it.

In the copper glow, the bald dome of his head, encircled by a horseshoe of duckling feathers, was a full moon rising from a fermented ocean. Not quite bald. Where the hairline used to be, three single hairs stood straight up, waving gently like seaweed caught in a drift. It was a wide head, with a strong forehead, far too big now for the rest of the face which was thin and drawn. The skin, amazingly smooth for one so ancient, cleaved to the prominent cheekbones and jaw, so that etched against the dark background, he appeared to have no cheeks at all. His eyebrows, an unbroken tangle of barbed wire, and his proud Roman nose, protected eyes sunken with age.

He gave a couple of sharp raps on the table with his forefinger, a sign of impatience which gave me my clue. He wanted an argument. I knew nothing about China or bats, and he waited for my comment on either. It was dark now and he couldn't see my reaction, so I let him wait.

He rapped again irritably, and reached for the brass bell that was always by his side.

The resonance of it faded until only the memory remained and I heard the clink of ice as he took a sip from his glass.

A door opened at the end of the room, the great chandelier over the table came to life, and in limped a mirror image of himself. A polite greeting to me, and Jacob stood humbly. His bearing was that of the faithful retainer, but I knew these two had shared a lifetime of adventure, adversity and affluence, and were like brothers. They might have been twins, even to the swollen arthritic knees, except that one was positive and one was negative.

'I wanted only light, Jacob,' said Hudson Knight. The other shuffled out, and I could delay no longer. His anticipation was palpable.

'And pandas too,' I said.

He glared at me for a moment, then the eyebrows descended, his thin mouth split, revealing toothless gums, and he thumped the table and cackled.

'Checkmate!' he said. 'Go tend your family, my girl. I'll see you tomorrow.'

Pat Fletcher

Isolation

Commended Poem 2005

He moves darkly through his days,
sees nothing good in anyone.
Curtains closed, locks secure,
he huddles in his chosen gaol,
prisoner of the proofs of love
that he sought,
bought.

Gifts to bind her,
a constant reminder
of his desire
to chain her, change her
to a passive replica
of his ego's projection.
Created for admiration,
manipulation.

Until
discerning the game,
with rules only for her,
she turned, challenged;
met retribution
that scorched her wellspring,
forged a cylinder
bold and red,
cold and dead.

Enraged he roared:
'Then die or go away'.
And she went,
not to die, but to live,
leaving him
to flounder in his isolation,
spitting vengeance,
malevolence.

He clings to his possessions,
victim of the web he wove,
the love he craved
choked by his obsessions.
Solitary phantom
in a hollow opera -
estranged,
deranged.

Pat Fletcher

Published – Allsorts KWC poetry anthology - 2019

Natural, Unnatural and Supernatural

Highly Commended Article 2018

The house perched on the crest of a slope, a guardian presiding over its domain. It gazed benignly down at the myriad saplings which, in time, would become a forest that screened it from the thunder and pollution of a freeway. Its diamond-pane windows collected the sun's early morning rays, transforming the house into a golden beacon shining above a pristine landscape.

From those windows we observed the passage of that freeway heading northwards, contraction of the wetland through landfill, ponies in spiders practising for the Trots, men and tractors tilling and sowing.

We saw the seasons change. In forty-degrees, no careless spark was needed for the peat to ignite spontaneously. A wisp of smoke in the reeds at midday became a roaring blaze by mid-afternoon. With no way for fire brigades to reach the flames, we could only hope that the wind would not turn, drenching us with thick pungent smoke and paper-ash.

On its hillock, the house was safe from nature's forces. Not necessarily from man's. Winter's flight path took aeroplanes to and fro over the house. Most flew high, some resoundingly low, one terrifyingly so. It headed straight for the house, growing closer, larger. Closer, no higher. And strangely, no noise. Across the swamp it came, as we wondered how it stayed aloft and when the pilot would pull out. No time, now, to race downstairs to safety. No safety anyway, if the plane plunged into the house. I screwed shut my eyes, heard the roar, and opened them, to see the underside pass over like special effects on film of a starship moving overhead.

In daylight, most sensations were visual. At night our senses switched between visual and aural. Below, devoid of colour and still dewy from evening watering, young foliage blinked reflections to the stars and moon.

At middle distance, the swamp was a black expanse from which noises of the night drew visions in our minds of clandestine pursuits. Screeches, howls, ducks driven to squawking flight by a sudden report - all heard but never seen - contributed to the mystery of the night. In winter, frogs in harmony called to their mates with melodious 'boings', sounding like an oriental orchestra without tympany.

Beyond the swamp, the sparse scattering of pale streetlamps led into a view of suburban glitter, on to the distant southern horizon where we could just discern one red and one blue light on the tallest of the city's buildings.

Sometimes mist or fog blotted out these views, the only sign of civilisation our driveway lamp, casting opaquely against a wall of moisture. On one occasion there was not even that. So thick was the fog that with no house lights to bounce reflection, and even the whispers of the night deadened to total silence, it was as if the world had come to an end and only we remained.

Then, unexpectedly, we would happen upon a rare occasion of stunning beauty. One night, through the bedroom window, above the darkened terrain, an orange glow extending in a huge arc. Mindful of wars and of spaceships, we stood transfixed and watched as the saffron edge of the full moon appeared. Rapidly, it rose, its roundness swelling, until the outer edges were as wide as the window. We moved forward. Still, it grew, and we watched until the entire gigantic orb became visible, transforming the eastern sky into golden sunlight-bright. Never before and never since have we witnessed a more splendid moonrise.

No moon shone on the night of our most eerie experience. After a day filled with storms, we woke to a strange silence, broken by intermittent cracks like someone chopping sticks. We twitched aside the curtain and saw, on the other side of the swamp, a flash of green light, then another and another, like camera flashes in a dark stadium. There followed three reports. A pause, a flash of green, an explosion. Four more. An interval. Another three. For a while we watched, imagining fireworks, guns, missile testing. But fireworks are multi-coloured, guns shoot yellow, missiles leave trails. And then - a book remembered, read in final year at school. The Day of the Triffids by John Wyndham. We closed the curtains, and hauled the blankets over our heads.

The house is now concealed in its forest, no longer lord of the plantation. If the sun reaches its windows, the vision is not for others' eyes. Close by, medium density housing eats at the edges of the once rural area. Developers lurk, awaiting official sanction to buy, clear, subdivide. The house will go, to make way for lesser dwellings that will never stand sentinel or play the morning sun in their windows.

Pat Fletcher

Marlene Fulcher

In The Stillness

Commended Poem 2008

Mt Ainslie
Australian War Memorial
close now, but still too far away.
Every time I read one of the post cards
From Somewhere in France, the feeling grew.
The ink fades but you become more real.
The knowing of you grand-dad
comes from between the lines.
I need to place a scarlet poppy
on the honour roll,
next to your name.
One foot on the bottom step - main entrance
commemorative pool, eternal flame
my heart beats faster.
Above white walls,
arches frame the Roll of Honour.
I place the poppy, take photos,
finger your name, fight back tears.
In the stillness I recall your words.
September 19th, 1917.
'I know you must be lonely,

I can tell you I am
and will be glad
when I can get home with you again.
Now Dear I will close, our big day is tomorrow.
Love to all .... kisses for dear little Edie and Dulcie
not forgetting your Dear self.
I am always your own loving hubby William
You express pleasure, relief almost,
at receiving three letters from your beloved
before going into battle
mention having written
a long letter the day before.
Did you know somehow
A soldier pipes the last post
I stand tall –
Regret we never met.

Marlene Fulcher

Sestina of a Letter Home – 1917

Commended Poem 2011

I write to you from war-torn France, dear Dad
assure both you and Mum that I am safe.
So few remain; the wounded shipped back home,
the fallen left to help wild flowers grow.
We hear the shells exploding night and day,
and disillusioned men, who fight for peace,

their freedom, country, pray this hour for peace
to not relive the horror, pain. Dear Dad
I pray this war ends soon, await the day
our brave Australians are once more safe,
released from fear and sadness, free to grow
beside their sweethearts, loved ones left at home

Here only old folk stay, defend their home.
I'm sure this land is beautiful in peace
when fields, unfenced, turn green as grasses grow
with spring and trees bear fruit. But sadly Dad
the Germans torch those trees. It keeps them safe, delays our
Aussie troops at least a day.

These people labour long and hard each day,
to cultivate the soil, protect their home
and farmlands knowing they are far from safe.
Equipment here is out of date, so peace
won't bring relief from heavy toil, but Dad
these folk resist, earn our respect and grow.

My girls improve of late, I'm told they grow
in health and strength, more beautiful each day
since leaving Albany. I ask you Dad
and Mum to visit soon my wife and home.
Please tell me all is well, it gives me peace
to hear my Jane, my little girls, are safe

I end this now and trust that you are safe.
Ask Mum to write me how her roses grow,
at summer's end. Her letters bring me peace,
as do my Jane's. They give me hope the day
will come when families will live at home
as one. For now my darling Mum and Dad,

I wish for peace, my dear ones to be safe
and pray, dear Dad, as scarlet poppies grow
I will return one day to heart and home.

Marlene Fulcher

Come to Mummy

Highly Commended Short Story 2013

'What's your excuse this time? And don't tell me you were working back.'

'Arguing isn't going to help.' Ben glared at you. 'Just look at the kid.' Pete's soft mouth quivered. 'Besides, it's useless trying to discuss anything with you.'

You moved towards your son but when Ben marched out of the room, Pete, as usual, ran after his dad.

You're confused. Press your fingers to your forehead. You thought Pete would need you but he turns away.

It was the lawn-beetle last week. One twist of your foot, squish. It was dead. Pete should have left it alone but he never listens.

Silly boy. He moped for a couple of days then you found him talking to the budgie.

You expect, almost pray its heart gives out, but it flutters, flaps for ages before you grab it, feel the tiny snap.

Pete was fascinated with the stupid thing. Shut you out like Mother did. She blamed you when Father walked out. Couldn't see you needed her.

This time it's Ben's fault but Pete blames you. Hasn't spoken to you since his father left.

'Sorry son, Daddy has to leave.' Ben hadn't heard you enter the room, spun around mouth agape. 'The firm's opening a branch in Sydney. Want me to set up.'

'When were you intending to tell me?' You pointed to his suitcase.

'There's a letter on the bed.'

'It's another woman, isn't it?'

'I'll ring.' Ben picked up his suitcase. 'Look, you'll be all right.'

Pickets twist into your ribs as you lean over the fence for a better view.

Pete and the grey-haired man laughed and talked over the fence a few minutes ago and it wasn't the first time.

You watched him walk to the corner. Brakes screech. Someone screamed.

The old man had to die but you didn't think wishing it would make it happen. If only it had been that simple yesterday.

Squeals of laughter came from Pete's room. You watched him play with Moggy.

Moggy, the cat that used to be yours.

By afternoon the tablets had worked. Poor Puss

Your head hurts.

You're at the curb; smile as the man is placed into an ambulance. Pete stands beside you. You take his hand. He'll need you now.

'It's all right, darling. Mummy's here.' You squeeze his hand. 'I'll look after you. We can play hide and seek, maybe read your favourite story together.'

Pete pulls away, runs home. You call. Follow him inside.

'We could play let's pretend.' You struggle to remember the game but Pete fingers the TV buttons. Cartoons flash, flare.

You try to focus. His attention centres on the screen

You walk across the room.

There's a crackling and the television goes black.

You shrug, check switches, plugs.

Now you're his only friend. The only one he can turn to.

Tears track your son's face. You open your arms but he runs to his room.

How are you going to keep Pete to yourself?

What's going to happen when he starts Kindy?

Marlene Fulcher

Spin of the Wheel

Commended Short Story 2013

It's the dead of night on the open freeway, her image floats before me. I shake my head, gun the accelerator. Headlights! Tyres squeal, metal crunches, glass bites.

I scream. The road burns my hand and knees. I grope in the dark, drag myself along the gutter and up the curb.

Grey fog rolls, strands me at an intersection. I search for familiar signs. Nothing is clear beyond arm's length.

Shadows shift, shape, solidify into a framework of buildings.

My right arm throbs. I unzip my jacket, ease leather off my shoulder, expose torn flesh and bone. The pavement moves and a ball of heat sears my gut. I can't breathe. Air, I need air.

Sirens wail, doors slam. I see familiar uniforms. The girl, do they know about the girl? Then hear. "You'll be right mate." I prop myself on one arm, swallow against the pain in my chest, cough, taste blood. Wrapped in a warm blanket, I'm carried away.

Amid a veil of ghosts I try to hear above the pounding of my heart.

A noise, soft as sneakers on carpet, alerts me to others in the room. Footsteps mill around me. My lungs labour faster.

Grey shapes, silhouettes mingle. They have no faces. Only eyes, above a blur of faded green, but no mouths. I need to ask questions but how will they answer?

I'm raced along a clean, white corridor, hurtled around several corners. My stomach heaves, settles.

Under bright lights I sink into blackness, hear the murmur of forgotten souls. I float up, watch nurse apply gel, the doctor ready with paddles. My body shudders.

My life rushes.

Cigarette smoke snakes through haze, lingers near a high ceiling.

Images coalesce. A spinning car, roulette wheels, finger-nailed playing cards; lines of razor fine powder, rolled fifty dollar notes; the glint of a blade; glass shards in pools of wine and blood.

A naked woman, on stained sheets, her breasts curved,

eyes sunken, lips parted, blue.

Blood ebbs from my heart. My chest aches.

The dead swarm up from black caverns of darkness. Yellow fumes cannot hide flames, faces glowing in coals, or the rushing descent.

Vapours coil from slimy water. A sulphurous stench overpowers my lungs, rips my throat.

Cerberus' howls echo above the knell of bronze.

From across the river a shadow calls my name. I want to scream, run, but my legs drag me step by step closer to the water's edge.

A tall figure looms. A lantern lights hollow eyes, streaks a tangled beard clinging to faded purple robes. A sneer reveals uneven blackened teeth. The putrid smell of death invades my nostrils.

A skeletal hand beckons.

Too late, I fall to my knees, pray forgiveness. I didn't mean to

The Ferryman poles his boat across the river. His laughter reverberates, mocks me as he demands his coin.

Marlene Fulcher

Robin Giraudo

Goldfield's Children

Special Mention Poem 2011

Moulded by the savage heat
of a relentless sun,
across the scorched earth,
swift brown lizards, we ran our careless way.
Among the bush flies, the red dust, the dry bone glare,
we grew and flourished.

In our playground
of open mouthed prospector shafts,
grey slime dumps,
slag heaps and dusty streets,
carefree and unconcerned,
we conquered our arid world

Our Wongai friends were two ancient crones.
Earth's marrow filled their bones,
nature's sap coursed through their veins,
Lady Jane and Annie Poor Bugger,
called themselves by their white man names.
We gathered twigs to boil their billy,
stole bread to fill their belly,
Sat with them under eucalyptus tree,
while they discerned its spirit.

Industrious, tireless ants,
we laboured through the priceless days.
Wielding awkward shovel,
heavy crow bar, rake and spike.
to dig out our underground cubbies,
Small willing ponies all,
through many days,
we'd drag an old cart full of branches,
out of our bush land paradise,
to build the bonfire for Guy Faux Night.
Then fearless of dangers unforeseen
plunged our overheated bodies
into Paddy's muddy dam.

We were the Honey Bees,
So busy, busy, busy, Eager,
dedicated, focused, living wholly in the moment.
There was no tomorrow, our time was forever.

Ah! But time proved fickle.
Glimpsed briefly, my childhood Self,
silently with little fuss,
vanished with my dark friends,
into the mists of time.
Would that I could return
to your world,
to your way of being.

Robin Giraudo

Fran Graham

Review of an Exhibition: Russell Drysdale 1912-81

Commended Article 2012

In a career spanning four decades Russell Drysdale painted fewer than three hundred paintings. Russell Drysdale 1912-81 was the first major retrospective exhibition of one of Australia's most noted artists. Between December 1997 and November 1998 it toured to four states and the Northern Territory. I visited the exhibition in Hobart at the Tasmanian Museum and Art Gallery. Put together by the National Gallery of Victoria and curated by Geoffrey Smith, seventy-seven paintings were on show.

Russell Drysdale came to Australia with his family from England at the age of eleven. He began his working life as a jackeroo and only decided to be an artist in 1933 at the age of twenty-one. His identification with the landscape and its inhabitants was a deeply personal one and his images of rural and outback Australia, combining the ordinary with the heroic, and landscapes of beauty with scenes of devastation, had a significant influence on defining a national identity at a time of tremendous social change in Australian history (Potts 1997). Spanning depression, war and unprecedented immigration from the 1940s to the 70s, his paintings reflected the essence of Australia and its people.

The exhibition shows twenty-three paintings from the period between 1938-44 which deal with ordinary domestic life with occasional scenes of social life and recreation. The very first painting in the exhibition, The rabbiter and his family is one such domestic scene. Its bright colours and its pyramidal type arrangement of the figures strike a somewhat serious chord in contrast to the humorous elements of everyday life, like the children's bare feet, the pom-pom slippers on the wife, and the dog scratching himself.

Fig. 1.

Other early paintings depict such simple scenes as a man reading the newspaper and a man feeding his dog, followed by some social scenes such as Moody's pub and Going to the pictures.

Fig. 2.

Moody's pub became one of Drysdale's most famous paintings and demonstrates his sense of humour in observing scenes from everyday life with four elongated, laid back figures smoking outside the hotel. The presence of the car and the names written on the buildings reveal Drysdale's interest in social commentary and story-telling in his work. The intense colours from the blue sky to the red buildings create strong contrasts in this dramatic depiction of Australian country life (Catalogue 1997).

From 1941 the war begins to make an appearance with The medical examination, his first painting to explore this theme and show Drysdale's preoccupation with the subject of Australia at war.

Fig. 3.

The enormously elongated figures of the semi-naked and naked men form a stark contrast with the officials who are not just fully clothed but quite formally so in shirts, ties and waistcoats. This is accentuated even more by the formality of the room, polished floorboards, long windows and the many paintings on the walls. It could be seen as a somewhat humiliating scene, but as Drysdale himself was found unfit for military service due to poor eyesight, perhaps it represents the trauma of this rejection mixed with guilt that many of his friends would be going to war (Catalogue 1997).

A very large full-length portrait of a soldier is representative of a number of Drysdale's depictions of soldiers going off to war. Soldier, shows a young man rugged up against the cold, hands in the pockets of his army great coat, kitbag by his side, waiting for a train. The soldier's form fills the canvas looking tired and solemn as he leans against a wall highlighted in red giving the image a somewhat sinister feeling. It is monumental in its simplicity (Catalogue 1997). This painting, along with others of Drysdale's works depicting soldiers at Albury Station, again demonstrate Drysdale's preoccupation with the war.

Fig. 4.

Another theme to emerge from the exhibition was that of drought. In 1944 Drysdale accompanied a Sydney Morning Herald reporter thousands of kilometres through outback New South Wales to cover what was considered to be the worst drought in Australia's recorded history. Many of his drawings from this trip became paintings.

Fig. 5.

Deserted out-station was among the first of his remarkable series of drought landscapes. It has a somewhat surreal presence with the dead tree trunk on the left appearing to transform itself into something almost human with sagging knees and a flailing arm indicative of surrender. The sharp edges and twisted shapes of the collapsing corrugated iron also suggest suffering against the deep space and emptiness of the Australian outback. Another really startling image from the drought paintings was Dead Bullock. This is a powerful image of the rotting carcass of a victim of the drought. The carcass almost fills the canvas as a shocking reminder of the tragedy of drought. Dead trees, dead animals, and remains of buildings depict a harsh, desolate landscape and yet Drysdale's apparent understanding of extreme hardship gives such images a dignity that is unique to his work.

Fig. 6.

Another important aspect of Drysdale's work was his paintings of children. The broken mill shows two children playing amidst the ruins of a windmill. The presence of the children in the outback landscape and the more muted tones is much softer than his earlier harsher images of drought.

The exhibition also has Drysdale's most famous painting of children. Two children is almost classical in its formal composition. These are children of the outback in whom Drysdale has managed to capture an inherent shyness as well as a strange combination of fragility and toughness. Although standing together in an empty landscape their eyes speak eloquently of the consuming loneliness of outback life (Catalogue 1997).

Fig. 7.

I am always very moved by Drysdale's portrayal of country women, my favourite being Drover's wife. These paintings also marked a change in his style from the long, skinny elongated early figures of his war paintings, to very rounded, robust and quietly strong women. I love the way the Drover's wife is larger than life in the foreground while her husband is hitching the wagon in the distance for the obvious trip to town. There is so much significance in the suitcase; it gives the painting, and the woman, absolute intent. Her face is expressionless just like the Woman in a landscape and Portrait of a woman in all of whom we see a calm and simple dignity; and yet they demonstrate a sturdiness and a resilience that lies solidly beneath the surface which is the power of their survival (Catalogue 1997).

Fig. 8.

In 1953, Drysdale began a series of paintings which included Aboriginal subjects. Drysdale was the first artist to portray aborigines as ordinary people. The fifties was also a time when they were being forced to integrate into white society. The painting Shopping day shows women and children dressed in what society would have considered clothes for going out. However, one woman carries a sack and all are bare footed. This speaks rather poignantly of their sad situation of being trapped between two cultures. This is no doubt Drysdale commenting on the sense of displacement of the Australian aborigines at this time (Catalogue 1997).

Fig. 9.

However, for me, the most striking and memorable thing about the exhibition is Drysdale's use of deep russet shades to give the landscape that sense of claustrophobic heat and dryness. It is most obvious in Red landscape and Broken mountain. Red landscape depicts twisted and fallen trees with tangled branches and rocks painted in vivid colours from deep red to pale orange. Drysdale himself said that this painting depicts an area of Australia where the spirit of the outback is unrestrained, and the stretches of land so vast that they seem devoid of life (Catalogue 1997).

Paintings like Broken Mountain reveal Drysdale's sympathy for and spiritual affinity with the landscape. There is a harmony and absolute unity in his use of colour and variation of tone. The light gives a ghostly affect with the boulders in the foreground looking like they are neon lit. The presence of the young aboriginal man is solid yet subtle as he blends in completely with the landscape yet we know he is there. The white of his shirt and the white on top of the mountain perhaps identify these two figures as the main subjects of the painting, with the giant, bright yellow boulders being significant but secondary. The few brightly painted smaller rocks in the centre of the painting connect this trinity of leading characters, and give this very large painting an exquisite balance. In this painting, perhaps more than any other in the exhibition, we can see that Drysdale's landscapes are more about the spiritual condition of the land than its physicality.

Fig. 10.

This was an inspiring exhibition triggering in me an awareness of parts of the continent that is supposedly my own and yet so much of its character and soul are still unfamiliar to me. As a narrative it tells a story of the many dimensions of country life, interrupted by war, challenged by drought and yet surviving through the strength of its many heroes, particularly the women. The story of the aborigines' struggle to survive disenfranchisement is also a poignant part of the story. Drysdale's sensitivity to the spirit and character of the land is eloquently expressed in his use of colour, be it muted tones or an intense rich palette. His paintings are an articulate interpretation of the Australian landscape.

List of References:

Catalogue 1997, Russell Drysdale 1912-81, Curated by Geoffrey Smith. National Gallery of Victoria, Melbourne.

Potts, Timothy 1997, Director's foreword in Catalogue Russell Drysdale 1912-81, National Gallery of Victoria, Melbourne.

List of Visual References:

Fig. 1. The rabbiter and his family. 1938 Melbourne, oil on canvas, 61.5 x 76.7cm. National Gallery of Australia, Canberra.

Fig. 2. Moody's pub. 1941, oil on plywood, 50.9 x 61.4cm. National Gallery of Victoria, Melbourne.

Fig. 3. The medical examination 1941, oil on wood, 38.1 x 45.7cm. The Agapitos/Wilson Collection.

Fig. 4. Soldier 1942, oil on composition board, 59.5 x 40.0cm. Arrow Pearl Company.

Fig. 5. Deserted out-station 1945, oil on canvas, 86.4 x 111.7cm. John Fairfax Holdings Limited.

Fig. 6. Dead bullock 1945, oil on composition board, 55.7 x 65.8cm. The Honourable J.F. Nagle, AO QC.

Fig. 7. Two children 1945-46, oil on canvas on composition board, 60.6 x 50.8cm. National Gallery of Victoria, Melbourne.

Fig. 8. Drover's wife 1945, oil on canvas, 51.3 x 61.3cm. National Gallery of Australia, Canberra.

Fig. 9. Shopping day 1953, oil on canvas, 59.7 x 75.0cm. The Art Gallery of New South Wales, Sydney.

Fig. 10. Broken mountain 1972, oil on canvas, 101.6 x 127.0cm. Private collection, Sydney.

All images retrieved on from:
"http://www.ngv.vic.gov.au/drysdale/paintings/01.htm"
http://www.ngv.vic.gov.au/drysdale/paintings/01.htm

Fran Graham

After a Week of Teaching in Jiaxing

Winning Poem 2014

The humid day settles on layers
of evening calm and cool stillness.
Outside my apartment
phantoms evaporate over Qin's canal.
On the breeze, my triumph
echoes all the way to town.

Storm air like burnt biscuits
breaks against the bonfire
of darkening clouds.
I breathe the slow release of raw belief
I'm in China, I'm in China.

Brown barges like rusty ornaments glide
under Long Feng Bridge.
Baked images from a smog sky hover
pixelated in the haze and I remember
clean water down crisp creeks.

In the courtyard
dragonflies, reckless as Blackhawks,
spin and rock in a death reel.
Children whack with tender bamboo
the thrill of kill festering in their palms.

Fran Graham

After the Blast

Winning Poem 2017

He's done two tours of duty in Iraq.
Now he's doing a tour of the local clinic.
He's lost something; he's not sure what
or even if he ever had it. Or had it
but was unaware he had it. Either way
it's eluding him, running away like gunfire.

He thought he was happy to be there until
the roadside bomb blew the tank he was driving
clean off the ground. While seeing to his commanding
officer's bloody face and eyes, it occurred to him
he didn't want to be there anymore. But he
had to finish his tour so just a part of him deserted.

Several years on, others began to notice.
He couldn't smell the flowers or charm
the fish. The atmosphere was wooden.
He couldn't see colour; everything was
sepia or black and white. Black mainly.
He rocked back on his heels and was stuck.

His speech became hard to understand, like war.
It buzzed, rippled, echoed, but remained
camouflaged, bunkered down.
It became the enemy. He had to keep on
repeating himself. It caused embarrassment. Like defeat.
It was beginning to look like a hill he had to climb.

He was afraid of parked cars and wheelie bins.
His wife was burnt out trying to help.
He was a shadow she didn't recognise.
His baby daughter was unsettled by his strangeness.
Finally panic set in and he wept   desperate.
So they admitted him to the clinic   hopeful.

We stand vigil while he looks for himself   expectant.
His search will be painful, but in solitude he might
lose the phantoms and find laughter again
forget the madness, his and the world's, and articulate
clearly that he's come through, flying like a bird
the ceasefire resting easy in his head.

Fran Graham

Claire Grose

Green Gums and Gravel

Winning Poem 1993

In spring

imaginings are everything.
The mind inclines to travel south
down country highways gravel-edged,
where eucalypts green-tip the sky;
their sculptured trunks like columns rise
to colonnade the forest floor.
Beside the road where saplings sprout
young gums, new-leafed, are shining red
and wildflowers launch themselves in space
earth-popping through their underplace.
The white clematis starry-eyed
climbs twining rampant round its host
the drooping fissured peppermint,
while lechenaultia, pink pimelia
each colour-code their artistry.

A half-way stop to stretch and stare,
a jarrah cabin nestled there
where bush paths lead from gravel tracks,
the smell of wattles, forest mulch,
the feel of damp and gravel crunch,
the thought of billy tea and lunch,
the curling smoke from burning twigs.
To live here, though, would be to fear

the smell of bushfire ever near.
The ibis in the creek can fly–

not I.

I watch to see the fire die
then back en route in hot pursuit
of that white line which leads me on.
The Ludlow forest takes me in –
it comes to meet me like a friend
embracing with its outstretched limbs.
The car eats up the road between
where lacey tuarts filter sun
to pale green-gold and faerie cool
and takes me past the bunyip pool.

The wind in wires, the sound of tyres
on country roads which lead through towns,
I hear the sounds and picture scenes
of shearing sheds and wineries
and cottage crafts and potteries.

I see the loam-red cattle range
in bare green paddocks with raised dams
and dandelions and burnt-out logs.

Time out for swimming togs.

Down further south along the coast
the ocean silvers in the sun,
a soothing salve for tired limbs
as surfers dart from sun-hot sand.
Along the beach blow balls of fibre,

dead seagrass rounded by the tides.
The crashing waves on Isaac Rocks
crush snow-white spray to bales of cloud.
The foam-mouthed sea, the smell of salt,
the rugged coastline beckons me.
Then winding back the gravel track
beyond the sandy coastal strip
through wooded pastures, dappled shade,
the senses quicken at the sight –
the burgeoning of spring is seen
in native forest undergrowth.
The green is magic to the eye,
a scenic walk, I cross the bridge
where banks are rugged steep and damp.
A robust remnant, sandstone house,
reflects its pioneering past

at Margaret River.

Young jarrah forests steal the light
from rustic rammed-earth cottages.
The redgums weep. The magpies call
in woodlands near the river deep
and, near the dam where water flows
the hooded lily stilted grows.
The streets are quiet, no high-rise
to pierce these virgin country skies.

Imaginings are sweeter when
I pack and drive down south again.

Claire Grose

Tina Hentisz

Throw me a rose!

Commended Article 2015

Have you ever delighted in the look of a beautiful rose, then anticipating its heady fragrance, sniffed, and sniffed again, but nothing? Absolutely nothing! No sweet perfume! You can't believe your nose. This is no rose, this is a clone! Some clever rose farmer has propagated all the smell out! It is so disappointing. It makes your heart bleed. The very thing, that is so essential to roses, the thing that brings them to life, their very expression is missing. It is like a butterfly without wings, a bird without a song, or a man without action.

Throw me a real rose!

Have you ever looked at a man with happy anticipation, impressed by his stature and looked forward to his speech? But then, when he did talk, the words were all wrong; because he didn't talk from the heart, from his own natural being? It is such a shame. This can happen anywhere, at a party, a social occasion or when participating in a political rally that you looked forward to so much.

A rose is a rose and cannot pretend. The essence of the rose is its sweet perfume, you can't see it, you can't hear it, but it fills your head with sweet dreams and inspiration. The rose has been a symbol of beauty, love and precious promises throughout the ages.

A fragrant rose needs no words; it exists only to inspire

expression in man. What greater prompter is there and its message is always new!

It is a pity, but we have to face it, man is far more complex than the rose; we would be bored silly exuding fragrance only. And we can't walk around town with our nose thrust in a bunch of roses, hoping to be inspired. So what inspires us, after we have smelled the roses?

Usually it will be the everyday events, the morning sunshine, fresh air, scenery, friends, the job and the situation at home. But, it can be hard at times to see the beauty of the day, for instance; when you are at the office, it is pouring rain and you have mud all over your shoes because they are digging up the carpark again.

Your boss tells you; "You have to work smarter; business is slow, we need more orders delivered and coming in!" Easy for him to say, he is not out there on the road; so now you are in a hurry to fill the orders and you are stuck in a traffic jam. 'Oh no, suffering Socrates; not another accident further up the road! That's all you need'… As well as that the fellow in the car beside you tooting his horn and shouting obscenities through the open window, because you cut him off at the corner!

'Of course, your customer won't commit, he wants time to think it over; you have to be pleasant when you would rather tell him just where to go with his dithering and messing around! Does your boss care, oh no, he just sits in the office calculating profits.'

At the end of the day you drag yourself through the front door, home at last! Peace, a glass of wine, some good food and perhaps a little television. But, it is not a good day, the wife is cranky and has a headache, the kids are squabbling again and the dog is hiding behind the sofa because he has chewed up your favourite pair of slippers.

This is reality, all of your illusions shattered, all your dreams into disarray. You sink into an armchair and hope that the drink in your hand will relieve the suffering. Dinner may never come, and you hate take-aways. Probably pizza again and it is never your favourite. "Oh, somebody; throw me a rose, please."

How can you be inspired with that slave driver at work, the maniacs on the road, customers who dawdle and can't make up their mind, and now… this bunch at home!

But, hold on a minute, haven't you forgotten something? Something so vital, so all important! Wasn't it you who smelled the roses? Wasn't it you who created the pictures of beauty and love? Wasn't it you who dreamed the sweet dreams? The dream is still there you know, in fact you are sitting right in the middle of it! It is not as sweet as you thought, in fact, all of the people in it seem to have the words all wrong! It was supposed to be much nicer; you were supposed to be the hero, with the happy homecoming. "Hurrah, dad's home!" Your blue heaven, where roses bloom…

But this is the hard reality, no wishy-washy, half-cooked notions, but real life with mud on your shoes. You could close your eyes and pretend it is all rosy, but it won't get dinner cooked and you may have to be the one to pick up that awful pizza.

Will the real hero stand up please?

"Alright possums, let's get some action here. Put on the kettle, get mum a pillow, and son, this is your opportunity in the making of a super, duper, spaghetti a la maison. Today, you will learn of the secret ingredient that has been handed down for generations… No ifs and buts, let's get started!"

You dance around the kitchen, clattering the pots and pans, singing Italian Opera; making a great show of the whole thing and before you know it, you're having fun. And then everybody wants to get in on it, they all want to help. It is crazy, it is bedlam, even the dog has stopped feeling sorry for himself and yaps excitedly standing on a kitchen chair.

All of a sudden, the whole house smells of roses!

You made the difference. Without your imagination, your action, the rose is nothing and you realized it just in time.

Without you, the rose would be just a thorny bush, growing in the wild, amidst a myriad of bushes. Who is to know, who is to care? Be glad for all of our discoveries, be glad for the roses, silent sentinels of love that they are.

The rose farmer knew what he was doing all along, he recognized the potential, saw the quality and diversity. In fact, he got over enthusiastic in trying to create the perfect rose. Mother Nature plays some crazy tricks, you can always depend on her to come up with something new, and it may not always be what we want, or what we dream of.

The rose farmer is busy, working hard to bring back the fragrance and it is an awful job. Standing knee-deep in cow manure he sometimes curses the whole project. But he keeps on working, because he knows that without his action, without his participation, the world will be a lot poorer.

It is that way for all of us. Follow the dream and make it happen!

Throw me a rose!

Tina Hentisz

Stella Hewson

Woosh Wish

Runner-Up Poem 2014

I wish I had a Porsche…a purple Porsche…
with gold leaf where all the chrome
should be, and windows tinted black.
Just once, by night, I'd cruise the highways
and select my victim…a handsome young man
driving alone in a suitably fast car…a Jaguar or Pontiac.
Beside him, in the next lane,
absorbing the dual subjection to speed, wheel for wheel,
thrust for thrust, bend for bend…
watching his aggression unseen behind the dark glass!
Being an excellent driver at speed,
he'd be convinced I was another man!
Drawing up at the lights, on his left-hand side,
I'd halfway lower the electronic window,
and slowly extend an exquisitely red-tipped hand
and naked be-jewelled arm …
dropping with great panache, a heavily perfumed,
lace-edged handkerchief
on the hood of his machine!
During his dilemma to retrieve it or not,
the purple Porsche would race off down the
the avenues of light, leading him a dazzling dance of speed,

to the forest in the hills,
the tantalizing tail-lights always just around the next curve.
Then, turn on the turbo, and pressing the diamond on the
dash marked 'Whoosh',
the car would mood the road with clouds of purple smoke,
and disappear to some dark heart.
I wish he would,...I think he would,...remember me.

Stella Hewson

Gold

Highly Commended Short Story 2019

Orange. Yellow and Orange. Russet grass, ochre trees, the golden river meandering like lager through the jaundiced bull-rushes frothing gently at the bends. The dark tawny clouds integrating from amber, through sulphur and lemon to the palest cream on the fluffy edges.

Spinifex tussocks in coppery khaki stood in sheaths on the flat citrus-coloured mud floor; the released spiny bundles bowling slowly with the wind to no-where in particular.

The shafting sunlight brightened the buttercups and primroses from carrot through apricot on the sandy banks Rocks pierced the earth haphazardly looking more like cork than stone.

Ginger scanned the scenery in awe; the golden vista unbelievable. She looked down at her hands; her mustard coloured skin and topaz nails took her breath away. Holding out her skirt, which was usually buff, she saw it had become tangerine; her favourite white blouse now saffron. The familiar old natural straw hat that she held, glowed copper and the strands of blond hair that blew across her eyes now shone henna-coloured and flickered like flames in the breeze.

The scene was amazing, like nothing she had seen before. The whole landscape was of a gilded nature, yet all the tones of orange and yellow were as they should be; the hues merging or individually standing alone but all together pleasing to the eye in their balance and blending. It was an environment uniquely spectacular; extremely beautiful and orderly in a most unusual way.

She fingered the orange-framed spectacles with canary-coloured glass.

'What a wonderful therapist to have prescribed these to cure her Dyslexia?'

In her hand the parchment-like letter with gold letterhead, prescription and details of her practitioner, was clear and precise in orderly tawny print. She stared at its clarity, absorbing its meaning and significance for her. She panned the beautiful glowing landscape once more and then took off the orange spectacles.

The landscape returned to normal, green and muddy with indistinct forms, blurred edges; figures only just what they should be, might be, colours blending inappropriately. Sighing, she looked down at the letter, now in black and white print, the letters malformed, some backward, some missing, gaps with distorted characters.

'Which of these choices is reality?' she pondered. 'Maybe both; maybe neither.'

Taking one last look at the blurred, muddy-green, distorted scene, she allowed a large brazen smile to slowly spread across her face. Replacing the orange glasses on her eager face, she strode off into her new golden world.

Stella Hewson

Helen Iles

Resolutions

Highly Commended Short Story 2004

She stood on the edge of the platform looking down its interminable length. In ten minutes the 9.15 train would come hurtling through from Causham. Shortly after that, the silver streak of the non-stop run from Epsom to Durridge would fly by, whizzing her hair and scarf into a riotous mess.

She strained to see the lights in the distance but the 9.15 train was still too far away, and there were numerous bends between Cumbridge and Causham.

She sighed, deeply. Ten minutes and a minuscule second was all that was left of this worn out, decrepit old hag of a woman. Ten minutes and a brief shunt was all that held her from her maker. Nine minutes and thirty seconds.

She edged a little closer to the sudden drop. People further along the station milled about, waiting patiently for the 9.20 that would take them to the city to arrive. A group of teenagers ballyhooed each other in mock argument, then laughed.

How grand it must be to be young, she thought whimsically. How grand it would be to have the time to undo all the mistakes one makes in life. Unfortunately, she realised, not for the first time, the older she got, the less time there was to rectify the horrid mistakes she made.

Now time was too short. There would be no undoing. She

would go to her grave without resolving her errors – the errors she'd made could not be undone.

Glancing down the platform, she checked that no-one was aware of her closeness to the wooden rim of the station landing. Her toes were almost nipping over the edge of the wood.

Nine-ten. Five minutes.

She had chosen this exact time to remedy her errors the only way she could, purely because if she felt weak-hearted at the nine-fifteen, she had the silver streak close behind it. One slip and it would all be over.

She wondered if Simon would ever find out. She wondered if there would be any great reaction. Then she shook her head. Probably not. How could you love someone you didn't know? How could you miss them?

She glanced down the platform again. There was a light in the distance. This was it!

As the light grew larger and brighter, she shuffled almost inconspicuously closer to the drop, below which sat the insidious steel tracks. Briefly, she wondered what she would feel as she was crushed and shattered and severed beneath the iron wheels. But she pushed the thought back. She mustn't think! She mustn't imagine! She must just step out. She must step out at 9.15.

A huge white ball obliterated the distance, and the bends, and the tracks, and the station. All she saw was the hurtling light of the 9.15.

For a second, she saw Simon. She saw Simon at the moment of his birth. She saw Simon at the moment he was first laid in her arms. She saw Simon handed back to the nurse for the last time. She saw Simon being placed in his crib and his crib carefully lifted into the back seat of a car. She saw

Simon at five years old. How smart he looked in his short pants suit, his hair slicked neatly back and covered with a cap.

She saw Simon as a young man making his way in life. She saw Simon opening his new offices on Rochelle Street and the smart young lady that now graced his arm. She saw Simon walking tall down the boulevard with reporters chasing after him. How well he handled himself in public. How proud a young man he was.

She saw Simon as she saw him on TV, the congressman, the lawyer. She heard the slander sheet reporters questioning his past, his heritage and heard Simon say how he was endeavouring to find his family. One day soon he would find his family.

The bright white light now filled her vision. One day he would find her.

She saw Simon, his dark wrath of hair ruffling, his white teeth gleaming as he announced he had news that would soon enable him to be reunited with his mother. Oh, Simon, she thought desperately. Why couldn't you leave well enough alone?

The white light now filled her mind. Nine-fifteen. She stepped out.

Someone shouted.

A dark shadow raced across her as the child was ripped from her mindful arms for the last time.

The newspapers next day reported, "A bag lady, known to all around Rochelle as Give-a-care Annie, slipped tragically to her death from a railway platform last night. Authorities are investigating how the accident occurred. Congressman Simon Dalton said last night that Annie's death could have been avoided had Government-approved the funding for the Homeless of Rochelle.

"Annie was a regular face around the streets of our city," he said. "She will be sadly missed."

Helen Iles

Battle Beach – 6th of June

Highly Commended Poem 2005

The red, dead sea at Omaha
ebbs out, seeps in
litters lives upon the beach,
lingering lives,
lives fragmented
fear demented,
shaking, screaming,
praying
bob in surf, sit limp, stare lifeless.
Fish gag, shrapnel fins flap
as life ebbs out from the red washed sand
where life stains the land blood red.
Fish flip and flop like men
then airless, flop no more
drowned in guts
smothered in gore.

Bomb barrages
splatter the sand
their red display of target spray
drowns screams
shatters dreams.

Life shattered, splattered,
on the beach men tattered
sink heads to Tommy gun rattles
and they cry, Momma,
Momma, they cry.

"I don't like Omaha, Momma,"
the young child cries
as the soldier dies on the screen.
Before his face he's had a taste
of war.
He will play that game no more.

Helen Iles

The Birthday

Winning Short Story 2007

Enid Bellamy sat in her comfortable chair, in her comfortable room, in her very comfortable house in Wiggam Street. She knitted, for she was waiting, and what better way to while away the time than to lengthen the garment that clung supportively in a hundred or so places along the breadth of the needles. The clock on the cabinet behind her read seven o'clock precisely, the time not overly pressing at her conscience for the family were not due until the half-hour.

Looking up, she noted her appearance in the mantel mirror, a glorious long hanger with fluted edges and a smoky image of galleons and oceans in the lower-left corner. It was an heirloom and she liked where it was displayed for at any time of the day she could touch up her hair or face, or just assure herself that health was still predominant on her features. She assured herself of just that now as she touched her hair and straightened the set of exquisite pearls that graced her neckline. Her blue eyes dropped back to the soft woollen creation that was to be a matinee jacket for the newest family member-to-be, and she pondered whether it would be a boy or a girl - but only briefly: Sandra and Carl already had one of each, and as long as the grandchild was healthy, it mattered little what gender was increased. For safety, she had chosen a lemon colour.

The clock now read seven-zero-five, and she completed the

next row and laid it down; went to the rather meagre kitchen and made a pot of tea. They would be here soon and she didn't mind admitting that she looked forward to their visit. The children had not been around for some time, but she understood – they had lives of their own to lead, and husbands to tend. Her own marriage had been a perfect one for half a century, and if her own children could be blessed with even half of that she would be very happy. It was their joys now that she could share in, her own having come to a rapid stand-still with Albert's demise five long years ago.

She carried the tea back into the lounge and put it on the small oval table by her chair, her eyes drifting momentarily out through the window to the street, to a passing car, but it wasn't them; not Sandra and Carl; not Judy and Simon; not Barry who had taken the notion to remain single and travel the world without restriction of wife or child, and who had taken special consideration to return to his homeland in time for her birthday. Not that he had said that, mind, but she knew that he had. He was a good boy, and she pondered that the next project would be a new sweater for her oldest, in blue because it matched his eyes, and he had inherited her eyes. Sandra had Bert's eyes, she smiled solemnly, had Bert's every mannerism of face and mind, and his temper, and she was thankful Carl was a placid man. Judy, on the other hand, resembled none of them. Dark and broody, yet bright of mind and 'arty', Judy didn't talk much, but she was a keen listener and a deep thinker, and would probably one day be somebody special; what, she didn't know, but she would be. It was a mother's intuition to sense those things.

Glancing back over her shoulder, the clock showed ten past the hour, and she wondered if one of them would come early: Barry maybe. He had no family to hold him up, and he would relish the thought of not having to cook for himself. But then,

Barry always had places to go and things to do, rushing here, rushing there. No, she decided wistfully, Judy would be the first for Sandra would be tied down with the infants, and with Carl, for the man seemed to do little for himself, the product of an overly doting mother; something she was thankful that she had never been with her own. No, she considered proudly; she had been wise enough to let them find their own way in life, guiding them only along the paths of righteous belief, telling them the difference between right and wrong and leaving them to decide the road they would take. They had all taken the high road, and that made her proud.

The garment gained another inch and the clock another five minutes.

Soon, she pacified her anxiousness. Don't hurry the children. They will arrive soon. Her gaze flicked up to the dining table. It was ready, neatly set with an array of delectable dishes for supper; the usual cold dishes of chicken and salads, ham and slabs of lamb; nibblies of pretzels and peanuts and chips; and the trifle for Barry which he loved so much because she would always overladen it with sherry and wine. It was all there, all ready, and she was satisfied with the presentation. But they would need to be on time or it would all go warm and not taste as nice. For a moment she deliberated returning it to the refrigerator then decided not to worry. The clock said seven-twenty and another ten minutes would chill it no further than it already was.

Another inch lengthened the tiny jacket, the constant click of the needles tapping away with the seconds on the clock. Presently, Enid put down the bundle that busied her hands, patted her grey-gold hair into a more organised position and stood; she smoothed the sheeny cotton floral that she reserved for such occasions and, although a quiet thought told her not to, she wandered to the window to survey the tree-lined street below her sloping lawn. The clock clicked over seven-thirty, and at any moment one of them would arrive. Maybe even the next set of headlights coming down the road would turn and climb the driveway and stop beside the house.

None did, and for a long while no cars even came down the roadway. The street was dark and lonely, and soon not even the trees were distinguishable in the gloom. She noted her mood was rapidly beginning to match that of the atmosphere outside her window and she turned away and let her eyes take a slow wander over the room, a room where she seemed to be spending more and more time of late. Briefly she wondered if the children had felt as comfortable in this house as she had when they had moved there a decade ago. It was just she and Albert then, the children having grown and taken homes of their own. She consoled herself with the notion that they had seemed to have accepted the house though it hadn't been immediate, and she remembered the horrified looks on their faces when they had announced that the family home was to be sold, being far too large and difficult for her and Bertie to maintain in their senior years.

But they had gotten over it, she reflected lightly. They were good children, and only wanted what was best for her and their father, and now that it was only her, for her. A car appeared at the far end of the street, its golden cat-eyes casting a wide beam of light in its path, directing the way closer and closer to her daisy-strewn street verge. She watched keenly, waiting for the yellow blinker to flash its turning beacon, but it didn't – the car swept on past to become two minuscule slits of red until they too faded in the blackness. She sighed and glanced back to the clock on the cabinet. It was ten minutes to the next hour and she frowned, the motion adding to the creases already marring her otherwise unblemished face.

A nag of worry tinkered in her head as she turned back to

the table, to the limping lettuce and sogging pudding. Scowling, she waited a few minutes more, took a nibble of a small morsel of bird, a peck of the wine-sodden cake, and returned the whole array of decorative bowls back to the ice-box. By eight o'clock, the needles were scraping and clicking noisily away again but this time without love-incited fingers: there was a greater need to be fulfilled inside her now, a need to alleviate the growing concern and quiet hint of annoyance. The hint grew rapidly to a more apparent thought that the needles did little to remedy. Had they forgotten? she wondered icily. And when had it been discussed that they would gather on this particular night, at this particular place? Or had she by chance taken for granted they would turn up as they always did, for none had ever forgotten her birthday before, and this one was special for it was her seventieth. Not sixty-eighth. Not sixty-ninth. But seventieth! And of course they would come! Maybe she had just mixed up the time, and they would be here soon. Maybe it was to be at eight. Of course, it was to be at eight. The children were seldom late, and certainly never all of them.

And so she waited, the needles again poised but inactive, her ear tuned to the silence on Wiggam Street. It remained unbearably so.

By eight-fifteen, she rose and poked her head hopefully into the kitchen, minor thoughts flitting to the teapot yet overshadowed by more pressing ones that prayed the lounge-room timepiece was wrong. Remorsefully, she sighed. It wasn't. Her knitting discarded to her favourite chair, she stood hollowly, fingers rubbing lightly up and down against confused temples, teasing out the slight but rising tension nagging at her brow. Turning, she looked forlornly about. It was eight-thirty, and obvious that she would have no visitors tonight, no-one to share her birthday with. Not her children. And not dear

Albert, though memories of many better, fuller days of celebration glinted in and out of her reminiscences and made her smile.

There had been so many beautifully shared birthdays, so many filled with laughter and caring; what did it really matter that they had forgotten this one. She was not a selfish woman, she told herself as her hand found the light switch and dimmed that room, her knitting left to ponder the darkness, as alone as she herself felt right at that moment. No, she was not selfish, but she recognised that little pang of disappointment that hovered between her love for her children and her need to still be considered very much a part of the family, the part that kept them all together. She sighed deeply. It was time for this tired old lady to put herself to bed.

Tomorrow, she would be seventy and a day.

Helen Iles

Just a Doll and a Story

Commended Short Story 2007

It was just a little Kewpie doll, skirted in mauve netted-lace, spangled with a silvery-purple glitter, its hair painted golden like the tall hooked stick it came on. It hung from that hook on a rod at the back of the carnival stand; had hung there for days, maybe years the way the old man's luck had been running. Nobody wanted to try their luck at his stall these days, he mused as the crowd passed by on their way to more modern amusements. Nobody wanted to toss the ring and loop themselves a prize … or maybe the game was just too simple to pose a valid challenge anymore. But still he smiled and hollered above the bedlam the side-shows created:

"Try your luck; three throws for a dollar. Everybody wins." But the walkers didn't listen, just kept their eyes to the front and kept going. If business didn't pick up soon, Old Jobe Garrick wouldn't have one, he noted, acknowledging his life was dwindling away into nothingness – had been going steadily that way since Pearl died. And if Old Jobe was down on his luck now, it had started from that sad day. In a few more tomorrows, he would close his tent and wander, for he was barely making enough now to scrape together a meal, let alone make a sustainable living. He just wasn't cut out to be a Carnie anymore. Maybe he never had been, for this was Pearl's life – she'd had the gift to woo the crowds their way; had the smile that drew them to the stand and held them there. She was a mighty special woman, and everyone loved her. Hell, he'd loved her. Still did.

"Try your luck! Three throws for a dollar."

Yep, his luck had gone to the grave with Pearl all right. She'd been the light for both of them, and now he was just a withered old shell with no reason for battling on. He looked up and surveyed the stand critically. It was a lonely place without that woman. He spied the doll, felt a pang of remorse touch his heart with the memory. Above all the little pieces – the fluffy dogs, the china cats, the goofy bears – Pearl loved the Kewpie dolls best; she would spend hours at night spangling their plastic bodies, tidying their netted skirts, organising their order on the rack so their colours harmonised. The stand had looked grand then. It was dismal now; dismal, dreary and lonely.

"Try your luck."

Damn bloody luck, he hissed to himself. Without Pearl he couldn't raise enough to replenish the stocks to keep the stand half as good as she'd had it. Hell, he was down to his last of everything: his last meal, his last carnival, his last cigarette, even his last damn Kewpie doll. He had no money to buy any more anything.

For a moment he considered closing the stand right then; take the rest of the day to go and visit Pearl. He spent a lot of time in the cemetery when he came to this town. She'd like this town; said it was bright and held a hope she could feel. Hell, he couldn't feel any damn hope for nothin' no more.

"Try your …"

"Look, Daddy, look!" a little girl's voice touched the air, her finger pointing at the old man's red striped stall. "Look, he looks like Grandpa! Oh, and look, there's a doll, Daddy. It's the purple one. I haven't got the purple one."

Old Jobe peered through the passing crowd as it parted like a sea, allowing a tall man to make his way through. In front of him, he pushed a wheelchair, in it a child of early age. Jobe assessed her to be about six, maybe seven.

"Please, Daddy, may I try? I do so want that doll."

"Try your luck! Three throws for a dollar. Everybody wins." The old man smiled with hope.

The tall man looked weary, rubbed a hand tiredly across his face then pushed it deep into his pocket. "Well, okay …" he heaved a deep sigh, "but this is the last one, Poppet, the last dollar I have on me, so you'd better make it good."

"Oh, I will, Daddy. I must. I must have that doll."

"She collects them," he told the old man with a smile, excusing her brash enthusiasm.

Jobe handed the child three rings as the man lined her up to his counter. He took the dollar and dropped it into his own pocket, wondering what was more important to buy, the cigarettes or something to fill his nagging stomach. Strange, right now he didn't much care, for Life just wasn't going to get any better.

"She have an accident?" Jobe asked, studying the wheelchair.

"No, she has a bone disease," her father said softly. "Doctors don't like our chances, but we have faith. We must keep hoping."

The little girl looked up, her big blue eyes like china pools in her sweet young face. "You look like my Grandpa," she said brightly, "but he died last month."

The old man smiled down at her. "We all got to go sometime, sweetheart. All got to go some time."

"I love your doll," she said with a determined smile, "but she looks so lonely."

"Then you'd better throw your rings and get all three to

hang on the hooks over there," Old Jobe prompted her gently. It was an easy game and he had no doubt she'd succeed. In readiness, he lifted the Kewpie doll down from its rod.

The little girl tossed the first ring, her eyes beaming as it hovered then fell over the highest hook on the board. "I did it, Daddy! I got one."

The man smiled at Jobe. "She's determined. That's why I know she's going to make it."

The second quoit was on its way; it clicked against the backboard and fell over a hook in the middlemost row. Blue eyes sparkled at her achievement. Her father smiled wider. "Now slow down and take your time, Chicken," he warned.

"I have the doll. I know I have the doll." Her hope exuded from her as she flicked the last loop across the distance. It seemed to take forever to reach the back of the stand, seemed to hover indefinitely in mid-air before teetering above the bottom-most row, her throw barely reaching the board. Then it tipped the hook, swirled around a few wobbly revolutions then fell to the shelf below with a dull deafening thud. The hook lay empty.

Old Jobe looked at the girl with sympathy, her forlorn face almost shining with tears. Her father shrugged with empathy. "Well, you tried, sweetheart. You can't win all the time."

He nodded a thank you to the old man and eased the chair back into the crowd, the little girl's eyes misting over. "I did try, Daddy ... and I did so want that doll. She's so beautiful."

"Never mind," the man said, his voice mingling then fading in the surrounding din.

The ever-wandering masses quickly swallowed them up, and they were soon gone from sight, leaving Jobe standing there looking at the doll in his hands. How Pearl had loved those dolls too! he sighed dismally, his loneliness returning.

The tide of heads flowed further down the laneways, their

routes diverging and digressing down different paths. How she loved this town, he reflected again. There was hope in this town. Well, he didn't think so, but hell, that little girl had hoped.

In a burst of compulsion, he swung his crooked legs over the counter, his wrinkled hand releasing the cord that dropped the red striped awning across the opening. For the first time in a long while, he joined the crush of merry-makers and was carried along in their wake, going where he didn't know but hopeful of finding that unfortunate child. He tucked the Kewpie doll tight in to his chest to avoid it being damaged.

Coming to a fork in the path, well distant from his tent now, Jobe was jostled heavily, the foot traffic deviating in a chaotic mingle as walkers battled to take their chosen line. Amid the battering, he lost all hope of finding the little girl and her father, was now just concerned with getting back to the safety of his stand and closing it for good. Struggling to exit the throng, he found a clear patch of ground ahead and pushed his way forward; came to stand on a strip of grass at the fork's centre. From there, he turned to survey his whereabouts.

A few feet from where he stood, pulled well back from the hard shoving flow, was the man, the child and the wheelchair. Nodding his gladness, Jobe wobbled forward, his old hands holding out the Kewpie doll in front of him.

"Here, please take it," he said to the child. "I'm sure she would be far happier with your other dolls than hanging in my tent alone." The girl's eyes beamed widely, her smile sending a glow of radiance across her pretty face.

"Oh, Daddy! Look!" She looked up and behind her to her father, "I told you he was like Grandpa!"

Jobe only smiled, but the expression on the man's face brought it to a quick demise.

"No, we really couldn't," he said, reaching out to stop his

daughter's hand from grasping the doll.

"Please, I want her to have it! She tried so hard, had so much hope …"

The man looked unsure, his hand gone to his pocket, groping, delving into its depths. "I would really rather pay for it," he said, "but honestly, she has played me completely dry."

"I want no money," Jobe said firmly. "I do this because my wife would do this."

The man looked thoughtful. "Please … I have nothing with me to reciprocate but would you honour us by joining us for dinner?"

Jobe looked surprised. "You don't have to …"

"Please, Grandpa. Please come." The little girl took his hand in hers, her other clutched the doll safely to her.

"Oh, so it's Grandpa, is it?" Jobe smiled up at the man, then looked down at the child. "And what am I to call you, may I ask?"

"Pearl," she said pertly.

An old man sat rocking on the verandah swing, its rhythmic squeak lulling him slowly to sleep. A child of ten sat on the steps across from him, a box of dolls beside her on the porch. Standing, she walked across and sat on the swing beside him.

"You gave me this one, Grandpa. Do you remember?"

His grey eyes misted as time took him back. "Yes, Pearl. I do remember," he answered wryly. "It's just a little Kewpie doll, but my, it tells a wonderful story."

Helen Iles

Brave Molly

Commended Poem 2008

The steady plod of solid feet
upon the distant sands
where soldiers rest upon their seats,
mates guided by their hands
across their backs their rifles slung,
not needed at this time
They stand to face the enemy's gun,
wait for orders down the line.

And then it comes, "Fall into line!"
they swing to line abreast
their horses champing on the wire,
this charge will be the test.
For who will hold their courage,
their line held on the run
and who will beat the barrage,
and charge beneath the guns.

"Fix bayonets!" comes the call now,
metal clinks as this is done,
and now the horses stand there,
manes tossing in the sun.
Chestnuts, browns, a dun or two,
each tired from the sands,
from walking endless hours
to make this final stand.

For water now they're desperate
and it spreads beyond the guns,
their life hangs in the balance
and for this they make their run.
The captain gives the order
and the riders ease the rein,
the horses all move forward,
not one of them detained.

They march as one along the sand,
picking up the pace,
till Captain shouts the order
that starts this final race.
Sand kicks up from the desert,
a dust cloud rising high
as the horses gallop freely,
to succeed or else to die.

Across the burning desert sands,
the soldiers make their run.
The horses bravely galloping,
their coats reflecting sun
as bullets whiz and plop around
destroying targets large,
as soldiers duck their heads and yell
on the Tenth Light Horse last charge

Mick was riding on the flank,
his Molly in full flight.
His hands were trembling on the reins
when he felt the bullets bite.
The impact knocked him from his horse
with a loud resounding whack;
he hit the sand, lay deathly still
till Molly trotted back.

She stood with him beneath the sun
as the battle raged around,
her body casting shadows
over Mick upon the ground.
At times she gently nuzzled him
in asking him to rise.
And Mick looked up and blessed her –
to him she was a prize.

He'd picked her out some months ago,
this roguish chestnut mare,
so wild of eye, she'd challenged him
to 'ride me if you dare'.
They had some fights, some breaking
of the man, the horse and saddles.
Till one day she'd agreeably
let Mick stay full a-straddle.

Until that time had happened
her strength and courage bound
meant sometimes Mick was mounted,
the next upon the ground.
Yet something 'bout this chestnut mare,
in his heart she held the place,
'tis where he kept those cherished things,
now his fingers stroked her face.

She nickered soft and deeply
as her muzzle touched his cheek
as she tried to push him upward
but he was quickly growing weak
for the bullets passed right through him
and his head was pained and addled
But Molly lay beside him
to help him in the saddle.

"Good on you, mate," he told her
as he barely swung astride
"We may have had our differences
but, girl, you've done me proud,"
And up she stood with Mick aboard
and gentle made her tread
back to the line from whence she came,
too late though – Mick was dead.

But Molly Girl was treasured
for the role she played that day
in bringing home her Hero
from the sand where he had lay
A part of war-time history,
the Tenth Light Horse last run
when they charged through hails of bullets
in the desert 'neath the sun.

Helen Iles

Behind the Scenes

Highly Commended Article 2009

The music starts, the lights dim, the spotlight swings across the grass and up the castle wall. The entrance bars of music pierces the night, the arched doors open, and out into the arena surges a big black charger, its black mane flying, astride it, the Captain of the Kings Troop Royal Horse Artillery in all his resplendent glory. Behind him gallops the Bugler, and behind him thunders the team of heavy blacks hauling the three-tonne gun. They peel to the right as the spotlight finds the finer team of browns hauling another gun. They peel to the left. The spotlight pulls back to flood the field with brilliance and colour. The Captain draws his sabre, holds it erect, barks an order, and the musical ride begins.

The crowd is transfixed, wincing as the teams haul the heavy guns around the field, mirroring movement, swing them through wild loops and curves, then, galloping the diagonals miss each other by inches, three tonnes of heavy gun ready to bring them down and take their souls if the timing isn't perfect. If one horse baulks, the performance will be tragic.

We grimace behind the scenes, pray the gear holds, and ready ourselves for when the guns are disengaged and our teams gallop out to stand behind the grandstands out of sight. We leap into action, grabbing their bridles, keeping them from bolting as the cannons fire ceremonial retorts. On that cue, we release them and they gallop back to centre stage to retrieve the guns and surge back out of the arena. It seems only minutes since they left, since we released them for the very worrisome ride down Riverside Drive in the thick night traffic, to jog to the Esplanade for their grand and frightening entrance, these horses that are doing this for the very first time.

Soon they will be back for a costume change, the Kings Troop saddles and gun harness stripped, square high-backed saddles and velvet robes donned for the Knights of the Royal British Armoury. They will now have to endure the creak and crash of armour.

The ringing clash of metal on metal echoes around the enclosure as the horses are made ready, the two knights rehearsing the strokes they'll play in battle, then they double-check their carefully shaved lances, and it is time. They mount, girths are tightened as they haul down their helmets, visors raised until the full-on joust. We step back and bid them well, and again pray the horses stay safe.

So how did we get here, standing behind the stands at Supreme Court Gardens, peeking out through the centre stage entrance at a huge castle replica complete with turrets and opening double arched gates? It started from a simple phone call asking for assistance. The Mounted Section of the State Emergency Service had been noted for its horsemanship and discipline at a recent riding display, and our help was required by the organisers of the Perth International Tattoo. Being good little volunteers, we jumped at the invitation to be involved.

This spectacular event would consist of the Kings Troop Royal Horse Artillery reproducing their world-famous musical ride – a performance of sixty-three horses and ten three-tonne cannons – and a team of jousting knights to replicate the Days of Olde. Our role in this great plan was to find enough suitable horses and train them for those tasks in six months. And so we began.

The word went out, and soon horses of all descriptions began arriving at the property allocated as the training centre. All were dark-coloured, a requirement of the Kings Troop. Ron, the Equestrian Coordinator, offered a couple of Friesians, which he intended to showcase throughout the event. The difficulty was, Friesians were scarce in Perth, so, to aid his cause, two were imported from over east, one of them unbroken. Newly breaking a sizeable light draught horse and having it ready to perform in public under floodlights beside a percussion band in less than six months was impossible for the best of trainers, but, in the absence of an alternative, we started work.

Horses were trialled and 'binned', trialled and accepted, then trained for their role, which varied for some. The Friesians were the harness horses that would tow the three-tonne guns, and would also carry the armour-clad knights down a narrow lane of bunting while a jousting lance bore straight at them.

'Not a problem!'; we rolled our eyes.

But we only had four horses of one team, and the Kings Troop gun team had six – a millionaire's combined driving team, a kid's Pony Club horse and the unbroken gelding didn't even make one team, and the two part-bred, badly trained horses were far too dubious of character to risk the others. And we still needed a second team – and no more Friesians available. What else could we use for a gun team?

Ron said he knew of some standardbreds (that's those trotting horses that race at Gloucester Park) that worked as a carriage team in Kings Park. We could train them to tow a gun. Surely we could find two more!

Then we needed more horses for the Captain and the Bugler to ride. And the horses would also need to tent-peg because the Kings Troop had accepted an invitation to tent-peg against the WA Police Mounted Section. It was hair-tearing time: this handful of mismatched horses had to learn to tow the guns and accept the clash and clang of armour and having lances bearing down at their faces; they would never be able to tent-peg as well. We simply had to find more horses and fit them into our training programme. Did I mention anywhere that we were volunteers?

So in came more donations – horses for the causes, more testing and rejecting until a core group of horses looked halfway suitable. We began to mould and shape the horses in our charge, teaching the gun horses to work as a pair, the left horse ridden, the right-hand horse led and obeying the bat. The bat is a small white stick with a rope loop each end, which is used to keep the led horse up with and close in against the left horse. This was all new to us too, never having ridden a carriage horse before, or used a bat. Next, we worked them as a four, not yet harnessed together, selecting the staidest two as the wheel horses. This was Jordy, our Pony Club horse, and Grundgeon, would you believe, our newly broken gelding, who was accepting everything amazingly well.

Six months and a lot of dilemmas later, twenty-two horses were stabled up at Noalimba, the accommodation and training centre for the next month. Our international guests arrived shortly after – eight riders from the Kings Royal Horse Artillery, two Knights from the Royal British Armoury – all delightfully British lads who were eager to please and definitely determined to put on a cracking good show.

So the training and hiccups continued. The old World War II horse harnesses that were on loan for the performances were so decrepit they fell apart the first time used, almost pulling down the team – which was now an acceptable four – and the second team had not yet come to fruition. We explained to Ron what might happen when you hook four ex-racing standardbreds together and put them under floodlights in front of a crowd, but he just couldn't imagine it.

In due course, the riders became familiar with their mounts. The gun teams slowly became more settled. The jousting horses were less and less frightened by the lance and clang of the quintain, and we became quite proficient in centring that medieval device. The tent pegging horses were getting faster and faster and veered less and less from the white pegs in the ground. All was looking ready.

"Can you get me some big watermelons," the Captain asked one morning. "We might add in a sabre run to simulate beheadings."

So I go out and buy a half dozen watermelons and haul them back in a crate.

"What are they?" asks the Captain.

"Watermelons," say I.

"But I only want them about this big." He indicates the size of a rockmelon.

"This is the smallest they had," say I. So daily, we cut them in half and stuck them on the sticks. You just wouldn't get a ripe watermelon as small as that.

Dress rehearsal came and looked magnificent. The only problem was the Captain couldn't see with his busby on – he was totally blind – which apparently was common. They remedied this by the Bugler calling out instructions: "Go faster, Sir. Go slower, Sir. Halt there, Sir."

So here we were on the grounds at Supreme Court Gardens, twenty-two barely trained horses, a riding-blind Captain, a brand new set of harness per team, made through the nights by a bleary-eyed Kings Troop Saddler and a local saddlemaker, a team of Friesian horses hooked together and extremely touchy, a team of four standardbreds just waiting for the lights and music to race each other, a team of ten partly trained tent-peggers, and our rabbly group acting as backstage grooms, squires and crash team dummies ready to leap to the cause to save a horse or rider – with strict instructions: "Don't cut off my armour! It's terribly expensive."

We had vets and chiropractors on hand for any mishap and a good supply of Rescue Remedy with which we liberally laced the horses (and some riders) before sending them out the gates and down the road to Riverside Drive, the bright, sparkling lights of heavy traffic showing only silhouettes of two teams of magnificent horses towing two three-tonne cannons like professionals.

In those quiet moments, shattered only by the clashing of one broad sword against another in the background, I wondered if the crowd in the stands had any inkling of the effort and challenges suffered and overcome by a handful of dedicated people to bring this spectacle together, that, as the castle doors swung open and in charged the blind Captain of the Troop, big black Mandy veering with fright all the way down the centre of the arena with the Bugler saying: "Left Sir. Right, Sir. More Right, Sir. Halt, Sir."

In amongst that gun team was Grundgeon, wheel horse extraordinaire, undaunted jousting horse of the callous Black Knight. Our newly broken gelding had taken up the challenge and learnt as much as we had, performing to a level of excellence night after breath-taking night.

By the end of the week, with memories stored for a lifetime, we agreed whole-heartedly with the White Knight: We all had a cracking good time.

And mine will be the first hand up if they ever do it again.

Helen Iles

In Bradley's House

Winning Short Story 2010

She walked down the street carrying only her long grey shoulder bag, the tattered fabric matching her long loose trousers and long-sleeved, thigh-length overshirt. Her drab green floppy hat was pulled down over dark brown eyes, overlong dark hair that she had, as usual, pushed crudely up inside to hide its beauty and protect it from the harsh rays of sunlight beating down upon her back. She walked silently, retracing the steps she'd often walked from the town in the late afternoon, the limestone edges almost rutted by her single path. Su-Lin's path, Brad had called it.

She pushed the thought away. She did not want to think of Brad right now. Now was not the time.

Moving further off the road as a black car swept by, she turned her head to avoid the swirl of dust and litter; kept her head turned until the car disappeared round the bend. She tried not to think about where it was going. It would make little difference.

Soon enough, she reached the curve and, far across the pasture, saw the house, a house with many windows, its two-storied elegance nestled in the cove of towering magnolias where one summer they had erected the garden swing.

The fields were deep in grass, the tips browning slightly with the season, the surrounding fences standing crooked with neglect. She reached the driveway, its edges overgrown by red

Bergia and dog-rose, the house sulking at its abandonment, its boards chipped and shedding the white coat Brad had lathered on it. The purple wisteria that had trailed across the balconies and ornate latticework were now skeletal – and she thought about Brad again, and pushed the thought away.

Ignoring the three black cars parked out front, she followed the drive to the back of the house, stepped up on the wide slatted verandah and entered through the open back door. Inwardly she smiled – he had not put up curtains in her kitchen even though he had often threatened to. Maybe he too liked to look out the window and remember what she remembered, the freshly mown fields spreading out like rice paddies, each paddock coloured different by the separate days of mowing, each looking like terraces of paddies on the mountains of her home. Some days they made her sad and she longed for the palm trees and the umbrage of jungle growth around it. Some days she couldn't wait for the fields to grow and hide her long term memories. Those days she wanted to hang curtains and hide the view in total.

But not today. Today the curtain-less windows meant so much to her.

She turned and faced the kitchen, a large room bordered by many cupboards – cream cupboards in a pale green room – a bright room now buried in dust and leaves. Had no-one shut the door in all that time?

She heard footsteps on the stairway coming down, clunking hollowly as they always did, and voices carried in the next room. She pulled the hat from her head, shook the tresses loose and laid her bag and hat on the huge wooden table, not bothering to sweep it clean. She would have enough time for that much later.

A light flicked on in the next room, its glow shining through the gap beneath the swinging door. A shadow crossed the room, and she turned her back on it and opened the refrigerator. Every shelf was choked with ice, its solid crystal whiteness binding every metal tray to the next, and in amongst it she thought she could see a beer can. Brad liked his beer cold. She noticed too the open can of dog food just within the frozen boundaries of the lower shelf, and that was all. She wondered if Maska was even known of.

She turned to the table, pulled out the three pies and an apple she had purchased in the town, the voices becoming louder as she unwrapped two pies.

From the cupboard, she took the old chipped plate, set one pie upon it, and placed the plate on the edge of the verandah. Pulling a few large leaves from the magnolia tree, she set the other pie across them, decorated the leaves with a few carefully placed blooms from the garden and a quarter of the apple and placed it as an offering on the grass beside the step; she knelt and bowed fully. Rising to her knees again, she looked up as a shadow cast across her.

A man stood on the verandah, staring sternly down, his face surprisingly familiar, maybe even handsome if he did not scowl so much. She rose to her feet, bowed slightly then, the customary pleasantries dealt with, said:

"I Suey-Lin. This my house. You go now."

The man's scowl was replaced by wide-eyed rage, no sign of surprise at her presence. "No! This is my brother's house! You have no right being here."

She shook her head, her long hair swaying with defiance. "I no leave. My house," she insisted as she climbed the steps.

A woman stepped out to stand behind the man and Su-Lin brushed past her. Two more men standing in the kitchen moved aside as she entered.

"You all go now. You no belong here."

The man stormed in after her. "If you don't leave now I'll

have you thrown out," he bellowed at her back.

Su-Lin, her head bent, pulled the broom from the cupboard and began to sweep the floor.

"Did you hear me?" he bellowed again.

She heard the woman's voice, saw her ease the man back to the doorway. "John, leave this to me. I'll talk to her. Go on out, all of you."

Su-Lin felt relieved that the anger in the room had gone. The offering for peace and prosperity on the doorstep was working again. She kept sweeping.

"Su-Lin, stop," the woman said. "We need to talk."

Su-Lin looked at her. "This my house," she reiterated firmly. "Su-Lin live here long time."

"I know. But you left here. You left Bradley and went home. This house belongs to Bradley's estate and will go to his family."

"I Bradley's family," she said softly. "Bradley say this Su-Lin's house. This Suey-Lin's kitchen. Suey-Lin's verandah. Suey-Lin come back now."

"But you left him. You are no longer entitled."

For the first time, tears touched her eyes and she looked straight at the woman. "I no leave Bradley! Mr Winston call Bradley home. Say 'You come home now and no bring that whore. I no whore. I Bradley's wife." She started to whisk the leaves from the table. "I wait long time for Bradley come home. He come for short time then go again. He change. He very different. Then he send me home. I no understand but I go. He very different."

"Bradley was sick, Su-Lin," the woman said. "He got sick in the war and needed his family to look after him."

Su-Lin was silent. She knew the things that happened in the war; she knew the devastation on the men who'd fought on both sides, the devastation on the land. She had met Bradley in Long Dat before the last assault and spent time with him in her village while the damage was repaired. He had promised her they would make a life in America. He would get them a nice little farm where she could grow her vegetables and work the fields to her heart's content. He had brought her here and they had shared their lives, for years – until his father called him home. Then, after his last visit, he'd sent her back to her village high up in the mountains.

Then the letter came. He was very ill – he needed her to take over his affairs, to take over the farm, their farm, and if the worst happened before she arrived, her farm. She had used the ticket he had sent and returned, praying she would be in time.

"War a very bad thing," she said. "War in your family very bad too."

The woman looked sympathetic. "I know," she said. "They are rich and don't like outsiders. Even I have trouble fitting in. But I know they won't let you keep this place. They'll fight you every step of the way."

"They fight all they like. Su-Lin live here in Bradley's house. Bradley say I stay. Su-Lin have letter."

"They'll fight you with lawyers. You have no chance of winning, Su-Lin. Just leave now and save yourself a lot of heartache and money, money they know you don't have."

"Su-Lin have money. Bradley sent much money."

Footsteps on the verandah turned her head and a moment later the angry man strode back through the doorway. "Okay, I've had enough! You, get your bag and get the hell off this property. I've called our lawyer and he's preparing documents to bar you from being here. You have no right to this property whatsoever, regardless of what you think."

Su-Lin flicked a glare back at him.

"John, Su-Lin is Bradley's wife. They were married."

The man snorted. "No pathetic marriage service held in a pox-ridden village in a war zone is going to hold up in any court of law. Where is the paperwork? It could be just what she says … Brad wouldn't in a blue fit …"

"We marry here in America too," Su-Lin said as calmly as her temper allowed.

The man slapped his forehead with the heel of his hand. "Damn him. How bloody stupid could he be?!"

"Bradley good man," Su-Lin defended. "Not coward like brother. Honest man. Made good husband. Would have made good father."

Myriads of moments of her life with Brad flicked through her mind, moments she would treasure to the end of her days. Moments too she had envisaged of the future, the whole family playing together, laughing under the magnolias.

The woman turned to her, frowning. "What do you mean?"

"Su-Lin heavy with Bradley's child when he send Su-Lin back to village. Say he no want son to see him with sickness. Want his son to grow up strong and good like people in my village; not want son damaged by Winston family. Better off alone he say. Su-Lin see how angry Bradley is with family. He not want go home – only went because he sick. Bradley love Su-Lin and Kai. Not want leave us alone. We go on now without Bradley."

She saw the redness grow on the brother's face and hid the pain from hers; looked up as a familiar scratching came from the verandah. "Maska?" she cried. "Maska?"

A tall wiry deerhound appeared in the doorway, its tail wagging its whole grey body. "Oh, Maska!" Tears fell freely now.

She had felt so alone for so-so long. Leaving Kai with friends until she was settled was heartbreaking, leaving Maska, the wonderful dog Bradley had given her as a pup, behind when she left for Vietnam was devastating. But losing Brad had destroyed her soul completely. But the farm, Kai and Maska could restore it for all were part of him.

She straightened her back as the dog bounded towards her, felt the life coming back into her soul; her family evolving; she could see them all laughing beneath the magnolias for Brad would always be here in this place with her.

"You go now," she said to them all, unafraid of future consequences. The offering on the verandah was working fully, working strong, all good things coming back into her life. "You fight me however long you want, but you not come here again. This my place. This Bradley house. Bradley house where I belong."

She knew, standing beneath those grand magnolia trees with Maska leaning gently against her thigh on one side and the faint sense of Bradley on her other, watching them drive away that they would never return to destroy the dream she and Brad created. Her family would grow strong, and she would grow whole again in Bradley's house.

Helen Iles

Kimberley Dream

Special Mention Poem 2011

To wake in my swag with a wide-stretching yawn
and be gently caressed by a Kimberley dawn
in a camp that I pitched by a cold rippled stream
is only a part of my Kimberley dream.

White birds overhead that are bickering anew
wing far, far away in the Kimberley blue,
to where cockatoos rest in Albizia trees
take my memories soaring on the Kimberley breeze
of crouched round a fire in a mustering camp
huddling to keep warm in the Kimberley damp;
of lying flat out on a pool crystal deep
soothing the skin in the Kimberley heat.
of droving the cattle across the vast plain
or cleansing the skin in the Kimberley rain
or when stepping to ground from a horse that I trust
to sink my feet deep in the Kimberley dust.

When I left this land long time my heart sorely hurt
till I lay my swag back in the Kimberley dirt
In the Kimberley sun or the Kimberley flood
the life in this land is my Kimberley blood.
And now in my swag watching black clouds form
I know it's the first of the Kimberley storms
The changes are coming, no seasonal regret
it's time for the winter - the Kimberley wet

When rainfall eradicates land's steamy haze
giving relief from hot Kimberley days
where far and wide such magnificence seen
rolls on and on in new Kimberley green.

After droving long years in this glorious land
I'll give my bones up to the Kimberley sand
To die in the Top-end's a sure-fired must
so my soul can drift on in the Kimberley dust

And now that I've lived to Life's journey's end
I let my soul fly on the Kimberley wind
I lie on my swag as life passes me by
'neath a boab tree 'neath a star-filled Kimberley sky

Helen Iles

The Remember Game

Runner Up Short Story 2013

Daisy picked her way through the hummock and spinifex as she headed down to the stream, a small pale hand encased in hers. "We gunna play remember game," she said to the child trudging along beside her. "We gunna turn dis ting round."

They reached the stream that rippled slowly towards the distant gorge, its pebbly base glinting like diamonds where the water coursing round the curve had deepened the stream to calf-deep. Here Daisy had built a containment pond, where she soaked Zamia seeds for February eating. The water gathered in the pool, swirled around before swelling up and trickling over rocks to continue on its way. She scooped the still rock-hard Zamia seeds out of the small round pool and laid them on the bank, freeing the pool for the game.

"Okay, you take off dem old boots and put 'em up on dis big pella rock. I don't want your Dad gettin' narky at me ip you gettem wet."

The child sat in the red dust and peeled off her scuffed, brown boots and orange-tinged socks, and sat them on the rock as Daisy said.

"Okay, now you go in da water dere, and take dat basket wib ya." She scooped some of the basket's contents out into her orange-stained, floral skirt, gathered up the hem to her waist and climbed onto the boulder beside the stream. The child waded into the stream which swirled gently around her knees, eradicating the smudges of red dirt that had gathered on her pink skin during their walk from the homestead.

Daisy turned and sat, her calloused bare feet sticking out on the warm ochre surface further heating in the sun. "You ready," she grinned. "Me pirst." She thought for a moment then said … "I remember …" Her head tipped slightly as the past filtered to her mind. "Yeah, I know … I remember dat day you tried to cut across da home paddock to get to the muster camp across da riber and dat bloody old big pella bull Bossman put in dere chased you right up dat skinny gimlet tree. I still remember da way your skinny legs looked turning circles like Curly's old bike, ya ran so fast, and how ya had to lift 'em high to leap above the tall brown grass. Geez, I had to hang on to da fence to stay standin' up ya looked so bloody funny."

Her big white grin gleaming from her ebony face and the way her plump high cheeks lifted invoked the child's wide smile. She stood looking up at Daisy, all sweetness and dusty brown curls. "Dem legs just went round and round and round," Daisy added, grinning wider, her arms churning like huge locomotive wheels as she emulated how the wildly flailing legs moved. Her actions made Missy giggle.

Then Daisy remembered and plucked a flower from the folds of her skirt, held its stem in her fingers, twirled it then let it fly spinning through the air until it drifted down and settled on the water. It lingered a moment then was picked up by the swirling flow and danced around the pool. "Now, it's your turn," she said, glad of the child's glee.

Missy watched the flower bobbing around on the pool. "I remember … I remember," she sifted carefully, so many memories flooding in, "I remember when you taught me to tie my bows." Her eyes lit with the joy of that moment so long ago. "… and you got my finger stuck in the laces, and you said

… 'Well, how did that happen?' And so you showed me again … and you got my finger stuck again! And you pulled a funny face and I laughed and laughed and laughed."

Daisy started to chuckle too. "Flower! Flower!"

Missy picked a flower from the basket and carefully laid it on the water, watched as it swirled around and caught the same circular motion as Daisy's.

"My turn," Daisy grinned, images already dancing in her mind. "I remember da first day I taught ya how to make bread. You got more of dat belly flour across da table and up da kitchen walls than ya got in the bread dough. Then Bossman came in and roared with laughter 'cose you had dough on ya face and flour in ya hair and he grabbed ya round the waist and whirled ya round and said dat ya looked good enough ta eat. You remember dat?"

Missy squealed: "I remember that," gladness painting colour back onto her face.

"Oh, I laughed and laughed," Daisy remembered.

She picked another flower from her skirt basket, held it up, twirled it and let the wind take it to the pond. Missy watched it soar, spinning on its descent, followed its arc down to join the others. Missy laughed too. Then she said: "I remember when you tried to teach me to ride and Mr Magic started running fast, and I went bounce, bounce, bounce and bounced right off his back onto the ground. And you ran over and picked me up and said: 'Now, how did that happen?'And you made me laugh when I really wanted to cry because it hurt so much – and I'm sorry I wouldn't let you try to teach me again. Then Daddy said he would teach me to ride, and you could teach me later when you learnt to ride first. I really, really liked it when we finally got to go out riding together."

Daisy sighed deeply. "Yeah, dat was real nice."

Missy picked another white flower from the basket and laid

it gently on the water. It drifted and bobbed and surged around the pool to join the others.

Daisy was deep in thought when Missy called out: "Remember another one, Daisy. Remember another one."

Daisy nodded, enjoying the images that poured into her head. She grinned widely, pulled out the next flower and gazed at it. "I remember da first day you come to Kyeema in dat beat up old Landbrover. It done pull up in a big bloody cloud ob dust and you climbed out coughin' and wheezin' and cubered in dirt. We all be standin' on da verandah and you looked up at dat big old homestead and said: 'Oh my God!' We done taut you'd get straight back in dat bloody rattly car and go back where you come from. I always remember da look on your face dat day." She smiled but a tear rose to the corner of her eye and she sighed then sat staring out across the mulga plain on the other side of the creek.

"Your frangapelli, Daisy … Throw your frangapelli."

"Frang-i-pan-i," Daisy corrected, remembering how Bossman had taught her the names of the flowers in the homestead garden, this giant tree constantly spattering the ground and its canopy with white and yellow blooms. She loved lying under the thick shady branches staring up at the sun when Boss Lady had nothing for her to do. Sometimes she'd sit out there with her too.

"Daisy …"

Daisy snapped back to the moment, selected the largest flower and twirled it onto the wind. Missy watched as its wide curved petals turned elegantly as it made its way down to the water. The flowers had now all gathered near the bank where Daisy had laid the Zamia seeds, each turning on the gentle motion of the water like ballerinas pirouetting on pointy toes.

"Your turn."

Missy sighed deeply; sighed again. "I remember when you

got sick …"

"No! Not dat one," Daisy ordered brusquely. "Something else … you hab to remember someting nice."

Missy thought for a short time. "I remember," she said wistfully, "when you used to tuck me into bed and read me a story, and when you were finished you'd kiss me goodnight right here." She pointed to the middle of her forehead, "… and I'd put my arms around your neck and give you the big, big, biggest hug."

Daisy smiled; smiled ever so slightly. "Dat one 'serbs two flowers," she said.

Missy carefully picked two beautiful yellow-centred blooms and laid them on the water. Their dance joined the corps de ballet, and around the pool they twirled. "Aren't they beautiful," Missy said, watching them bob and whirl and partner off in a gentle, graceful waltz. Finally, she said, "Your turn, Daisy!"

"Okay, last one but," she said, "or Bossman gunna wonder where we got to." She edged herself from the rock to stand in the cool wet sand. "I remember dat day when Bossman sold all dose big pella bulls. He was so bloody proud he picked you up and spun ya round on da big verandah and you and Bossman started dancin'. Geez, you dance funny, all slow and twirly and squashed in togedda." She spun around with one arm in the air. "I'd neber seen dancin' like dat before."

"Daddy calls it waltzing, like waltzing Matilda."

"Yeah, like we better be waltzin' back to da house," said Daisy, wading into the stream. She stood with Missie watching the white flowers dance around them. "You ready set dem mem'ries free? Let dem fly to the bush so all da spirits can hear all da happy stories?"

Missie nodded, her curls bouncing across her shoulders.

"Okay, you say a wish now and we let 'em go so dem stories

can be told all across the land. You got a wish?"

Again Missie nodded with excitement.

"Okay, say your wish." Daisy lifted a rock and let the stream pour out through the opening. The current picked up the flowers and carried them round in a circle and out through the gap; took those dancing frangipanis floating away down the river, a row of ballerinas twirling on their points.

"I wish you will always be happy," Missie said, watching the flowers glide away, each one a beautiful memory she would always remember. She looked up at Daisy, waiting for her wish.

"And I wish *you* always be happy," Daisy said, looking down at the little girl.

They watched a moment longer then Daisy dropped the Zamia seeds back into the soaking pool, helped Missie pull on her boots and together they wandered back through the scrub to the homestead, the little girl skipping at times to keep up with Daisy's long stride. "Do you think we can bring Daddy to play the Remember Game next time?" she asked Daisy cheerily. "I think Daddy would like to remember Mummy too then maybe he won't be sad anymore."

Daisy squeezed Missie's tiny hand. "Dat's a real good idea," she said solemnly, looking down at the child and appreciating the life coming back in those big blue eyes. "Dat's a real bloody good idea."

Helen Iles

Moments

Highly Commended Short Story 2013

You stand on the edge of the wide concrete balustrade, your toes nipping at space as you stare at the blackness below. The water is down there somewhere, way down, swirling murky and brown around the massive concrete pylons before it sweeps away to the sea miles away. You know all that because you stood here yesterday, feet on the cracked grey pavement though as you stared down, watching it roil, wondering where else it touched. You calculated you will wash up on the pretty little inlet by the boat sheds across the river and that it wouldn't take too long for you to get there. Once in, the water's rush would finish you quickly, either the current dragging you under or the fall killing you outright. It would be like hitting concrete. You have calculated your path from the height of the bridge, the strength of the flow and the action of the tide around the headland. Therefore you would most likely be found on the shore, or floating nearby. It wouldn't be fair on Claire if you just disappeared out to sea – she'd think you ran out on her – betrayed her – left her holding the baby, rather than meeting with this ... accident.

All you have to do is sneak your toes out further, wriggle them in your shoes, shuffle, shuffle, till you feel nothing beneath the balls of your feet, as you do now … then tip a little forward. Would it feel like flying? Would the agony of hitting the water flat on be horrendous? Too late to think about that now … What would it matter!

You glance along the bridge. That old homeless bum you just emptied your pocket to is scuffing along the walk, shambling along in his baggy grey pants and oversized coat, the smell of old ale and urine strong on the air around him. You grimace that he followed you onto the bridge, a witness that will see Claire get nothing from your efforts. And you don't have time for this!

The old man stops at the railing, glances you up and down.

"I don't have any more money," you say. "I gave you my last dime."

"Just come to say thanks," he says, folding his arms on the railing. Seems like he's settling in to stay. "Mighty generous of you, sonny."

Mighty generous, be buggered, you think. It's just that you have no need of loose change anymore. You will have no need of anything from this moment on. You half smile, not wanting to engage in conversation, and stare blankly down at him.

"You know, I wasn't always like this," the man says, maybe a little embarrassed. "I was real successful once - had a great job, got paid better than most – had big companies trying to woo me over to their payroll. Drove one of those big, flash, black Mercedes and parked it up in my garage. Yeah, I've had my moments. And didn't I shine."

You think: Yeah, I've had my moments too. Life was good when I was shining gold. But shine doesn't stay. It's like, one minute you stand in the sunlight, the next the dark clouds come and tarnishes everything. Only you weren't ready for the storm – you didn't see it coming and got stuck in the deluge without a frigging umbrella.

Understanding a little of what the old man feels, you lean back from the edge.

"Yep. Had a real nice house too," the old man nods. "…

two-storey affair up in Glenford Heights, with a great big yard where the kids hung out all day in the pool; the wife there waiting for me every night when I came home for dinner."

Yeah, you think, your toes sliding back from the airiness of space. You know what that was like. Sefton Park, a gated community only the rich and famous could afford. A five-by-three split level bungalow with three car garage, and an indoor pool and gym. You heave a sigh. Not anymore though. Not anymore.

You stare at the blackness below; glance at the old man again. Is this where you're heading if you don't do this? Is this where this spiralling decline will lead?

"How many kids?" you ask, wondering why he is here on the street. Why is he not with his family?

"Two girls and a boy."

You think that even if the girls don't take him in, he would have a special relationship with his son. He must have done something pretty bad to not be with his son.

"*Had* a son," the old man corrected. "Lost him in Iraq. One of those roadside bombs."

You both remain silent, imagining the mayhem, the loss, imagining the news being delivered home. "That was the start of the end of me and the wife," the old man says. "I supported him joining the Army, she didn't. Didn't take long after our loss for her to finish it for good."

You sigh at his news. At least your lot wasn't that bad. No way would Joel join the Army or Navy. If it wasn't an all-out slaughter on the computer screen, he wasn't interested. Maybe that's where you should have put your foot down, you think. Maybe if you'd pushed some issues he'd have grown up with some sense of loyalty to family. Some concern at least. You doubt that he will even notice you've gone, or care. Would any soul care?

"Lost my faith in a bottle," the old man says, looking down to where the mighty river rushes away beneath you. He looks up again, his gaze lingering on your eyes. You wonder if he can see the desperation in them; you wonder if maybe he had stood here once. He gazes back out into the blackness of night, maybe picking up the twinkling of lights over on the headland where you will eventually wash up. Had he maybe also calculated ending it here? It seems he knew what you intended coming up onto the bridge at this bitter cold hour of night. So what do you do now? He obviously isn't going away. If you leave it much longer you won't do it. Just jump, you think. He's too frail to stop you.

"Mmm," he adds. "Lost my faith for a long time. Couldn't see then that things happen for a reason … everything, son, happens for a reason."

He pulls the collar of his coat higher and you realise you are shivering, that a fine spray constantly wafts past, wetting your hair, dampening your clothes. "Then I realised why I had to go through that …"

You look down at him. Why does anyone have to go through such pain, such absolute despair? Life is just too hard. You sneak your toes back over the edge of the railing. The wind blustering at your back will make it easy to let go and fly. You can do it, because you simply can't go back to being nothing. You had it all, and in your effort to have more you made stupid mistakes. In your effort to give Claire and Joel everything, to have everything you ever wanted, you took too many risks. And you lost. Lost it all. Oh boy did you lose. You lost the house, the cars. You lost your son's respect. You lost Claire. There was absolutely nothing left ... except your policies. You are at least worth something on those pieces of paper. Claire will realise you did it for her. She could pay off your debts and still be comfortable. You sneak the balls of your feet back out into space. The old man wouldn't tell - he sees your desperation.

The old man sighs. "I needed to realise that all that wealth doesn't make happiness, son. I needed to let that all go to learn what was important in life - that life is about being here for people. Life is nothing without people." He sighs again. "I remember one cold, dark night, I stood about where you are now, wondering why life had let me down, not able to see that things in life steer your purpose."

You stare down into the blackness where the river runs; try to shut out his words. It would be too hard to start again; too hard to win back Claire's respect.

"There was this homeless woman, what we then called a bag lady – she followed me up on this bridge," he says. "Started talking, telling me her sad, lonely story. You know, son, in that moment of giving up I realised I could help her. I could make her life a whole heap better. I realised that helping folk was worth much more than high falutin' houses and fancy cars. I been here helping people ever since. This is my purpose, and losing all that stuff was necessary to bring me here to this bridge." He pulls his coat tighter around him. And you lean out again, loosen your grip on the world.

"And you won't wash up on the cove from here," he says. "The current turns in the middle of the river, and," he skids his palms across each other, "you're straight out to sea."

That will mean Claire won't get a cent, you realise. There won't be anyone to look after her. She will have to pay off all your debts and she'd have a real hard time of that. Your grip locks back on the rail. You pull yourself back in. Sneak your toes back onto solid concrete. A deep, heavy weight drops in the pit of your stomach.

"The Lord works in mysterious way, son," the old man says. "And there is always a way out of your problems. You just need people to help you get through it. Why don't you come down from there and we can walk a while; find somewhere out of this cold blessed rain."

Rain? Is it raining? You plop back to the pavement; feel even more a failure that you couldn't even do this right. Nevertheless, it just means better planning next time – like everything else you should have done.

"Come on, son, there's some fire drums over near the alley on the corner. Some nice folk to chat to as well. I can introduce you to Annie. Get you a coat. Light will shine on your day tomorrow," he says as you walk back off the bridge. You can see a gathering of homeless warming their hands perilously close to the dancing flames, an elderly bag lady standing aside watching for the old man's return. You wonder if this was his saviour.

"No, I think I'll go home from here," you say, praying you can sort this out some other way, praying Claire will give you one more chance. You head in the other direction, hands in pockets and bunched against the cold. "Thanks for the chat."

The old man calls after you. "Hey, sonny, you want back your change?" He holds out the fistful of coins.

"Nah! You earned it," you say.

You imagine him, as you walk somewhat defeated, standing around the drums telling all how he'd just stopped a jumper leaping from the East Street Bridge; that he'd just had his greatest moment of all in the sun.

Helen Iles

Hoops

Commended Poem 2014

You
train me
to jump through hoops
wear flowers in my aura
flaunt feathers and finery
to lift the eyes from tattered skirts
you dress me in

I
spin within your hoops
camouflage my thoughts with joyful smiles
wear purple warmers on my wrists
to hide the scars
caused by your eternal domination

You
spruik to crowds
who watch my daily act
watch me spinning in your rule
gyrating to your constant requirements
as I lose my identity
in an ocean of regret
and fix the smile rigid
to hide the thoughts within

I
founder
torn between first love and marital duty
wrestle with a pride too long suppressed
and try to stay afloat
knowing that all you see
is the size of the ring that binds me
never knowing that …

You
are the hole in my boat
and
I
drown
'neath the weight of your expectations

Helen Iles

Island Time

Runner-Up Article 2015

Christmas Island is a rare and hidden beauty, a paradise in the middle of the ocean. It moves with a slow and gentle grace that can only be appreciated from experience.

We flew to the island on a Friday in early November, hopping across the ocean from Learmonth to Cocos Island then on to the third most dangerous airport in the world. Sheer cliffs border the tarmac, rising up on our left to another plateau, dropping down into the ocean on the right, leaving no room for human error. Any mistake splatters you across the cliff-face or drops you into the drink. There is no radar on Christmas Island so landing is attempted only with clear visibility. Any fog and the plane diverts to Jakarta. We will be here for a week, there being one flight in and out, on Fridays. Empty seats on the plane are loaded with precious food, and trucks lumber along the tarmac to collect the island's supplies.

We are here to deliver Cliff Rescue training to the Islanders, an intensive four day course which leaves us three days free to explore the jungles and coastlines. Hire vehicles are waiting at the airport and we stow our luggage, toeing aside a few red crabs playing Customs with our bags before heading for the VQ3 Lodge down in The Settlement. November is the start of the red crab migration so, driving down the steep mountain road, we not only have to watch out for other traffic but also have to dodge every red pedestrian crab. If seen driving without due regard to crabs, Parks and Gardens officers confiscate the car.

Crabs on the road come in two varieties: runners and squatters. Those that squat usually survive. Runners become an easy feed for the massive population of feral cats.

Christmas Island is layered in five plateaus, the first beneath the ocean so everywhere you travel away from the coast you take the mountain road. This curves back and forth around tall cliff walls as it heads up the mountain - one lane up, one lane down, the lanes divided by a double white line. In crab migration season these lines are disregarded, only applying to oncoming traffic when no crabs hamper forward movement, otherwise you veer anywhere you like to avoid crunching tiny little bodies under the wheels. The migration occurs at breeding time when the crabs sidle out of the jungle and trek down the mountain to the coast. Reaching the sea, they perform a comical, ritualistic dance, lay their eggs, and crab-walk back to the jungle. On many roads low plastic buffer guards channel the flow of crabs away from the road, but when the full onslaught is on, these are useless and most roads on the island are closed.

We reach our lodgings and soon realise crabs are everywhere; they even climb the steps to our quarters. Thankfully they are timid creatures that scurry out of the way though I did during an idle moment encounter a cluster hell-bent on untying my shoelaces.

The weather on Christmas Island is warm and humid, the hotel room air-conditioned and meeting our basic needs. VQ3 is a friendly place where lodgers sit and chat on balconies and look out onto lava rock-faces, which are also daubed with … red crabs. We soon learnt they climb cliff walls with far more ease than the Cliff Rescue team we are here to train.

Our bags tossed into our rooms, we reconnoiter the island for likely cliffs to throw rescue bodies off for the night and day activities. It's not hard to find cliffs here – but we need to check the height of each cliff and its stability – most of the island drops steeply to the sea with few places to safely land a boat. One safe place is Flying Fish Cove.

Skirting Flying Fish Cove, we pass the Malay kampong on our way to the Governor's Mansion above the bay, reached by a narrow wiggly road that juts out on steel girders from the cliff-face. The cliff face is garbed in heavy wire mesh which attempts to hold back rock-falls that would easily push a car over the edge. We drive fast, noting even the crabs don't come here much, rather climbing the cliff-face to the plateau than taking the road. Our first cliff accepted, we head for Poon Saan.

The island is populated mainly by Chinese and Malays, with a few Europeans. Most of the inhabitants work at the Phosphate Mine or for National Parks and Gardens. The Malays live mainly in the Kampong on the coast, and daily the sound of their midday prayers and music echoes across the cliff-tops, a pleasant sound at first, becoming annoying as the hour drifts on. The Chinese live at Poon Saan or higher up the mountain, each nationality choosing to live in separation since settlement began. Most Europeans live at The Settlement north of Flying Fish Cove, their simple houses looking out to a blue horizon that seamlessly fuses sea and sky. The sea is calm and sleepy now though some damaged buildings lay skeletal from a cyclone that ripped across the coast years ago. Whether kept as a reminder of the weather's fury or just not yet repaired is hard to tell, for time on the island moves slow.

We soon find out how slow. We need food, but shops on the island don't open till 9 am. They close again mid-afternoon. Wanting to buy lunch, we must wait until 4 pm when their doors open again. Then we can eat until midnight.

The Rumah Tingii Tavern has the best steaks on the island (maybe the only steaks as they fly meat in on Fridays). We dine there many times, walking back each night along quiet roads that skirt the cliffs, accompanied by the gentle kitcher-kitcher-kitcher of red crabs scurrying into the darkness. We encounter our first Robber crab – also known as Coconut crab for its skill of carrying fallen coconuts back up the tree and dropping them; they then feed off the contents through the broken shell. We warn ourselves to stay away from coconut trees. When one giant beast wandered out of the bushes looking more like a turtle than a crab my counterparts moved to the other side of the road, not wanting to incite its nastiness. Unlike our friendly red crabs, this crab attacks and can sever your Achilles with its hydraulic-like claws – claws big enough to feed a small family. They, like the red crab, are protected, so we quietly sidle by.

On our first day up on the cliff face, our students prepare us for our days of exploring. "Watch out for Pandanus," they say, "also known as Walking Tree. Brush leaf this way, okay. Brush that way, tear big holes in skin." We avoid the giant Pandanus. "Watch out for Maruta Vine," they say, "… called Stinging Bush. Thorns give you rash, make you itch. More you scratch, more you itch." I begin to wonder if going into the jungle is such a good idea.

We go nevertheless as soon as our trainee friends are happily qualified in Rescue from Heights, and I am happily spared from being thrown over any more cliffs.

We become proficient in weaving our way up and down the mountain road, dodging crabs and rusted cars, at swinging round at the ring road that cuts the mountain road onto the coast road. It is now time to go exploring. But the sign at the ring road states all roads, bar one, are closed due to the crab migration, meaning most of the island is now inaccessible.

We drive up to the massive, disused Casino, which is showing signs of decay, the metal on many buildings corroding from the constant sea spray that lashes up the cliff face, laying salt over everything. We visit temples and cemeteries, lookout towers and beaches, Dolly Beach the most memorable. After walking five kilometres along higgledy-piggledy boardwalks through the jungle, the structures built to protect the red crab burrows, and hearing crashing of waves bashing the coastline for much of that time, we eventually stand on a clifftop looking down on a glorious beach, its pristine sands unmarked. Coconut palms sway in the late afternoon breeze as they wait for the sea to wash their feet. Feeling like Tom Hanks must have felt

in The Castaway, I capture a hundred photos before the tide urges us back up the concrete stairs to the cliff.

We stroll back through the humid jungle, appreciate enormous Birds Nest ferns in treetops, edge past serrated Pandanus, gush at porcelain blue crabs and awe the life in the jungle.

We visit The Grotto, a cave flooded by sea-water whenever a wave crashes on the coastal cliffs, the current surging into the cave then receding back. In the afternoon heat and humidity, we are tempted to swim, but the rope to be held for safety looks rotted and the old adage comes to our mind: Who rescues the rescuer when the rescuer needs rescuing. Not wanting to be sucked out through the back of the cave and having our trainee friends pull us out of the sea, we move on.

From the lookout on the western cliffs, we watch prehistoric-like Golden Bosun, birds found only on this island; they drift on thermal currents escorted by Frigate birds until they settle on their nests on cliff tops.

That night we taste Robber Crab, poached from the National Park by our miscreant friends. It's a delicacy of grand proportions, obviously the reason they are protected. We dispose of the shells furtively, not wanting to run foul of Federal Police who have jurisdiction over the island.

On our last day, we visit the Japanese Cemetery on Phosphorous Hill, where headstones have been reverently restored, the jungle cut back so each fallen soul can receive visitors. The ethereal atmosphere is added to by the stifling heat and surrounding crush of Pandanas that rise like church walls, sunlight pouring through the cramped tree canopy like rays through a stained glass window. I feel the movement of souls still walking here.

Our last meal, we gather with our friends at a restaurant in Poon Saan and sample every Chinese dish, a sumptuous but low-cost banquet.

Our time up, we pack for the midday flight, pray for clear skies, and sadly bid the island farewell. The last few days I have missed patting a dog – only two live on the island – and the sound of country music – of that there was none. We wave the red crabs goodbye, board the plane and soar off the cliff ledge into thick white clouds, leaving our Island Paradise rising from a sleeping ocean until our blissful return.

Helen Iles

Breaking Full Circle

Commended Article 2018

She huddles in the corner of the dilapidated cubby, knees pulled up to her chin to avoid the rain pouring through the roof where his fist has made a hole. In the darkest hours of this cold stormy night, she sinks into depression and contemplates death: she simply cannot go on like this anymore.

She has not slept in four long nights, not since he threatened in the darkness of her room that he will come while she is sleeping, bash her head in with a shovel, and bury her in the garden. She has lain for three nights peeling paint off the wall, anything to keep herself awake. Maybe, if she stays awake he will not come. But now, so sleep-deprived, she feels death would be better than this nightly torture. She is eight years old and luckily has few options available to achieve her self-destruction.

So mentally distraught, she eventually lashes out, and is hauled along to Child and Adolescent Mental Health Service (CAMHS) where she tells her story of verbal and physical abuse and relentless torment, of a stepfather who beats her, belittles her and a mother who turns a blind eye. Here she prays for the help she needs, but is betrayed: rather than coming to her aid CAMHS reveals to her parents her accusations and she is taken home to more beatings. She is then traipsed around a plethora of doctors until one labels her

ADHD and administers mind-management pills in the hope her mind will settle enough that she can concentrate at school and learn what she needs to progress in life. But she cannot learn: the fear of returning home from school each day occupies her mind to the exclusion of all else.

For the next five years, she struggles to learn, and after school hides away in her room, coming out only for meals. If she is unseen, she cannot be abused; she cannot be blamed or ridiculed; she can avoid suffering the pain that her mother sits there and does not stand up for her. So secluded, she loses the ability to interact socially; has difficulty retaining friends; doesn't sleep and develops low self-esteem.

The abuse continues. She cannot escape it. In absolute desperation she retaliates; fights back with violence. Anger, verbal abuse and lashing out with fists becomes her normal behaviour. She resents her half-siblings who do not suffer any of the treatment she deals with.

At fifteen, the lid blows off her world and, unable to improve her situation, unable escape anywhere, she breaks mentally. Manic and depressed, her personality splits into three: she tries to survive by becoming the persona who can cope with the situation at the time. And when that doesn't save her, she suffers a full-blown nervous breakdown, which provides her escape from the home environment. Eventually, she becomes a child of the streets.

At sixteen, she attracts a mate, but her lack of social skills prevents her from seeing she has fallen for a duplicate of her abuser – a vicious, manipulative, controlling sociopath who continues to beat and torment her, emotionally, physically and sexually. This is now the new normal in her life. She is now degraded, defiled, alone. And she stays for the sake of her newborn child, not seeing that this will become the life for her offspring as well. She does not want a broken home for her child to suffer the way she has suffered at the hands of a stepfather.

This results in a volatile environment and the infant grows in a household of screaming abuse and bashing, and threats against them both, till the mother flees, a natural instinct to protect her offspring at all costs, saving her.

But the damage is done. Socially inept, her anger wielded like a weapon, violence becomes a necessary part of her. While she thinks she is worldly-wise, she has not yet been out in the world to understand its risks. Betrayed by those who were supposed to love her, she knows not what love is, and therefore knows not how to love.

Research by McGill University (2015) showed that emotional abuse of a child may be as harmful as physical abuse and neglect. It found that emotionally abused children exhibit a range of specific signs. They often feel unhappy, frightened and distressed, behave aggressively and antisocially or too maturely for their age; they experience difficulties with school attendance and achievement, find it hard to make friends, show signs of physical neglect and malnourishment, experience incontinence and mysterious pains.

Glaser's research in 2002, noted that adults emotionally abused as children were more likely to experience mental health problems and difficulties in personal relationships. Many of the harms of physical and sexual abuse were related to the emotional abuse that accompanied them, and as a result many emotionally abused adults exhibited a range of complex psychological and psychosocial problems associated with multiple forms of trauma in childhood.

While this girl, now a young woman, has survived, she exhibits all the traits mentioned above. An MRI of her brain taken after the nervous breakdown in adolescence reveals all the pockets of her brain relating to the emotions are dead or dormant, most probably caused by mental trauma of some form or another. Whether, under perfect circumstances, the brain will repair itself is unknown.

The saddest part of all this, is that, not knowing what a normal childhood should have been, she now becomes the tormentor, her children the victims. The deprivation of all good things a child should experience in life becomes, to her, 'Tough Love', the beatings 'Discipline.' It is how her mother had explained it.

One report on filicide in Australia found that fifty-two per cent of the child victims of filicide were killed by their fathers/ stepfathers, while 48 per cent by their mothers, however it must be stressed that there are gaps in the data and research and overseas evidence indicates a higher proportion of mothers are responsible for filicide.

Research undertaken by the Australian Medical Association in October 2016, revealed that 'between July 1997 and June 2008, 468 children (under 18) were killed, with the overwhelming majority of these child deaths (62 per cent) perpetrated by a parent. Data and research on the motives behind filicide (death of a child attributed to a parent or step-parent) is limited. We do know from filicide research that men and women kill children in different circumstances and for different reasons, however understanding these gender differences is complex and the findings contradictory.

And just as sad, violence will again breed violence and another generation of abuser is formed. Where will this vicious cycle end?

Thankfully there are organisations that deal with child protection – one being The Department of Child Protection (DCP), now called the Department of Communities. Their primary role is protecting children, each case starting with someone reporting harm being inflicted on a child. Depending on the findings of the initial assessment and investigation, other agencies, such as Police, may also become involved.

Where possible, the DCP work with the family to determine the circumstances of the alleged abuse, remedy the situation, provide support to the family to correct the behaviours and ensure the child's safety. Two field workers investigate the report, possibly talking with the child and checking them for injuries, often before the abuser is approached. In the case of emotional abuse, they look for behaviour indicators in the child that may indicate the trauma they have suffered.

In their Annual Report 2016-2017, the DCP reported receiving 85,025 calls regarding abuse or harm to children and youth. They issued 19,758 notifications, undertook 12,954 assessments for the safety and wellbeing of a child, and were granted through the courts 1,093 protection orders.

Unfortunately, in the instance of our case study, the report to DCP resulted in the referral to CAMHS, the diagnosis of ADHD, allowing this child to slip through the cracks.

Hopefully, with this new generation, family, neighbours and teachers will pick up on the behavioural indicators displayed by the children and be instrumental in creating an early intervention. Certainly, if the abuse is allowed to continue, particularly during the children's formative years (between 1 and 5 years old), the behaviour will be ingrained and will become the normal behaviour in their growing years and into adulthood.

As a member of the community, it is your responsibility to report any cruelty against children, whether verbal, emotional or sexual, in an effort to break the cycle of violence. Certainly, no child should ever live in fear, especially fear created by their own family/protectors.

It would be difficult to exist if a tragedy occurred knowing you could have done something about it. A simple phone call, always kept anonymous from the abuser, could save a child from ongoing harm.

If you see or suspect child abuse in any of its forms, please save a child and make that vital call. You may be instrumental in breaking the cycle of abuse and saving future generations from this unforgivable suffering.

Helen Iles

Chasing Tadpoles

Commended Poem 2020

There's a frog outside the window
that takes me long time back
to happy days
when we floated car tops on the swamp
you long-poling through rushes
Bro stabbing for gilgies
and I – too young – chasing tadpoles
on the peaty bank

I would watch your auburn crown
meandering above brown bullrush heads
praying it remained there
fearful you would both fall in
and alert Pa to our antics
invoking his wrath
and him forbidding us our sanctuary
My tadpoles so far had saved us
from his knowing –
we were only chasing tadpoles

Distance   time   life
removed us from the swamp
just like my tadpoles maturing
hopping away to climes unknown
only to hear their occasional croak nearby

We flew too   separated
not brother and sisters
but individuals
raising our own tadpoles
who also hopped away from us
We rarely hear their occasional croak

As I sit here now
holding your hand
wondering where all our tadpoles hopped
wondering if the frogs will come to see you
to remember all the good times
to treasure tales of our escapades …
But Bro is gone
lost to us when Ma's passing destroyed us
And now you …

As you take your last breath
I hear a frog outside the window
and I am left, long poling alone
floating on an island
in a swamp of memories
still chasing tadpoles.

Helen Iles

Elizabeth Pappas

Judas at Their Table

Winning Short Story 2019

Our villa rattles and groans. Shutters break free from their latches cracking like whips against grey walls. Roof tiles shift as the night storm weighs down upon our home. Frightened by the intensity of the gale, I snuggle in bed beneath my blankets. A branch taps at my window. Its eerie appearance resembles the long arthritic finger of a timeworn witch. From the light of crashing thunderbolts, sheltering on my windowsill, sits a *koukouviya* (owl). I spring from under the blankets to retrieve it from the storm. Flinging wide the window, a mighty gust blows the bird fluttering onto my dressing table. There it sits wide-eyed, trembling.

Closing the window, I realise what I have done. I have let in a *koukouviya.* According to the villagers on Corfu, someone dies when a *koukouviya* enters a home. Why, I curse, are the Greeks so superstitious? The bird continues to perch on my dressing table, blinking. As the storm rages, I sink into a fitful sleep.

A long ray of sunshine falls across my face warming my cheek like the touch of a gentle kiss. I open my eyes and recall the shivering, wide-eyed bird. I look across the room; there is the bird. It's still wide-eyed and shivering on my dressing table. Trying not to frighten the bird, I get out of bed and pick it up. Flinging open the window, I discharge it from its overnight shelter. It ascends into a clear blue-sky hooting as it departs.

At breakfast the news breaks that a life was stolen in the night. Our neighbours *Yiayia* (Grandmother) died. Her transparent soul winged its way through the stormy night to the mysterious sorting yard where all lifeless souls wait.

"I knew it, I knew it," I say to myself. "It's my fault. I shouldn't have rescued the *koukouviya*."

I decide not to mention the owl. Later I join villagers and visit Yiayia's family. At her villa, I'm invited to join the mourners. We perch on assembled chairs set around the lifeless woman's body where she lies flat on her bed.

Before I or others arrived, Yiayia's body was prepared and laid out. Special *moirologia* (mourners) had embarked on a sequence of bereavement rituals. The women washed her body with vinegar, then dressed her. They placed candles at the head and foot of the old woman's brass bed. The icon of her name saint, her treasure, rests on a now still heart. The women placed two gleaming gold sovereigns in her eye sockets. These will pay the ferryman. Even in this Christian community, her passage to Hades is considered. Is it God, or do the Gods throw the dice? An evil eye on a white ribbon entwined with garlic hangs from a bed knob close to her head. More pagan measures against evil forces.

Now in the halo of the wavering light of candles and lanterns, I experience the ancient phenomena of *moirologia*. I'd never seen this ritual. The tradition heralds back to the Iliad: The Odyssey, the 8th century BC. Yiayia's female friends embody the skills of expert mourners. When the principal *moirologia* begins her lament, the other women, one by one follow suit, and wail. Their voices flow into a continuous chorus of crying. Their voices move beyond our world to the mysterious secret, sacred places where mere mortals cannot go until their time is ripe. As *moirologia* voices ascend, the sounds enter conditionally, a world beyond our own, the afterlife. During the lament, wearing no makeup, the women loosen their long hair allowing it to fall. It hangs wild and at liberty around their shoulders. Frequently yanking at their tresses, they chant and the pitch increases. Rocking and swaying back and forth, the women move in tempo with each other. Grief moves outward and into the spectators.

Amid subdued trembling light, *Yiayia* looks beautiful. Her braided hair frames her face in a decorative bun. Threaded beneath her white headdress, white ribbons entwine her braided hair in traditional Corfiot style. Her headdress falls in a short cascade over her shoulders. Only one ear, her right ear boasts a large gold earring. Bursts of colour emanate from blooms that negotiate her headdress. Yiayia's white blouse sits beneath a black velvet bolero jacket. Hand-stitched gold eagles mount its delicate front. An eagle perches on each breast symbolising Christian Byzantium. A gold Christian Orthodox cross hangs on a chain around her neck.

I recall how she wore this outfit on festival days; her black skirt ballooning from the many petticoats beneath. Now the outfit makes her shoulders and face appear tiny. An ethereal Mona Lisa smile traces her lips. The pale landscape of her skin is as wrinkleless as plump gardenia blossoms. Wearing tiny polished black shoes, it is as if she is a maiden off to a celebration in the village.

Friends bearing autumn flowers place them around her body. A generous bouquet of perfumed basil and lemon blossoms garnish her touching fingers. She's attended with unhurried love and care. Her hand-embroidered linen is on show around the room. They are a barometer of her life's effort embodied in fine stitches. Her daughter-in-law, hair hanging around her face, shows each masterpiece with pride. They are hers now.

Later, the smell of ouzo and brandy served on a small tray mingles with damp clothing and mothballs. Spirits are accompanied by Greek coffee in demitasse cups. A sheet of incense rests at head height as frankincense wafts unencumbered from *Yiayia's* crowded bedside shrine. Her much-loved icons sending out a final tribute to her from the light of her grandmother's crackling oil lamp. From time to time friends and family, overcome with grief, fling themselves over her still body. They wail loudly. It is as if they are endeavouring to call her back from where she has gone but they fail. White starched handkerchiefs pass along the row of chairs. Old bodies, once young, bend with effort touching her face with rough gentleness. Farmers hands gnarled and purple from olive picking. Even in the milling, a melancholic final caress from a once ardent lover. Past passions left to yesterday. Tears drop from above.

"The funeral, the funeral, we must speak of this," comes the voice of the daughter-in-law. It's time I left them to their arrangements.

During the night I have a dream about an icon I'd seen in a church in Corfu town. It depicts the dead plucked off heavens ladder. Devils pull at those ascending it by using every conceivable temptation. At the bottom of the icon, the dead scream in torment as the fires of hell engulf them. The Orthodox believe the soul of the deceased wanders the earth for 40 days after death. *Yiayia's* soul is on a journey through aerial toll houses. During this time *Yiayia* will reappear in places she frequented before her soul departs. If her soul fails its trials, demons will drag her to hell with tempting lures. I wonder if this will be my soul's destiny. A burrowing and unsettling malevolence hovers in the shadows of my dream and I awaken to wild pounding in my chest.

A few days later I join the solemn procession on its way

from *Yiayia's* house to the church. We make our way with the coffin held aloft through the olive groves. Upon entering the church, the familiar smell of incense; the flickering of icons. Tempered by the sound of chanting, before me is a scene of gold and silver. Juxtaposed against dark huddled bodies, sagging shoulders, the coffin lies unmoved. The mood echoing an image reminiscent of a gloomy El Greco painting. We pause before a now open coffin. It faces east in front of the alter. The priest's voice rings in my head.

"She is only sleeping; she will rise again."

I panic. Will she rise again and punish me for saving the *Koukouviya*?

Later, walking behind the coffin, the solemn congregation make their way to the graveyard. I walk with her family and I am cloaked in guilt. Golden autumn leaves rustle and swirl around our feet. Their colour contrasting with the blue sky. It is a serious scene as the sun emits rays warming us from the bite of the wind. Next to *Yiayia's* prepared grave, I see the remains of the former occupant. Not mere morsels of mortal remains, these discarded body parts are recognisable. Legs, spine and scull. They attend by protruding through clumps of sodden soil. They send shivers down my spine. I avert my eyes and whisper to Maria, my neighbour,

"Whose bones are by the graveside?"

Shuddering, she wraps her black shawl closer to her body. She explains,

"I don't know. The family to whom the bones belong must collect them. They wash the mortal remains and place them in an ossuary. This act of desecration allows *Yiayia* a place to rest until she's lifted out of the earth; placed into an ossuary."

Keeping her voice low Maria continues,

"In Greece cremation is illegal. It is not a Greek Orthodox tradition. We believe we will ascend again when Jesus returns.

As most of the population in Greece is Greek Orthodox, it's hard to find a space to bury the dead. Plots are leased for three years. When this period ends, relatives are notified to witness the removal of the skeleton from the ground. If they want to keep the remains in the grave, they need to continue paying rent."

Pausing to cross herself Maria reflects,

"If no one pays the rent on the grave or removes the bones from the grave, what remains is moved by the authorities. Then it will be dissolved in chemicals. The remnants get placed in a common burial plot. The Clergy believe incineration violates the mortal body."

I bow my head at this disclosure and turn my collar to the cold wind. Hesitating at *Yiayia's* gravesite, the priest shakes his head as he sizes up the coffin. He decides the grave is too small. After much conversation among the men, they exchange bitter words. The women discover what will occur next. They release primal howls. Appearing feeble and helpless, their rage sits in the air. Informed, the grave-diggers cannot dig a longer hole. If they do, her coffin will encroach into the sacred lot of another's grave. More debate and the priest insist the end of the coffin is to be shortened so it can fit into the ground. We stand waiting as one of the altar boys races back to the priest's house. He returns with an axe.

Pulled from the ranks of pallbearers, the priest commandeers a strong male. With shaking head, the recruit takes up his assignment. He must chop off the end of the coffin without damaging Yiayia's body. He fumbles for his gold crucifix. Finding it beneath his coat and jumper, he raises it to his lips, looks to heaven and kisses it. He prays out loud seeking absolution for what he is about to do. The lid of the coffin opens so the executioner may see where to aim his blade. Howling begins. Black arms haul women back in horror from the graveside. The blade of the axe shines in the sunlight. It strikes the end of coffin again and again. This desecration continues until the length of the coffin is the correct size. The priest, after assessing the scene, remains stoic. Yet, his steadfast face yields tears. But he must follow church rules even if it distresses his parishioner's.

When the task is completed, the priest signals the coffin to be lowered into the ground. With prayers, the priest pours olive oil over the coffin. Soil lands with a thud on the coffin lid. Yiayia lies beneath the earth. The scene before me is heartbreaking and I am to blame. I don't go to the *makari* (mercy) meal that follows. They wouldn't want Judas at their table.

Elizabeth Pappas

This Fat Piggy

Commended Short Story 2019

I deliver my daily mantra. "Mum, I'm hungry. What's for lunch?"

Her response,

"Bread and tomatoes."

"Oh no! We had that yesterday and the day before. In fact, we have it every day. Isn't there something else for lunch?" I complain.

"Nope." Comes her swift reply.

I've made my point. Every day I make my point. I make a point of it. It's not all bad. The truth is I love bread and tomatoes, but I'm not telling Mum. I want her to suffer, make her feel it's her fault that we eat this monotonous Greek peasant food. Yet, the bread from our local baker is lip-smacking good. His modest shop sits on the sloped street in Pyrgi village. Wonderful smells emanate from it. His wide-mouthed oven bakes bread six days a week and on big days, the villager's roasts. Our usual lunch, chunks of crusty white bread; soft in the centre served with slices of organic tomato drizzled with thick green olive oil and a pinch of salt. It's heaven, but I'm not telling Mum.

With bread and tomatoes eaten, I head to my friend Katarina's place. Her home is close to ours and forms part of our hamlet. We are both 12 and because neither of us go to school, our time together is often spent doing jobs around her parent's small farm or giggling about everything. Today is different. We are invited to watch an execution. Today the pig we've been feeding for months is going to be slaughtered. What remains of him after his execution will be shared among Katerina's family and her cousin Fortis family. Katerina and I loiter anxious near the well, waiting for the carnage to begin.

Soon others join us in the clearing near the well. We stand in an informal semi-circle with Katerina and Fortis family. The heavy pig is pulled snorting into the centre of our human horseshoe. I sense he senses what is about to happen. The pig's eyes widen, they appear human. I feel for the animal because there's no escape for him.

The men don't have much of a plan, only a knife and a few vicious-looking sawing implements. These are arranged on a tarpaulin that lies on the ground. Fortis volunteers to cut the pig's throat while George holds the pig steady with a rope. Fortis struggles to get his knife into the pig's throat. The animal is too strong and won't keep still. Frustrated, Fortis screams,

"Come on, George, give me a hand, you idiot. You can see he's not staying still."

George holds the rope fast around the pig's head to steady the beast, but the pig is having none of it. Again, Fortis berates George,

"You idiot, what are you doing? Can't you hold the animal still? How can I cut its throat if you won't keep the animal still?"

Red-faced and puffing, George retaliates, "If you'd hurry and get the knife into its throat, it would be over in no time. You are the idiot!"

The women laugh at the men. Katerina and I laugh nervously too. Without warning, Katerina's mother steps forward into the centre of the group armed with a brick.

Wearing wellington boots and a colourful house dress and apron she calmly brings the brick down on the pig's head with a thump. I am stunned, but the pig isn't! It releases a cry that could raise the dead. It's a horrible sound; I tremble. Taken back by the animal's reaction, the men cower away. Katerina's mother holds her nerve and steps forward again. The brick comes down on the animal's head. The pig repeats its cries of agony. Katerina and I look away in horror gripping each other's bodies. Still, even with our eyes closed, we can hear the thud of the brick on the animals' skull again, and again.

Eventually, the beast stops screaming. Relief ripples through the gathering. Katerina and I open our eyes and venture to look at the animal. Its mutilated head stares unblinkingly through a pool of blood. It's holding our eyes frozen, hostage, held in a holding pattern of guilt until we find the courage to wrench our eyes away. We look down and shuffle our feet. Clouds shift the focus of the light. How many times had I told this pig, when it was a piglet, that I loved it? Opportunistic chickens cluck and close in looking for something upon which to feed. A donkey brays in the background and moments pass.

The men reassemble and take charge; the pig's glare doesn't deter these accomplices. The silent animal is picked up as each of the parents grabs a leg dragging it in step onto the outstretched tarpaulin. Without pausing, they begin the task of hacking the animal's body to pieces. They divide the beast between families; squabble over its sweetmeats and head. Particular pieces of pork are kept to be eaten later while the rest of the meat is salted and kept for the long winter. Katerina's mother doesn't have a refrigerator, a square metal basket with a latch door hangs in their kitchen from the ceiling. It is here that nominated pieces of meat are stored for the day.

Returning home after the kill, I ask Mum, "What's for

dinner?"

She replies, "Our cheque hasn't arrived from Australia. There's a mail strike in Melbourne. Looks like it will be bread and tomatoes."

"Oh, no! Not again!" I reply.

Around dinner time, I visit Katerina. I want to make sure she's fully recovered from the day's trauma. Her family has grouped enthusiastically in their kitchen and are about to relish the luxury of grilled pork. They invite me to join them. The smell of meat cooking over an open coal fire flavoured with oregano and lemon juice is too much of a temptation for me. I can't refuse. Shooing a few chickens off a seat at the kitchen table, I join the family. I don't come to this feast empty-handed. I place my offering in Katerina's mothers' brown hands. My gift; a bag of fat ripe tomatoes.

Elizabeth Pappas

Enis Pearce

Chain Reaction

Commended Short Story 2010

Barbara heard the cold metallic sound of the key as it turned in the lock. She didn't need to see who it was – Oliver had been coming through that door for the last twenty-five years, dead on the stroke of six.

"I'm home, dear," he called.

Home. What a strange word. She repeated it to herself; somehow she felt a cold feeling register in her mind. Yes, this was his home, but not hers. She listened to the familiar sounds echoing around the hall – the thud of the briefcase as he dropped it to the floor; the swish of the silk lining as he took off his jacket, followed by the precise shaking before he hung it up. It was five-past six. She heard the muffled footsteps as he climbed the stairs then the final bang of the study door shutting her out.

She turned back to the stove. He would be down later, seven o'clock to be precise. That was the way he liked his life, in order. Of course, she should have been stronger in the past, spoken out, but that wasn't her nature. No, she couldn't blame him really; she'd made the rod for her own back. Strange to think his practicality had attracted her when they first met, mistaking his aloofness for strength.

He joined her for drinks at seven o'clock. She watched him

pour her a dry sherry, a sweet one would have been more to her liking. Even the glasses were his choice. When they married, he appeared to collate her along with his other work, something to be put in order. Any slight deviation on her part which spoilt the uniformity of his life caused problems.

Later they sat at the old walnut table, his walnut table, the one his mother had left him. He'd always liked it. Barbara served up the dinner. Disapprovingly, he looked at her over his gold-rimmed glasses.

"Barbara," he said quietly, "today is Tuesday. You know I like beef on Tuesday, so why is it chicken?"

She shrugged. "The beef at the butchers today wasn't worth buying – it was far too fatty for you."

"That is no excuse," he said in a resigned voice. "I have told you before you must learn to plan ahead."

Voices in her head said, 'For goodness sake, girl, where's your spirit? Answer him back. Do something!' She knew she should, but when she opened her mouth to reply, the same old words came out. "How was work today?" She always asked this in the false hope it might lead to a bright topic of conversation but it never did. His work for the government usually proved to be as boring as him.

"I'm writing an article for the students about the treatment of convicts in colonial times," he replied. "It's about the conditions and how they were used as slaves. Actually, my dear, you might find it quite an eye-opener to see how the women fared. Have a quick read through while I'm out. I'll be interested to hear your reaction."

Folding his napkin neatly on the table, he rose from his chair, saying: "I know you probably have other things to amuse yourself with, but it never harms to see what hardships other people have experienced."

She watched with a sense of relief as his back disappeared

through the door.

Clattering the china loudly, she cleared away the dinner plates. "Amuse myself," she muttered. "Experiences of others! Where does he think I live, in the middle of Disney World?"

A little while later, she picked up the stapled papers, settled into the leather chair and read.

Prisoners were often kept shackled with a ball and chain. She wriggled her feet. That certainly wouldn't have been very pleasant. *Wrested away from their country and loved ones, the women felt isolated and estranged from their families. The sea and distance between them was like an impenetrable barrier.* Well, she certainly knew how that felt, leaving her family behind to come out here with him. The distance seemed greater every year and the promised holiday never materialised, especially once the children arrived. She also understood the feeling of an impenetrable barrier, though hers was not the sea; it was the study door. Once closed, it shut her and the children out of his life.

She sighed and turned the page. It had been hard bringing up two children with a father who was never around. His office was his kingdom. Of course, they had left as soon as they were old enough – who could blame them.

"We need to experience life," they had told her.

She read on. *Female convicts were often employed as domestic servants.* She paused. 'I wonder if he is writing about me,' she thought. She cast her eyes down again. *Many of the prisoners were starved.* So had she been, in a way: starved of affection, thrown a little crumb now and again to keep her going. She had never been beaten though, she could be thankful for that – he wasn't violent by nature. Convicts in the service of the Government appeared to have had a better deal. They worked from six in the morning until three in the afternoon. The rest of the day they were free to amuse themselves or find profitable work. Well! They couldn't complain at that. She'd worked longer. However, one of the methods of correction for misbehaviour was to work until six at night without time for amusement.

'That sounds more like it,' thought Barbara.

The next heading jumped out at her: TICKET OF LEAVE.

This paper was certainly of interest, especially to her. It appeared with a seven-year sentence you could apply for a ticket of freedom, after only four years, and with a fourteen-year sentence, you could apply after six. She gasped and sat up in amazement. Look at that. Life imprisonment meant only eight years. Perhaps she should apply for one. After all, she had served twenty-five.

'What a fool I have been,' she thought. 'These people were trapped by the system, but I'm not.'

It was twelve o'clock when Oliver arrived home. The next chime sounded a new day, a new beginning. She listened to the coat ritual, then the footsteps, this time heading towards her. He looked startled to see her sitting there in the half shade of the lamp.

"Good Heavens, Barbara, I didn't expect to find you still up!"

"I've been engrossed in your paper," she said.

"Oh good, I thought it might interest you." He poured himself a drink and took a sip, peering over the top of the glass at her. "Well," he asked, "what was your reaction? You had one I hope?"

"Of course," she replied. "In fact, a very strong one, one that leads me to ask you about something very important."

"What is it?"

"I've decided to ask for a Ticket of Leave."

"Don't be silly, Barbara. What are you talking about?" he said crossly.

"I mean, I want a divorce."

"A divorce? What is this all about? Have you completely lost your senses?"

"No," she replied. "I have merely come to them and realised I have completed my life imprisonment terms by many years."

He stared at her in amazement. "I don't understand you."

"No," she said quietly. "You never did."

She glanced down at her feet. There were no visible signs but they were there all the same. Somehow it felt as though she was already unshackled.

Enis Pearce

Pawmarks

Commended Poem 2014

Now you and I have always known
dogs wear nothing on their feet.
But there are paw marks in the concrete
as you walk along the street.
Some poor old dog is plodding
with a new unwanted load.
Each step he takes weighs half a ton
as he wanders down the road.

Can you imagine his owner
when he leaps up to his chest?
Two plates of concrete hit full force
rip holes into his vest.
It will find a nice dark cubby
and try to gnaw it with his teeth
But it's a toothless concrete wonder
that will crawl from underneath.

Next a visit to the local vet
Who'll say, "I'm sorry mate,
I've taken thorns from out of paws
but never concrete plates.
I suggest you find some road works,
with a feller steady with the drill.
He might be able to help you
if you hold your dog real still."

I believe in happy endings
so to make this tale complete.
I'm sure it splashed through puddles
and washed it off its feet.

Enis Pearce

Silvano Preo

Venice, Bride of the Sea

Commended Article 2003

I loved her from my boyhood: she to me
Was a fairy city of the heart
Rising like water columns from the sea.
(from the fourth canto of Childe Harold)

No other city compares with Venice. Its watery ways, vibrant atmosphere and picturesque Byzantine and Gothic architecture, among other styles, make it unique.

Although many buildings now are in a state of decline due to time and salt-water erosion, the city still holds its fascinating charm and beauty. Poets praised this fabled metropolis and painters are inspired by its fine architecture and glorious atmospheric hues, which varies with season and time of day.

At the peak of its prosperity, when its strong naval fleet dominated the Mediterranean, Venice was dubbed 'Bride of the Sea', and every year, on Ascension Day, her wedding Anniversary is celebrated.

Festivals abound during the year. The most popular being the 'Regatta' and the 'Redentor'. In the Regatta, taking place in September, gondoliers race each other. A parade of richly decorated 'patrician' boats, previously owned by aristocratic families, precede the race. On the third Saturday of July,

Redentor Day, a bridge of boats is made across the Grand Canal, the city's main thoroughfare, enabling Venetians to walk to the Church of the Redeemer and give thanks for past deliverance from the plaque. Later in the evening they picnic on gondolas, watch a firework display on the lagoon, then row to the Lido to see the sunrise.

Venice stands on more than one hundred islands on the north-eastern coast of Italy. Its history begins around the 5th century, when the Hans and Ostrogoths ravaged northern Italy, forcing people to take refuge on the grassy isles.

Before buildings could be erected the unstable sub-soil had to be reinforced with wooden piles driven deep down to form a sound base. By 810 the city started to take shape, and by the end of the first millennium its foundations were firmly established.

Soon the Venetians acquired a taste for power and conquest. By the third millennium they controlled trade routes in the Mediterranean.

Due to rivalries, plague and economic lethargy, and following Napoleon's invasion and the Austrian domination of the mainland, the Venetian empire collapsed. In a plebiscite held in 1866 Venetians voted to join the new kingdom of Italy.

Evidence of the city's prosperous heyday (12th-18th centuries) shows in the beautiful palaces "rising like water columns from the sea' along the Grand Canal. As the vaporetto chugs on with its load of commuters, the handsome buildings, some of them now luxury hotels, gradually come into view, revealing their past splendour.

There are numerous churches in Venice, all abound in art. Paintings by Tiepolo, Canaletto and other artists adorn their walls in a celebration of colours. But the church of Saint Mark is the true jewel of the city. Built in the Byzantine style, its façade is an architectural masterpiece enriched with frescoes, sculptures and spoils from the sacking of Byzantium. Its vaulted and mosaic-rich interior has several alters, each catering for a different religion.

About four hundred bridges link the city's lanes across the many canals, the Rialto being the most imposing. This spans the Grand Canal in a half circle shape. Boutique shops run along the middle of its entire length.

Venice is joined to the mainland by a road and rail bridge over five kilometres long. All traffic stops at the city's western end. From there gondolas, motorboats and the vaporetto are the only means of transport. Deliveries into the lanes are done on foot using hand trolleys.

The networks of lanes and alleyways, criss-crossed by canals winding through this city of wonders, make it easy to lose one's way. But do wander off the thoroughfare at least once; experience the relaxed atmosphere of the back streets; walk under the dark porticos that hold secrets of the bygone era; hear the gentle lapping of water against centuries-old buildings. Be warned though, do not venture far off the main lanes or you are doomed to a long, tiring trek into a nightmarish labyrinth.

The Grand Canal

Silvana Preo

Ashan Rajan

Thirteen Ways to Count Your Chickens

Winning Poem 2020

I
Five hens scurry around the yard,
scratching and preening,
dust baths and dust ups.

II
I gather the eggs
one…two…three…four.
Starkly white, mottled brown,
or freckled like a young child's nose.
The hen watches me steal her labour.

III
I herd my children under my arm,
A mother hen,
even to these two grown men.

IV
When the rooster died,
one of the hens began to crow.
Will I crow if my husband dies?

V

My first roast hen was a disaster;
too many spices, not enough crisp glistening skin.
You can take the Indian out of the girl,
but the tandoori chicken remains.

VI

My insecurities have come home
to roost like proverbial hens.
They sit puffed and accusatorial on the fence.

VII

The only good thing about the cold
is huddling under the quilt.
I roll myself in the downy feathers,
imagine myself a hen
fussing in her nest.

VIII

Hens can fly, you know.
Short distances,
skirts hiked up, wings flapping.
They're much less graceful than bumble bees.

IX
Male birds denote human genitalia,
but hens are not vaginas.

X
My sister taught me to whistle
when I was ten.
You know what they say,
About whistling women and crowing hens.

XI
Once, my mother and I
watched my aunt,
mad as a wet hen,
chase my uncle,
a sickle held high in her hand,
threats of death on her tongue.

XII
I bought chocolates for the children.
"You look after them," they said,
Leaving a fox in charge of the hen house.

XIII

"What's a Hindu?" he asked,
but I heard "hen do".
"Lay eggs," I said.
We were both confused.

Asha Rajan

Frances Richardson

Destroying Monet

Runner-Up Short Story 2001

Today I destroyed a Monet. Oh – not a real one, but then what is real if purchased from a Red Dot Store? I was pretty sure it was a Monet before I began to ruin it: by the time I finished, I knew I was right.

I'm a frequent de-railer, a sign of schizophrenia they tell me – but please oblige. In *The Thomas Crown Affair (*the Brosnan version), there is a scene where Crown has taken the lovely Rene Russo (Catherine) to his pad. There, as they sit in isolated luxury, he gives her a painting as a present. Crown keeps asking her, "Wanna see it?" And the lovely Rene says "No." She, testing his affection, loyalties, and realities, places it in the fire. They watch it burn. She asks: "What was it?"

He replies, "A nice little Renoir."

"Oh, Renoir. Nice little copy?"

He smiles. "We'll never know will we?" I love it. I have seen *Thomas Crown* three times now, basically for the "burning the Renoir scene" but also the fantastic bowler hat Magritte sequence.

I bought the Monet at the local Red Dot Store. They didn't know it was a Monet. It had no title, no artist. It was in the Christmas pile of markdowns to $20. I was not shopping for a Monet. One day perhaps, but not in Red Dot. I wanted the frame. It was the right size, made of real, or very good, nearly real wood, and was a good warm colour. Not brassy. I checked the back and saw it would be easy to get the Monet out. It also had just the right colour mattboard. Mattboard half the size is $5 in the K-Mart here.

Taking it to the checkout the young man, while searching for a bag the right size said, "That's nice, isn't it?" I told him I thought it was a Monet, resisting saying I was only buying it for the frame, and the mattboard.

"Oh?" he said. "I like it," said he, meaning the painting.

"Me too," said I – meaning the frame.

So off home and, whilst the tea was brewing, I found on inspection that I needed a strong flat-like knife for the staples. And like the disorganized person I am – see above – side-stepped to find the etching I was going to place in the frame. An etching of Ramses and his wife. The king who had everything he wanted: and a beautiful wife to boot. Etched by yours truly, I had made a print on gold painted calico. Very proud of this I am, also apprehensive of ironing out the creases in case the ink runs. I told myself to think about this problem later. Held over the frame I could see it would fit. Great, I had been right.

So – with tea in hand – I found a screwdriver that would do the job. The painting was of people sitting in a garden with a house in the background. The light plays on the grass and the foreground is shaded. The house seems faded and rinsed of colour in the sunlight. The people seem to be sitting alongside a path and looking at a bush on the other side, which although a dark green colour seems to be solid. In fact, the foreground is very dark and I noticed that there was an arch that led to the sun and the house. The people are just idling the day away the day, as in most impressionist paintings. Boy, where were the workers in those days?

Thomas Crown – Brosnan – is a real worker, but of the corporate kind. In one of first scenes, we see him looking at a painting in the Impressionist section of the Art Museum. The custodian whom Crown calls Bobby is looking at "his" painting and Bobby tells him most people go first to the Monet. Crown glances briefly at the Monet (which he is going to steal) and turns his attention back to the painting he is viewing, telling him while he casually eats his bagel, "I like my haystacks." How come Brosnan is allowed to eat Bagels in what we are led to believe is the Metropolitan Museum of Art? They'd never let me do that!

Taking the back off my Monet, I uttered my worse swearword - bogger - on finding that the Monet lovers had not only stuck the print to the backboard but had stuck the mattboard onto the actual print. What sacrilege! So off I went to find a palette knife to separate the two saying - be careful of the matt-board - don't crack it! And I was. The mattboard came off just nicely. I know it is only a print but … below the print, I had torn away Monet's signature, which was above the title of the painting, *Parisians Enjoying the Park*. Not one listed in his major works!

Of course, seeing what I had done to it, taken some of the sides off and the tops of the trees, plus obliterating the enlarged signature, which of course was not actually on the painting but underneath, made me think, what a shame. The large signature did not matter because his signature, as always, was there on the print although hidden by the frame I had just removed. The year he painted this painting was 1879. Now this is when I really began to look at the painting.

If you like French Impressionism, possibly you would like this painting, but really, that foreground irritated me the more I looked at it. The line of the hill stretches right across from left to the right lower corner and is far too straight. It cuts right through the pathway so that one wonders where the path went. The yellow light on this, presumably grassy rise, is laid on thickly and – if the intent was to place dappled light on the hill – it fails. The painting began to look tres sinister to me. Actually, when I stepped back, there was a haunted quality about it. On closer inspection, the people seemed to be waiting – not just idling the day away - as in most impressionist paintings. What are they actually enjoying? If Monet entitled this *Parisians Enjoying the Park*, there is little sense of this. The focal point is a woman in black.

The Monet, which Crown eventually secures for himself, and places behind the Magritte copy of *Man in a Bowler Hat* in his study whilst congratulating himself on his achievement, is not one of his paintings done in France. It is of a sunset in Venice. This one I like. Why? Because it looks like a Turner! Now there was someone who knew about light! This Monet painting strikes one by the un-impressionistic use of a sunset, which – all orange – dominates the canvas. What I like about Crown is that he gives a Pissarro to the Museum to fill the space of the stolen Monet. The philanthropic touch. I like this because both painters, Pissarro and Monet were in London together in the early 1870s. And, of course, the Pissarro Crown gives to the Museum is a forgery painted over the Monet. One should remember that the going price for this Monet – according to the film – is "One hundred thousand bucks!" A little different to mine!

Now the interesting thing about my Monet is the year it was painted. This was not a good year for Monet. 1879 was the year in which his wife died. Is this why the people in this painting seem suspended? Is this why there is a sombre funereal atmosphere to their enjoyment? Monet was also not living in Paris at this time, which is not to say he could not have painted Paris, but there is something else that puzzles me. The house – I would swear – is very much his house in Giverny. There are so many photographs of Monet with his house in the background and here it seems to be a backdrop for my print. The house, seen through the arch, is a little incongruous in a park. I am sure that this is Monet's Giverny house right down to the roof and the chimneys.

Crown takes Catherine to the Museum. To the very room from which he has stolen the Monet. He asks her which painting she would have taken rather than the Monet and when she points out another typical Impressionist confection, we know he will steal it for her. In this scene, when they pass Magritte's *Man in a Bowler Hat,* she tells him that it looks like him, "The faceless man in a bowler hat." He smiles and says that he has a copy. We have seen Crown, the typical corporate raider, beautifully dressed, handsome, straight back, but with no bowler. That is to come.

My Monet has a man in a bowler hat. He sits almost unseen in the lower right-hand corner. He sits on the pathway, strangely, on what seems to be an individual chair and is looking out of the picture. He does not seem to be enjoying himself and does not look well dressed, although one cannot see too well. He adds to the disturbing air of the painting. We cannot really see him. He is not at all what a bowler-hatted man should be. He is overweight, small and untidy, and definitely alone.

The women who sit further along the pathway seem engaged in just sitting, perhaps talking. Then there are the people who are walking at the end of the path, framed – for effect – in the arch of the trees with the mansion behind them. The main is ignored by and is ignoring everyone. Alone, he seems to want to escape from the picture. It is a scene waiting for something to happen. But then, does anything ever happen in an Impressionist painting?

All the while I was cleaning the glass, the frame and getting the mattboard just right, I was looking at the Monet over my shoulder and feeling more unsettled - not about destroying it - but that it was not a Monet that anyone knew. My Monet was not one of the famous paintings! I had solved my Ramses etching dilemma but was still thinking about Monet as I had the water jug steaming and hanging my etching – very carefully – over the steam. It worked! Perfect! I let it dry and trimmed it to the correct size and voila! Ramses and wife framed. But the Monet with the ripped inch and half all round insisted itself and followed me as I went to get hammer and hook to raise Ramses to his rightful height.

In the great Magritte sequence, Crown bets on Catherine betraying him. And he is right. As he enters the Museum to replace the Monet, he stands in the entrance hall so that all the cameras can see him – rotates – and places a bowler on his head. He begins to walk. Long black coat a la Magritte, brief case, and hat. And within a moment, he has put his briefcase down, picked up another briefcase, and walked off. Another bowler-hatted man picks up the briefcase and walks away. And, of course, there are dozens of bowler-hatted men! It is a hoot of a scene.

What was Monet doing when he painted this picture *Parisians Enjoying the Park?* Was it just something to paint? Well, let me tell you it is not pretty enough for a "Monet." That black figure in the centre of the painting with her black dress and parasol dominates and the man who wants to get out of the picture should be allowed to escape. Perhaps he is Monet.

I am going to use the board, with the destroyed print, for a collagraph I am planning. In fact, I am off to get the acrylic just now.

Red Dot also has Van Gogh's sunflowers on sale for $25. Great frames.

Frances Richardson

Back to Aberdovey

Runner-Up Poem 2005

I can sit on that hill again
my back to Happy Valley
the estuary below silent in afternoon
 mud flats thick, oozing, warm
no-one on the strand

Houses below
cling to the hill rock
open their windows
to the spare sun
easing the autumn chill

The station
one platform and bench faces the hill
its back to the sea
no movement there

Was there ever a train?

The shed of the cinema/dance hall
shrinks with time's distance but was open that night
just once in the week to show a five-year-old film
to four people
me, a couple from Towyn and Miss Pugh

Quiet it is
'til the sun cools cloud-covered
A wind springs
to whip grassed dunes
The sea runs beneath the black rotted
sleepers of the jetty
leaving the mud flats faster
than my memory can see

I listen for the bells
but no bell rings on this tide

or do they only ring
for descendants of those
in that other Dovey
washed so long away?

Perhaps the deep currents
have swept the bells
from the submerged tower
to a bed of sand silence

But I hear that silent bell sound
reach across the world

It sets its sight
on me, wants to sweep me
to that far mud flat wash
a passenger on the outgoing run
immersed
free from time's mire
swimming to join the old hymns
a once singing congregation
in the long drowned church of Aberdovey

Frances Richardson

Matthew Madonna

Winning Poem 2011

(Madonna of Saint Matthew -Annibale Carracci)

Wings beat and the curtains over my throne are lifted toward
the approaching evening. I try to read,
but the reformed publican must record, ever record.

The child startles as Nature's Saint kisses his feet.
Perhaps his wounds will heal now. How rough his garment.
He is old, long travelled, and tired. Even John, who points
for you the way, looks tired. We are all tired - uncomfortable.
Why do we not rest?

When they go, the curtains must be drawn. The child will sleep
and I will descend from this cold marble pedestal to find
comfort in my book.

Giorno Madonna
(Il Giorno - Correggio)

Since the birth of this child, I am beset with angels.
I hear them almost continually.
They are always here, singing
playing, showing the baby all manner of wonders.

My days begin to merge
and I see the child growing before me
the future coming to visit.
All the Marys of the world want my child.
To touch, to hold, to feel the magic.

I try to keep my virgin look but fail
knowing I look like other virgins
who will not face the enquiring eye.
Jerome will, I know say my virginity will last forever
but I do not understand this.
He seems kindly and does much reading and writing.

The angel holds the book for my child
who is not ready yet but
who points toward the words. I look away.
I do not understand this book which is not written yet.
It is an angel's book.
Mary does not want to leave.
There will always be Marys at his feet.

Doni Madonna

(The Doni Tondo - Michelangelo)

Within a family circle, my child makes his first descent.
Behind us, the bay lies still. Blue hills fade
into a day of naked men who idle by the closed fountain.
The stone slab divides our lonely brilliance from them.

Young John watches us from the other side of the wall.
He will tell his parents. One can see him forming the
words and memorising the movement of others.

The child places his hands on my braids. I look up
holding my arms out for him,
fingers softened by the skin of his back and leg.
My earth-husband, the earth-father
holds him: supporting us both.

I have read all that I need to read of gifts from the closed
book in the folds of my lap.

Canigiani Madonna

(The Canigiani Holy Family - Raphael)

See, they are playing with the gold ribbon I use as a
bookmark. What made me look up?
Was it something they said?

How Elizabeth talks. She loves to come here.
To sit in the grass - to have our boys play together
to talk to my patient man who listens - however long.

He will shift his feet, as the sun moves
and the colours deepen to lean a little heavier on his staff.
I do not need to turn my head to know he will alter not his
gaze or let fatigue creep into his look
even though she will continue till the evening is pitcher dry.

No, it wasn't Elizabeth, or the children.
They do not heed me either. They play with my gold ribbon
sharing the delight of its colour.
How much can be conjured from a ribbon to make stories for
the future. How serious they are.

No, it wasn't Elizabeth, or the children.
It was the word in my ear
on my page. The afternoon air;
the words on the page, and the voice
in my ear.

I look out at the life around me;
hold the book open with my finger,
and listen.

Frances Richardson

One Day

Highly Commended Poem 2011

There will be flowers
I think
No waxed orchids
Detached, perfectly designed
No tulips, brilliant, stately
No, there will be
Daisies
There could be a sun
No Lucky Bay Indian Ocean sunset
But a Westvale sun
Letting you know it is there
Behind long lines of grey-blue cloud
Yes, there could be a sun
Timed to set in
About an hour
Perhaps a cello
Yes a cello
Playing Elgar or Barber
Maybe Walton
Yes Walton
Possibly my fingers
this would be special
will trace the silk skin
Of my mother's cheek

Her neck smell
Seeping in
She will laugh
One day
Somewhere near
I will hear
Young children
The same children
Running towards me

Frances Richardson

More Than the Sight of a Brancusi

Commended Poem 2011

To be able to give them
give them
more than
more than the sight of
a Brancusi

To fashion hands that reach
search
to find form
incise
the stone
discover movement in wood

To give them
more than much more than
the clarity
of white and black notes
in exchange
for grey angst

To create
perhaps
a deep-hued cosmos
dawn of romance
with new narratives
more than

so much
more than
the closing
of folios from the past

To be able
entering a room
to show them
vitality
which reaches
for the tool
to create
future shape

Frances Richardson

Bacon Rolls!

Winning Short Story 2013

Bacon Rolls! My daughter yells – no screams the words. Bacon Rolls for breakfast! This is going to be a dream weekend! She is jumping around in circles yelling her hoorays. Not if you keep yelling, I say slapping bacon in the pan.
– And I can stay in my jimjams? All day? And we can couch potato? And I can choose the dvds/videos/films? Oh I love it when the men are away – don't you Mummy?
– Well yes – and yes and yes, and it is nice to have a time where we do not have to listen to how the Dockers are doing.
– I hate – no loathe the Dockers. I really do Mummy.
– Trés unpatriotic Jenny.
– I know, I know.
– Do you think they say unpatriotic things about us when they are away?
– Undoubtedly. I could see her thinking what her brother might say about her. Any sibling betrayals. They do love us you know, I tell her.
– Yes, but Jeremy always makes fun of English doesn't he? Daddy wouldn't though. Of me, being tops, and books and The Lord of the Rings and HP. Wouldn't he?
– What about Les Mis?
– And Les Mis! But he hasn't read the book! It would change his mind!
As I turn the bacon, I wonder if Hugo's book changes people

still, whether Dostoevsky still made them stop reading while they howl.

I watch as my daughter finds the films she wants and I know we will be reprising LOTR's, HP's last two films and possibly To Kill a Mockingbird because she knows I had a "thing" for Gregory Peck in my English Life. Who would not want Atticus for a father? It was Jenny who divided my life into the English and Australian parts. She would say – in your English Life, did you ever …? Or, did you do that in your English Life? Poor Jeremy was totally confused when he was five thinking I had died in my English Life and come back as an Australian. I think that is still why he looks as me a pensively when his sister starts on about my English Life.

I wonder if most people who leave their country of origin feel this and divide their experiences into that past life and my now life? Some obviously would want to forget their experiences, but one doesn't does one? Those experiences can become not talked about and if something stirs a memory, it is quickly cloaked over. I did not have those dreadful experiences one hears about, but England was never the myth of picket fences, golden summers, and green lanes for me. There were good times and I shall be ever grateful for the history and literature which England gave to me and gives to anyone who opens their heart to it.

I feel Jenny at my side. She is like my other self and I immediately wonder what that means. She is buttering the rolls with too much butter – just as I do. She looks up and smiles knowing what I am thinking.

– Here it comes; I say and slide best back bacon onto the rolls.

– We could do some more if we really are hungry.

– We certainly can.
She has already plugged in the film and I question which one we are to watch first.
– Surprise – it's a surprise. I see the title on the case and smile.
– We can just watch the part where Matt Damon tries to walk across the road if you like. She giggles.
– No, let's watch it from the beginning.

We settle down to watch this lovely film. Both in jimjams, cushions everywhere.
– Bacon Rolls – she says – I just love Bacon Rolls.
And before I even think – I say it – it is so easy to please you.
My lovely daughter laughs.
– I am, am I not? Is that good English? Good BBC. I am so easy to please!
And I am smiling, laughing and loving her and knowing that for her – and me – it has always been the simple easy things which are most important. But I hear myself – you are so easy to please – it is all in the tone. And I know my tone has been one bordering on adoration. And as we watch Greg Kinnear and Matt Damon skipping through the snow, we join them singing We're off to see the Wizard, smell and devour the bacon rolls. With my Jenny curled by my side, and to the strains of Moon River, I slip, against my wishes, with that phrase, back to my English Life.

I am sitting on a bench. It is a walkway on Bankside. It must be about 5.30 pm because I have finished work and walked there. I am waiting and happy. Why? Because the sun is warmish. It seems to be smiling that this has been for the world: a good day. In front of me the Thames. I know that I am thinking about it being clean again and that there are fish, so you see all is not English gloom. If fish can return to the

Thames, anything is possible. I am happy also because tonight I shall be in one of the oldest theatres in London, smell that familiar smell, see a great play and watch great actors. Who would not be happy? And yet I know that somewhere, not to be admitted, that I am not as happy as I should be. And again one counts all the good things and this should make one smile. Life is fine, and things could be much worse: they are for many.

Behind me is a car park and it is where my husband will meet me. I have persuaded him to come into London for this, one last performance, of the play. He says he is looking forward to it and it will make the evening more special for me. It is early winter and that evening sun is beginning to cool – no in my English Life I would say - grow colder. I hug my coat and scarf closer and hope he will not be long. My thoughts of the Thames move to wondering if I like this part of the river or the part where my brother has a boat at Reading where still the river looks like the gathered images from all our sub-consciousnesses. I decide that this is my Thames because it has the Globe on it and that is enough – or should be – for anyone.

Jenny prods me and brings me back from the Thames.
– It's tone isn't it? Mummy! Are you watching? She has paused the film.
– When Matt says he will do it. Greg Kinnear i-s not listening, is he? It's tone! You remember the way he says it's what he wants. Greg should know Matt is doing it just for him. Greg Kinnear should pick this up, shouldn't he?
– I know, but later Matt says – it is time – doesn't he?
– Yes, but I still think Greg is selfish. I smile because I know I cannot move her on this and let's face it: it's a narrative ploy.

She has this thing about tone since one of her friends a couple of years back caused her many tears by transferring a best friend status to someone else. Jenny picked up on the way the girl had said we can still be friends. Through her blubbing she said – but she did not mean it – you could tell by the way she said it – she didn't mean it. I remember saying she was right and although people often said one thing, one could tell by the tone, they meant something else. Yes – tone she said – it was the tone of her voice – I knew she didn't mean it. So, now it was poor old Greg Kinnear who should have picked up on this.

I appease her and say he most certainly should have done and should we break for a cuppa? And so we do. To which we add muffins – English of course – with slathers of butter and marmalade. And then back to poor Matt Damon who soon will be trying to walk across the road without Greg's help to balance him.

It was no good though. I was still in that growing cold evening on the Thames, waiting for my husband. And, of course, he came. As usual my heart leapt and I ran to join him in the car.
– Did you have trouble finding it?
– No, but the traffic was awful through Palmers Green.
– We can leave the car here and walk. I know where we can get a sandwich and keep warm.
– No need. I left early and made some bacon rolls.

I can almost hear me now. Bacon Rolls! Just as I would hear my daughter. And, of course, I hugged him.
– Bacon Rolls, watching the sun go down by the world's best river, the great and mighty Thames, in a Lanchester (the great

pre-select old roadster), going to see a great play in a great theatre with great actors: even if it is in the Gods! I love Bacon Rolls!

And then my English Life changed.

– You are so easy to please.

And I laughed to make it easy. And what could have been easier? To do a Greg Kinnear and not hear. To pretend I had not heard. That is what the laughing did – continue to play the game which we played daily. The laugh that hid my failure. But tone is what went to heart of my daughter in losing a friend and it followed me through that evening and never left me until my English Life finished.

So here is Matt Damon, crossing the road to his loved one. It is our great fun part. Jenny jumps up and lurches with him in her well-practised Mattwalk. His tone is just right as he says Yes when May asks him does he want to go inside. We laugh and know he will be happy in his new free life.

Frances Richardson

cosmology and life

Highly Commended Poem 2017

she sits among missed moments
ponders on how time may curve
different definitions of light
why strings may take her through
relative mystery mechanics

today, her discussion
on Fermi's Paradox
was ignored or patronised
while others applauded
their efforts on spectroscopy

with a wave at the laptop
– wishing for Hubble's brain
that the universe would slow –
she sees black holes
swallow her new years

Frances Richardson

Jo Robertson

Sewing Mistress

Highly Commended Poem 2014

In my youngblood days of sun
and sudden miracles
she stitched away her winters
one by one, insistent on a perfect patch,
a line of buttonhole laid straight
as matches in a box,
a grubstitch rose
unpuckered.
Through wartime years
she fleshed our skipping rhymes:
Huckaback and headcloth
Calico and twill
If the Japs don't get her
Then the Jerries will.
In my youngblood days of sun
and sudden miracles
shame pricked with blunted needles.
We mocked her flannel thighs,
slabbed bifocals,
guessed at breasts
like wizened walnuts,
preened ourselves
newbudded.

Huckaback and headcloth
Calico and twill
If the Japs don't get her
Then the Jerries will.
Now, in my coldlit days of moons
and questioned miracles
I recollect a ragbag life
patched with compromise.
Frayed promises accuse.
Past pupil of flesh and ecstacy
chastened penitent,
I sit and sew a grubstitch rose
unpuckered.
Huckaback and headcloth
Calico and twill
If the Japs don't get me
Then the Jerries will.

Jo Robertson

Shirley Rowland

Tea for Two

Commended Short Story 2010

The Tea Rooms had been a landmark on the Swan River for nearly a century when Susan landed a waitress's job there. She barely believed her good luck at starting university, finding board and landing a part-time job all within the first week! Even better, all within walking distance.

Her first customer was an elderly woman who had walked straight past the 'please wait to be seated' rostrum and deposited her trim posterior on a chair at the most secluded table in the corner overlooking the river on two sides; although all the tables were arranged for river views. The woman had an air of faded elegance just like the Tea Rooms, Susan thought as she took her order.

"You're new here, aren't you?" the old lady commented when Susan returned with two cups of black tea.

"As a matter of fact this is my first day. How did you know?" Susan replied nervously.

"Because I haven't seen you before, and the other waitresses all know to hold back the second cup until Graham actually arrives. So he can enjoy a fresh, hot cuppa you see, dear," she explained with a smile.

"Oh." Susan hesitated, her hand resting on the saucer holding the second cup she had placed on the table.

"Graham's an elderly gentleman, about my age," the old lady added helpfully. "He'll ask for Elsie. That's me," she explained.

It was as clear as mud to Susan. "So you only want one cup of tea?" she asked, frowning in confusion.

"No; two," the old lady said emphatically. "One served now, and the second when Graham arrives. And stop frowning, dear. It's both unladylike and will give you wrinkles."

"Oh. Of course." With an effort Susan un-frowned and compensated by trying to smile as she picked up the cup and saucer and placed it back on her tray. As she returned to the kitchen she thought, I hope they don't get too many crazy old bats like her in here!

The manageress, her new boss, saw her coming. "I forgot to warn you about Elsie," she said before Susan had a chance to speak.

"Oh," Susan said again, feeling like a cracked record. "What does this man she's expecting look like?" she asked, feeling compelled to say something apart from 'oh' as she frowned again.

"We've never seen him. Elsie's been coming here every Sunday for at least a year and he hasn't turned up yet."

"So she only has one cup of tea. What about the bill?" Susan didn't dare say what she was thinking – what a rip-off to charge the old bat for two.

Her boss reached over and extracted Susan's order pad from her pocket. She quickly scribbled on it and then ripped the page off. "We only ever charge her for one," she explained, seemingly reading Susan's thoughts. "And we keep the docket at the cashier's station. Elsie's a special … er, customer. Another thing," she added with a smile, "She'll probably leave the money on the table; it's not a tip, it's her payment. She usually walks out without paying the cashier. That's why we keep the docket behind the counter. Just write 'Elsie' on it the next time you serve her."

"I see," Susan murmured. "Are there any other special customers I should know about?"

"No, only Elsie. Oh, and try to keep that particular window table vacant for her. Two o'clock Sunday afternoons. She usually walks in and seats herself." The boss glanced over Susan's shoulder. "There's a queue forming at the door. Off you go, and smile!"

Susan's smile was genuine by the time she reached the door. Time flew as she seated and served the historic Tea Room's customers. Sometime after 3 pm, she noticed the window table Elsie had occupied was vacant. She went over; the cup was empty and three dollars in coins sat on the saucer. Quickly she picked it all up, wiped the table and went to the cashier. "Elsie's payment," she said, handing over the coins.

"You learn quickly," the waitress at the till commented approvingly. "You didn't impress Elsie though, she's short this week."

"Oh? What do you do about it?" Susan suddenly had visions of docked pay.

The waitress shrugged. "Nothing. She'll over-pay another time, or her son will come in occasionally to square the balance. Remind me to show you the special account when it's your turn to learn the till."

"I'll keep it in mind," Susan said as she raced off to seat more customers.

*****

Susan worked part-time at the Tea Rooms for the three years it took her to complete her university degree. She enjoyed the job; it provided just enough income to cover life's necessities without impinging on the hectic social whirl of the student campus. During that time, she developed a friendship with many of the regular customers, but Elsie was her favourite. The old dear had a way of drawing out the details of Susan's life without revealing any of her own. After their exchange of pleasantries each Sunday, Elsie sat at the corner table overlooking the river, sipping her tea and watching the water, apparently deep in reverie. Susan often wondered what she was thinking, or perhaps remembering, but Elsie never shared her secrets.

It was during the pressured build-up to final exams that Susan suddenly realised she had not seen Elsie one Sunday. The following Sunday, it was raining and few customers defied the foul weather to visit the Tea Rooms. Susan had met Elsie's son several times previously and recognised him when he arrived at the door. "I'm not staying," he said when Susan approached. "I'm here to settle Elsie's account."

"Where is she?" Susan asked curiously. "I missed her last week."

"She died last Sunday. Her funeral was yesterday," he said bluntly.

"I'm so sorry. We'll miss her. My condolences," Susan replied politely, but she could not contain her curiosity. "Who was Graham?" she asked.

Elsie's son shrugged. "A figment of her imagination as far as I know."

"But that's who she said she was waiting for, every Sunday," Susan persisted, glancing around to see whether her boss was within earshot; she could be sacked for harassment but the puzzle of Elsie's vigil had become almost an obsession for her. "Perhaps her husband or an old lover?" she suggested.

"Dad's name was Brian. My brother's name is Sam and I'm

Daniel. There are no Graham's in the family to the best of my knowledge. As for lovers, dad always said mum was the only woman for him and the feeling was mutual. Mum never contradicted him. She seemed to lose her mind after dad passed away." He shrugged. "We don't know where Graham came from. Part of the Alzheimers, we think, but it seemed harmless enough to allow her to come here each Sunday. There's no such person as Graham to the best of my knowledge."

"I see," Susan replied, trying vainly to hide her disappointment. "Thank you for taking the time to explain it to me. I liked Elsie. I'll miss her."

"How much do I owe you?" he asked, obviously irritated by her questioning.

Quickly Susan checked the special account. "You don't," she said. "In fact it's six dollars in credit."

"Keep it," he replied curtly.

As Susan watched him walk away, she thought that was the end of Elsie's story. However, on her last working day at the Tea Rooms, she noticed an elderly gentleman standing hesitantly outside the door. "Come in," she invited. "Can I help you?"

"I doubt it," he replied. "I'm waiting for a certain lady. It's many years since we last saw each other."

"What's her name?" Susan asked curiously. Suddenly her skin prickled in premonition.

"Elsie," he replied.

"Oh!" Susan yelled in her excitement. She clapped her hand over her mouth in embarrassment. "I'm sorry," she added in a more subdued volume. "Elsie was my favourite customer. Are you Graham?"

"Graham Walter at your service," he said gallantly.

"So you are real! Elsie waited for you every Sunday, but you never came."

"When I ran away to sea, I never dreamed it would be so many years before I was able to return," he explained. "She's here?"

Susan heard sudden hope in his voice and tears prickled her eyes. "No, she died nearly a month ago."

Graham was silent for so long that Susan began to wonder what to say next. "Would you like to have the table she used to sit at?" she asked finally.

"Thank you, that would be most acceptable," he replied. "Tell me," he added as he followed Susan to the window table, "What did Elsie order when she came here?"

"Tea for two," Susan replied with a laugh. "But we always had to hold the second cup until Graham arrived."

"Then that's what I'll have." He lowered himself stiffly into the chair. "Tell me about Elsie," he invited.

"She came here every Sunday, 2 pm sharp, and always sat at this table."

"For how long?"

"I've been working here for three years, and she was coming here before that. From what her son told me, I think she started coming here after her husband died."

"Was his name Brian Cottle?"

"His first name was Brian; I never knew any surnames."

"Bastard," Graham muttered, so quietly that Susan barely heard the curse. She was debating whether to ask about his relationship with Elsie when Graham told her. "It was like this," he explained. "Elsie and I fell in love too young. We were both fifteen years old. We used to rendezvous here to drink and talk. Tea for two was all we could afford. We vowed to each other that whatever happened, one day we would meet here again on a Sunday at 2 pm. It was because of Brian that I went to sea. He threatened me and his father was a lawyer, so

I had to disappear quickly. His threat wasn't idle either; it has taken me five years of fighting the Immigration Department to return to the country of my birth!" For a moment, he sounded bitter. Then he sighed and looked at the peaceful river. "Time to bring me that cup of tea, love," he said.

Susan reddened as she hurried away. This might be her last day at work, but it was no reason to slack off! When she placed the cup in front of him, he asked for the bill.

"No charge," she told him. "Elsie's already paid for it." He raised his eyebrows and looked questioningly at her. "Her account was six dollars in credit after her last visit. I know she would have wanted to pay for you," Susan ended lamely. She didn't add that she would have paid for it herself to know the end of Elsie's story. Graham simply turned back to watching the river.

It was another quiet afternoon and minutes passed before Susan had another customer. More customers arrived and soon she was busy again. Several times she glanced at Graham; each time he was gazing at the river, deep in reverie just as Elsie had been. Sometime after 3 pm, she noticed he had gone. When she returned to the table, she discovered he had not touched the tea. The cup was still full. For several seconds she gazed out the window, watching the hypnotic river placidly lapping against the bank. A tear trickled down her cheek as she thought of two lovers who had tried but failed to meet one last time.

Shirley Rowland

For the Last Time

Commended Short Story 2013

He would never walk down this street again, Simon Blackburn thought as he pulled the front door shut, shouldered his duffle bag and strode the dozen steps to the front gate without looking back at his late parents' house; the house he had grown up in.

Only after closing the gate did he allow himself one last backward glance. He had taken the photo yesterday; actually fifty or more to show his children where he came from. His last tie to Dunoon had died with his widowed mother. The place he'd grown up in, although even as a child he couldn't wait to leave it.

He breathed in the dry, dusty air of the mid-western plain. Even here, he could taste only the salty tang of the distant sea. It had not been a conscious decision to run away to sea, it was simply where he'd ended up by chance, when a job on a prawn trawler had been his only immediate prospect of employment.

His wife and children had never visited Dunoon, while his parents had refused to accept his beautiful brown children or visit Fiji. They never understood that although he loved them, his soul belonged in the Pacific with his own family. Sometimes he felt as if the two disparate worlds were trying to pull him in half. He shook his head reflectively as he began the long walk the length of the town.

The place had barely changed in his long absence. A ribbon

of black bitumen ran between dead grass verges lined with paint-peeling picket fences and occasionally un-staked cyclone wire to deter wandering livestock and stray dogs. No kerbs, no gutters, no life. He could have walked down the centre of that black strip of tar in complete safety. Thirty years of bustling ports and crowded villages had conditioned him to remain on the footpath.

He reflected that Dunoon's greatest asset was also its biggest liability. Space unlimited. Room to move. Boasting a single main street literally a mile long. Pity the bus stop was at the far end and the Greyhound coach not due for another three hours. Probably a half-hour walk if he took it slowly. It would have been a pleasant diversion to tarry over a coffee or two, but the only café in town had closed years ago. With his luck there would be no shelter at the bus stop, and standing in the sun for two and a half hours was not his idea of excitement. Fortunately it was winter, the air cool and the wind almost absent for a change. It could have been far worse, raining hard or blowing a gale. The plains were infamous for their lousy weather.

A dilapidated 'For sale' sign in the front yard of a house caught his eye as he ambled past. The building looked forlorn and neglected, as if it had been vacant for years. He paused and glanced back at the gleaming 'For sale' sign he'd hammered into his late parents front yard a few days ago. How long before it found a new owner to care for and nurture it like his parents had? Or would it remain abandoned like this one? He looked more critically at the houses up and down the street. Most of them appeared derelict. It was a depressing sight.

As his scrutiny turned full circle, back to the sign that had originally caught his attention, a vague memory stirred and he stood still, allowing it entry. His childhood best mate Tim had lived here! Tim was the only boy in a household of girls, two older and two, or was it three younger sisters? For a moment a smile cracked the dust coating his face as the ghosts of high-pitched shouts and laughter played once more in his mind, like an old-half-forgotten melody.

Tim had shared his desire to head for Sydney as soon as they left high school. Then he remembered his mother telling him about a multi-car pile-up on the highway, where half the Pike family, including Tim, had been wiped out in a heartbeat.

Suddenly the wind seemed colder. Dust particles stung his face. He turned and walked on sadly. No childhood links remained; they were all gone, broken or dead. There was no-one to hold him here or bring him back.

Ten minutes later, as he paused at a junction with a laneway to a farmer's property, a voice hailed him.

"Hello sailor!"

The cheery voice was so unexpected he nearly dropped his duffle bag in shock. Spinning around, he saw a middle-aged woman with secateurs in gloved hands step away from a straggly rose rambling over a rickety wooden arch framing a gate interrupting the ubiquitous picket fence.

"Hello yourself," he responded.

"You don't recognise me, do you?" she challenged, stepping closer.

He noted peroxide-blond hair, probably permed, overly generous figure and a face that may have been pretty once. "Should I?" he said. He considered walking on as he weighed his options; standing chatting versus standing alone at a bus stop.

"I'm Tim Pike's sister Miranda. You're Simon Blackburn, aren't you? I must say it took me a while to recognise you. But I knew that I knew you as soon as I spotted you walking down the street."

"You're right." He allowed his surprise to show. "But I'm afraid I still don't remember you. Exactly which sister were … are you?"

She chuckled, a silvery, tinkly sound, unexpected but not unpleasant. "The second-youngest. I don't expect you to remember me, you and Tim were always running away and hiding whenever I tried to follow you!"

He laughed too. "I do remember that, but I still don't remember you; only an annoying little girl with brown plaits."

She threw her head back in a roar of uninhibited laughter. "That was me," she eventually acknowledged. "I've grown up and changed a just a teensy weensy little bit since them."

"Haven't we all," he agreed. Again he thought about walking on, but her next words stopped him.

"I was ever so sorry to hear about your wife. Your mama told me she died?" She sounded uncertain of her facts.

"Yes. Six months ago." He couldn't quite stop his voice from cracking. "Thank you for your concern. That's about the nicest thing anyone in this town has ever said to me."

"Oh, I'm sure it's not! Anyway, that Greyhound isn't due to pull in for hours yet. Why don't you come inside for a cuppa and tell me more? Your mama told me you have children. I couldn't have any, but my sister Poppy has six. I tell her she had my share."

Again the tinkly laugh, but he thought her eyes looked sad. "Oh," he said, unsure what to say and whether she expected an answer to her earlier question.

"Man of few words, aren't you. Don't just stand there. Are you coming in for a cuppa or what? It's time I put the kettle on anyway."

"Oh. Yes, thank you." He decided to accept the invitation. What harm could it do? "Do you always talk so much?" he asked as he allowed her to open her gate for him.

"Hazard of living in Dunoon with fewer and fewer locals left to talk to," she said cheerfully.

"So you never moved away? I remember hearing something about a car crash."

He noticed the tears she hastily brushed away. "That was a long time ago. All except Poppy and me was in the car. Tim wanted to show off his hot new wheels, but we were too young to go to the Royal Hotel so mum left us with our neighbours. Dad was the only survivor. I often thought it would have been kinder if he'd been taken too. He was never the same after. His injuries all mended but he was a broken man inside. Lost his only son, I think that's what hurt him the most. He loved Tim, you know."

"I knew he was proud of him, I was never sure why," Simon acknowledged as he followed her inside the house.

The interior surprised him; freshly painted in neutral tones and bold furnishings that had definitely not been inherited, unlike the ancient, shabby furniture in his parents' house. Somehow it relaxed him to have no visible reminders of his childhood as he deposited first his duffle bag, then himself on separate chairs. He watched her fuss with a sleek electric kettle and select two large mugs from a wooden peg stand. "Tell me about your children," she demanded.

Simon wasn't sure how it happened, but he found himself talking more than he had in years. Miranda seemed expert at extracting a person's life story. He related how he'd met his beautiful Angel, married and settled on her small home island north from Viti Levu in Fiji. He told her all about his children, their partners and the joyous birth of Angel's first grandchild shortly before the cancer took her life.

Miranda cheerfully admitted she had no idea where Fiji was, pulled out an old school atlas and demanded he show her. She fussed and bustled around the kitchen while she talked and

Simon could not remember meeting anyone who talked so much. Somewhere along the line he learned that she had been married and divorced twice. As she served lunch he glanced at his watch and realised he was about to miss his bus.

"Don't fuss about the bus," Miranda dismissed his concerns. "Eat up and then I'll run you over to the highway. It stops at the roadhouse for forty minutes, we can catch it up there."

Half an hour later Simon was a passenger in Miranda's car, speeding along that narrow black ribbon of tar defining Dunoon. She had a heavy foot, he mused as shabby and derelict houses gave way to the featureless plain where young wheat plants drew green lines through the brown earth to the flat horizon. His life had taken many unplanned u-turns in the past, and he decided it had just performed another one. Three hours ago he'd expected never to return; now he knew with equal certainty that one day he would indeed walk down the main street of Dunoon again.

"Penny for your thoughts," she demanded. "Or should it be cents? I never did get my head around all that political correctness nonsense."

He laughed easily. "I was just thinking about how three hours ago I was so certain I would never walk down the main street of Dunoon again. I guess it just goes to show you can never be sure that anywhere is the last time."

Shirley Rowland

June Smith

In Another Place

Winning Short Story 1986

The rain was pounding on the roof and the wind was rattling the windows and I was getting cold. So I put my tea on a tray and took it into the lounge.

Turning on one bar of the heater, I pulled my chair right in front and sat down. That was better. I found my old crocheted rug and pulled it over my knees. It was a great comfort to me, that rug. I remember when I made it. It took me ages - lots of nights in front of the fire, with Jack next to me reading one of his endless books. I never did understand most of them but he was such a brain, knew so much.

I finished my soup and picked up my knitting. Now where was I up to? Oh yes. The sleeve. I really should be doing this a lot faster but my fingers seem to be so stiff lately. Jack will be needing it now that winter is here. And he does love the jumpers I knit for him.

Especially the blue one. He wore it all the time and I had an awful job trying to take it away from him to wash. But he did look handsome in it.

A knock at the door interrupted my knitting. I got up slowly, waited a few moments for the feeling to come back into my legs, and went to the front door.

"I'm sorry to trouble you, Elsie love, but I just thought I'd better tell you there has been a storm warning tonight. I wasn't sure if you'd heard about it."

It was May Sullivan from next door. She was a dear, always popping in to see if she could do anything. And she was wet through.

"Thankyou May. I hadn't heard about it. I don't have my radio fixed yet."

"You'll have to let my Bern have a look at it. He's good with things like that. Now we'd better take your hanging baskets down. You don't want them crashing down in the middle of the night, do you?"

"Oh no. Thankyou May. Come in and take off your coat."

"Yes, oh, can you smell something burning? What ... oh quick, look at your rug!" May suddenly took hold of the rug and ran to the kitchen. When she came back she had a dark frown on her face.

"Elsie! You'll have to be more careful or you'll burn your house down and yourself with it. Look at your beautiful rug. It's all burnt at this end. You must have let it fall near the heater when you got up to let me in. Now, now, don't cry love. Here, use my hankie and wipe your eyes. It is clean. It's alright. It was an accident." May patted my arm with her chubby hand.

I stared numbly at the diamonds which were on her thick fingers. Forever, I thought. They're stuck. She'll never get them off. She was lucky her Bern had given her so many rings. Jack only gave me a wedding band. It was all we could afford when we got married. He …

"Elsie! Are you listening to me? Are you alright? I know it's upsetting, but I'm sure you can crochet another square onto it and then you'll never know the difference. Now, you sit tight, and I'll go and put the kettle on, and while it's boiling I'll take down your baskets. Oh, did you hear that thunder? This storm's going to be a beauty!"

I watched May go into the kitchen, and silence fell on the room again. She did chatter a lot, but a cup of tea would be nice.

"Did you say something, Elsie?" May's head appeared round the door.

"I was just saying a cup of tea would be nice."

"Oh. Won't be long then. You get on with your knitting."

"Alright. I'm trying to get this jumper finished for Jack. He'll be needing it with this weather coming on."

"Jack?" May's face appeared round the door again. "Jack?"

"Yes. I want to have it finished when he gets back from the country."

"Oh." May frowned. She did seem to frown and say 'oh' a lot.

The cup of tea was nice and I sat with it on my lap after May had gone, listening to the storm. I could hear the wind howling through the roof and then the thunder crashed loudly in the heavens. Lightning lit up the blackness outside. I hoped my Jack was safe.

The next day May came to see me again and she brought someone with her. A lady, very tall with red hair. She had it all piled up on top of her head and she wore thick-rimmed glasses.

"This is Mrs Hobson, Elsie. I've brought her to meet you."

I didn't like the way Mrs Hobson looked at me. She seemed to be able to see right inside. "Hello," I said.

"Hello, Elsie. It's nice to meet you. Hope the storm didn't bother you last night. It was quite a bad one."

"No. I don't mind when I'm tucked up in my bed." This lady had a very prim manner.

"And what have you been doing with yourself today?"

"Oh, mostly knitting this jumper for Jack." I held it up for her to see, but she was looking at May. They both looked back at me.

"Is Jack your husband?" Mrs Hobson asked.

"Yes."

"And … where's Jack now?"

"Why in the country of course. He goes often - it's part of his job you know. But he's usually away for only a couple of days."

"What sort of job has he got?"

"He's a salesman – takes boxes of clothes with him. He goes to all those little towns with no big shops, you know the ones."

"Mmm. Don't you get lonely?"

"Yes. I used to go with him but now my legs are so bad I can't go anymore. But it's lovely when he comes home. I cook a leg of lamb and we have a meal together."

"That's wonderful, dear. Well, it was nice meeting you. Do you mind if I come again?"

"No. I like to have visitors."

"Alright then."

"I'll see her out, Elsie, don't get up. Then I'll come back and make you a sandwich," May smiled at me.

"Thankyou May. I'll just get on with this knitting." They moved to the kitchen door and I could hear May whispering to Mrs Hobson, but I didn't take any notice. I had wasted too much time and wanted to finish the jumper.

"Do you see what I mean, Mrs Hobson? She's convinced he's coming home."

"Yes. She's in a bad way, poor thing."

"Well I'm doing just about everything for her. She's so forgetful and she hardly cooks any more. I really am worried about her."

"Of course. I'll certainly do my best. The first vacancy, I

promise you."

***

"Hello, love."

"Jack! Oh, it's good to see you. I've missed you so much."

"I've missed you too, my love. Here, let me give you a big hug."

"Mmm. That feels good. Look, I've got something for you." I held up the jumper and Jack smiled at me.

"Love, it's beautiful! As good as the old blue one! Do you remember it?"

"Yes of course. You used to look so handsome in that one. Now, come and sit beside me and tell me all your news."

Jack came and pulled up a chair next to mine. He tucked the rug firmly around my knees and patted my hand. "You look very tired my love. How've your legs been?"

"Not too bad. Could be worse!"

"Typical of you, Elsie. Never complain about anything."

"Jack, when can you take me with you?" I did miss him terribly.

"Soon, my love, very soon."

"Oh good. I do miss you Jack."

***

"Elsie?" May's voice called from the back door. "Come in May. I'm in the lounge."

"Just called to see if you need anything," May said as she came into the room. She was dressed in a raincoat and boots.

"Oh, I see you're knitting something else. What happened to the jumper?"

"I finished it. Jack thought it was wonderful, too."

"Jack … thought it was wonderful?" May stared at me, her

eyes very wide.

"Yes. It looks beautiful on him too."

"Is … is he home then?"

"Yes, came home yesterday."

"Where … where is he now?" May was looking rather cautiously around the room as if she expected to see him.

"Oh, he's not here. He's gone to the shops for me."

"The shops? Ah … yes, I came in to see if you needed anything from the shops?"

"No thankyou."

"Are you sure?"

"Yes, but thankyou for asking though. Maybe you'll run into Jack while you're out."

"What? Oh, yes, maybe. Well, I'd better go. See you later then."

"Bye bye." I watched May hurry from the room and wondered what had gotten into her. She had been acting so strange lately. Maybe it was that time of life for her.

***

It was late afternoon and I was dozing off in my chair in the lounge when I heard May's voice again.

"Come in," I said, trying to wake myself up. I felt very tired. Must be all the knitting I had been doing.

"Mrs Hobson has come to see you again, Elsie. Do you mind?"

"No, that's alright."

I sat up straight in my chair and tucked my rug around my legs. They were beginning to hurt again. I looked at my visitors and wondered why Mrs Hobson was back so soon.

"May tells me that … Jack is home." Mrs Hobson was smiling down at me. She seemed so tall.

"Yes. He came home yesterday. He loved the jumper too."

"That's nice, dear. Where is he now? I'd like to meet him."

"I'm sorry, he's not here."

"Not here? Where is he then?"

"Gone to the shops for me. I told May."

"But Elsie love that was this morning. He must be back by now." May was staring at me.

"No. He had a lot of business to do. Because he's been away you know. There's always things to do when he gets home. Bills and all that. You know."

"I see. What a shame! I would have liked to have met him before he goes away again. He … is … going away again, isn't he?" Mrs Hobson seemed disappointed. She would have liked Jack. It was a shame.

"Yes, he'll be going away again soon. But I'll be going with him this time."

"What do you mean, Elsie? Going with him?" May was looking very pale and was wringing a hankie round and round her fingers. She really ought to see a doctor.

"Well, he said he would take me with him. I'm looking forward to it too. I want to be with him all the time. I do get lonely on my own."

"Yes, well, maybe you'd like to come and live with lots of other ladies like yourself. They'd be good company for you, dear." Mrs Hobson patted my hand. I felt like a little girl.

"I don't know. I like my house and I don't know if I'd like a lot of strangers around me."

"They won't be strangers. They're lovely people and they like knitting too. You could even swap patterns. And there'd be someone to cook all your meals."

"That sounds nice. But I'll have to see what Jack thinks. Thankyou Mrs Hobson."

"All right. I'll come back tomorrow and you can tell me. I

know you'll like the other ladies." She looked at May. "Maybe you can explain about the home."

Poor May. She seemed so nervous. She kept looking from me to Mrs Hobson.

"Well, remember I may not be here. I'll be going with Jack."

"Ah, yes, Elsie, I'll remember, dear." Mrs Hobson took May by the arm and left the room.

"I'll come back tomorrow, May, and I'm afraid I'll have to take her with me."

"I know. What a terrible business! So sad."

"Yes, but it's the only way."

But it wasn't. Jack took me with him and he said I wouldn't have to be alone anymore or live with any strange people somewhere else. I could stay with him forever. In another place.

June Smith

Performed as a play by YAL Amateur Drama Academy 27/28.5.1995

Published in Society of Women Writers WA Silver Collection Anthology 2007

Published in the In Another Place collection 2019 by June Kingston Smith.

Afternoon Escape

Commended Article 2018

There we were, all gathered in the bowling club. Chattering. Laughing. Hugging. Faces, some instantly familiar, others a lovely surprise. Beards, moustaches, glasses, expanding waistlines, grey hair or no hair. It didn't matter. We were all young again.

Those who stayed invited those who had gone, back home. To remember. For one afternoon we abandoned the future and escaped to the past – to relive our happy days growing up in the little country town we called home, where life in the late fifties had been uncomplicated and carefree.

Everyone had a story.

As photos were passed around we reminisced about our old wooden school with its three amazing teachers who provided the education for years 1-7 which were crammed into three rooms. Their smiles hid the stress of controlling so many classes at the same time. A fireplace in each room created welcoming warmth in the winter and in summer we opened the windows.

In the playground we drank warm milk from tiny bottles (my friend added Milo to hers, thanks to her clever mum), played marbles in the sand and ate our sandwiches in the play sheds (one for girls, one for boys).

Going to school was sometimes an adventure in itself. As we walked (usually barefoot) or rode our bikes through an avenue of gum trees we occasionally had to avoid marauding magpies or clumps of spitting caterpillars which had fallen in squirming clumps to the road from the green canopy above.

In the main street there was a butcher shop, two stores, a bootmaker (who also sold a small selection of new shoes too – you were fortunate if he had your size), the town hall, a tiny one roomed-library, the CWA meeting house, a hotel (now single storey brick after a fire burnt the beautiful two storey wooden building with its big verandahs) and the railway station where the magnificent steam trains, hauling their carriages from the city, would hiss to a stop beside the long platform under the big timber bridge, then fill the air with the smell of steam and coal as they whistled and huffed their way onto Bunbury.

The 'vege man' had a little stall on Saturday mornings. Choices were limited to what he had picked on his property that day and were displayed on shelves behind the counter – you told him what you wanted and he chose them, weighed them and put them in brown paper bags (you didn't see the bruised items until you got home). He didn't use a cash register, just added everything up out loud and put the cash (no credit cards back then) into a leather bag around his waist.

But the heart of the town was the wonderful town hall.

On Friday nights Alan Jones brought his picture show to the hall (a newsreel, cartoon and two pictures) and on Saturday nights there was often a dance when the chairs would be pushed against the wall and the lovely timber floor covered with sawdust. The girls, starched petticoats rustling and ponytails flying, would be whirled around by their partners, their stilettos and polished boots resounding to the beat of the band (which often played out of tune). We recalled the flirtation barn dance (that was a favourite) as it usually lived up to its name.

Apart from pictures and dances the hall hosted wedding

receptions, balls and school functions, and once a month a professional hairdresser from Bunbury would set up a temporary salon in one of the little dressing rooms and we would happily queue for a new hairstyle. Sometimes a TV night (with a donation to charity) was held in the supper room for those unlucky enough not to have TV and we could watch The Perry Como Show or gaze at the gorgeous Clint Walker who was Cheyenne. The local RSL club also held their meetings there.

We remembered one of the two general stores (a deli by today's standards) where we bought Coke or Fanta, lollies (musk sticks, marshmallow poached eggs, and, Heaven forbid, fake cigarettes called Fags!), and delicious homemade minced beef pies. It was also where we bought our comics – Chucklers' Weekly, Archie, Phantom and School Friend, as well as The Daily News.

We laughed when someone said "what about ice-cream?" Available in vanilla, strawberry or chocolate. Oh, how we thought we'd died and gone to Heaven when Neapolitan arrived – all three flavours at the same time in a little cardboard brick package (which would fit into the freezer compartment of our fridge, along with the frozen peas).

The other general store sold food, clothes and televisions – the first to arrive in town (with their very high antennae). An indefinable odour permeated from the dimly-lit store and people believed it came from the overstocked wooden shelves and oiled timber floorboards.

We spent our lazy summer days swimming in the leech-filled river and doing 'bombies' from the tree at the edge of the water, while being watched by curious cows quietly chewing in the paddock nearby (sadly swimming is not allowed there now due to possible disease).

We talked about school fights, best friends, favourite

teachers, rock and roll, film stars, childhood sweethearts, teenage pregnancies and teenage marriages, and some admitted they had adventurously crept into the pictures without paying. We remembered our football club (some of the WAFL stars actually finished their careers in the country) which drew the town together on Sundays; and basketball, which some of the girls played on Saturday afternoons.

We even talked about milk which we could buy from a dairy at one end of the street (a billy, full of warm, creamy liquid) and bread, still warm from the ovens and smelling divine (white, brown, square, upright or tank in big baskets), delivered house to house by the local baker. No focaccia or ciabatta back then.

Our town also had its own hospital and doctor, a police station (and small gaol) with one policeman and a post office and telephone exchange. In those days the postman would ride around on his bike, announcing the arrival of letters in your box with a blast on his whistle.

And then there were the characters. Of course. Every town has them. There were a lot of giggles as we resurrected their names. Snowy, the cheery butcher who always made us laugh ("we don't have dead cats today" when I asked for a shillings' worth of cats' meat for my cat Whisky); Polony Bill, who visited regularly in his old van full of cold meats (he often gave you a piece of polony while you waited); and Les, the man who told jokes while cutting hair after his day's work at the mill (everyone got the same pudding basin style) and who also de-sexed tom cats when required. And naturally we had a town gossip who was always peering over her fence and missed nothing.

As the afternoon drew to a close we felt sad to think those wonderful times were long gone. Steam trains had been replaced, the timber mill which had once been the vibrant hub of the town with its whistle summoning the men to work, to lunch and to go home, and the smell of burning sawdust forever in the air, was now closed. The historic railway workshops, once bustling with men and noisy machinery, were now quietly brooding, ghosts of its past whispering in the gloom.

The post office, butcher shop, shoe shop and one of the stores had closed. The wooden school had been replaced by a modern brick one which was losing pupils, the hospital had been downgraded and people moved away. A big company stripped the nearby hills bare with their machines and chemicals and offered employment of a different kind. Some people became sick. More people moved away and empty houses were on the market for $70,000.

A town on its knees. Down but not out. The remaining store struggles amid deserted buildings. Silence stirs the dust and boards cover windows.

At the bowling club, while bowlers enjoy their afternoon outside on a perfect green, on a perfect afternoon, time was irrelevant inside. The bleakness of the future still loomed for some, but the threatening march of progress had temporarily stopped.

Phone numbers and email addresses were exchanged. The promise of another reunion, soon, was made with eager anticipation.

But we didn't know then that that would be our last reunion; that our town would soon struggle no more; that it would be consumed by the hungry flames of an enormous bushfire, with only the façade of our beloved town hall left standing – the heart of our town.

Memories, lingering like a summer day at the river. Memories, fading, but never forgotten.

June Smith

Wendy Stackhouse

Beneath Still Waters

Winning Short Story 2016

Hidden from view by the rocks, her breath caught as she watched him remove his clothes and lie on the dry sand. Taut muscles gleamed in the early morning sun and rippled over his chest as he turned on his stomach.

"I am in the presence of a god," she sighed, and edged closer, drinking in the perfection sprawled before her. With practised ease, she shed her outer garments before stepping over the rocky ground. Sharp stones bruised her tender feet, but she ignored the pain and crossed the sand to where he lay.

A shadow blocked out the sun and as he rolled over his mouth gaped open. A beautiful girl stood naked in front of him. Clouds of long black hair framed a perfect face and huge deep brown eyes gazed into his.

"Hello," he said, his voice a husky whisper. "Can I help you?"

She gave no answer but lay beside him and stroked his face. Soft hands continued to explore his body, and he gathered her into his arms.

Afterwards, they fell asleep in the midday sun and he woke alone on the empty beach. He called and searched for her until late afternoon. Only one set of footprints marked the narrow cliff path to this tiny inlet, and they bore the imprints of his own feet.

Half convinced it had been a dream he waited for her until the evening breeze stirred the sand, then climbed the path back to the cottage. Throughout the rest of his holiday, he visited the same spot on the beach every morning, but she never appeared again. Not wanting to appear foolish he never mentioned the incident to anyone on his return home. His mother asked how he'd enjoyed the holiday in his grandfather's cottage and he simply smiled and said "Wonderful."

Life settled into its usual routine and his 'dream' faded into a pleasant memory. Months after returning home he met Cilla, a graphic artist like himself. Long hours spent together at work developed into something more. In summer they became a couple, and he mentioned the cottage off the coast left to him by his grandfather.

"The island itself is a magical place," he said to Cilla, "perfect for us to get to know each other better." Enthused by his words she agreed and he went ahead with his plans, visiting an expensive jeweller then hiding the tiny box deep inside his hand luggage.

The plane dropped lower, and he pointed to a small island in the centre of a group of rocky outcrops. "Our home for the week," he said and caught up in his excitement she squeezed his hand. The cottage waited for them, neat and clean – a local woman from the other side of the island took care of it and stocked the pantry. The old generator needed an overhaul so at present no electricity existed for cooking or phones. They must rely on tinned and dried foods, plus any fish they caught.

Cilla's lips pressed together – like most successful young women her cooking consisted of taking frozen meals from the freezer to the microwave if not dining out. He assured her there were many delicious ways to make meals from the packets of legumes and tinned meats stacked on the pantry shelves. Privately she decided he could cook for the entire week.

The first cloud hovered on the horizon – Cilla's visions of a perfect island getaway did not include soaking dried beans overnight to create calorie-ridden stodge. Although not expecting to be waited on hand and foot the sheer isolation of the 'cosy cottage' appalled her. Surely at least one restaurant is open in the village across the island?

He roared with laughter when she voiced her concerns. The two cottages that comprised the village, he explained, could not be reached except by boat, which he didn't own.

"Mr Sinclair runs a small fishing boat and collects supplies from the other islands. He brings Mrs Sinclair here to check the place in my absence, and in return I send her things she can't get from the islands. Her daughter's family live in the next door cottage, but they'll be moving away as soon as the children go to school."

Furrows appeared on Cilla's smooth forehead. No mobiles, no restaurant, no hairdresser, no gym, and no theatres – the list mounted in her head. How on earth did the islanders live, it was not her idea of heaven.

The look that crossed her face sowed the first seeds of doubt. Unable to embrace solitude the way he did, it did not bode well for their future. For goodness sake he admonished himself, it was only the first day. Later, as she had more time to appreciate the place, she'd fall in love with it too.

That night as they curled up in bed his doubts faded away. The fire built from the logs Mr Sinclair stacked by the shed made the room as warm as their love-making. Later, while she slept the faint sounds of singing drifted through the window, but he dismissed it as part of the island's magic.

After breakfasting on oats cooked on the wood stove, they left the cottage hands entwined and followed the cliff path to the tiny beach. She chatted non-stop as she stepped easily down the steep track, helped by years of attending the gym. At the beach he led her towards the rock pools, a pastime of his since his childhood visits to his grandfather. Engrossed in the tiny miasma of life thriving in these microscopic worlds cut off from the ocean, he didn't notice her lack of interest.

Ignored, she wandered back to the beach as he reached a huge rock, a favourite spot of his. Although tall, he had to stretch on tiptoes to see the top, then found himself looking straight into the eyes of a massive seal. Motionless, he stared back, then noticed the infant seal by her side. The pup butted his mother's head in play, distracting her gaze from him, and in silence, he retraced his steps and caught up with Cilla.

"You must come with me," he urged her before she threw herself on the beach towel, "I want to show you something magical."

"Can't you tell me," she grumbled, "I need to catch a tan while the sun is out."

In his excitement, he dismissed her mood and caught hold of her hand to pull her along beside him. "This is something special," he promised her, "You'll love it!" I doubt that she thought, it'll be more of those slimy rock pool creatures he finds more fascinating than me.

They approached the rock, and he hoisted her above his shoulders, urging her to look. At once, she gave a loud scream, and he drew her back into his arms to comfort her as shudders wracked her body.

"For god's sake," she shouted, "do you want to get me killed? The animal is dangerous, those vicious teeth and hateful eyes – before you pulled me back, it tried to attack me."

Puzzled, he attempted to calm her, but as she stormed back to the beach, he turned to check the rock. What had scared her so much, he wondered as he poked his head above the top? The mother seal lay stretched out in the sun, relaxed and peaceful. From behind her the curious youngster waddled over to him and butted his nose like a playful puppy. He half expected the mother to react in defence of her baby, but she held his gaze without blinking and his heart filled with the wonder of the moment.

Later in the evening as he sliced tinned ham and opened a can of baked beans, he tried his best to assure Cilla the seal meant no harm. She pushed her plate away before answering him. "I know what I saw and you'll never convince me otherwise. The beast wanted to kill me. We will never speak of it again."

Regret filled him, his grandfather had encouraged him to be at one with nature but Cilla never could be. They had no future together, the jeweller's box hidden in his suitcase would be returned once this week ended. It was time to find another job, perhaps the graphic comic's he illustrated in his spare time might interest a buyer? Ever since the popular movies based on the Marvel comics hit the screens, demand for the comics had increased.

Late at night as she slept on the far side of the bed, the full moon shone directly on his face and woke him. As if in a dream, he dressed and walked outside the cottage towards the cliffs. Moonlight guided him to the rock. This time he climbed to the top and turned full circle, not sure of what he sought.

The beach lay empty, but as he looked downwards, he glimpsed the figure of a woman in the shallows. Shafts of moonlight outlined the masses of long hair floating like black seaweed around her naked body. In her arms, a tiny dark-haired infant wriggled and thrashed both arms and legs as if to mimic her swimming.

He slid from the rock and reached the beach in time to see the mother and child swim towards him. Deep brown eyes sought his, and she sang to him the same eerie song he heard through the window last night. The haunting tune ended as she and the babe disappeared from view around the rocks. With a start, he recalled one of the many myths his grandfather told him, but he knew now his grandfather's tale had been true.

"In my youth, I met a Selkie on this beach," his grandfather said, "a magical creature I caught changing from a seal into an enchanting young woman. To keep her by my side I hid her pelt, without which she could never return to the sea. The summer we spent together in my cottage became the happiest time of my life.

One day while I was out on my fishing boat she found her pelt. From the deck, I watched her wrap herself in the sealskin. With a splash, she leapt beneath the waves, never to return. Years later, I married an island girl, your grandmother, but I never forgot my Selkie maiden."

He remembered how sadness clouded his grandfather's eyes when he'd finished and vowed never to make the same mistake. The sealskin belonged to her, he would never take it and force her to live forever on land. She must stay as free to raise her son beneath the waves as she was to visit him on the island.

After this long week ended, and he returned to the city, he'd settle his affairs then make his home on the island. Comics could be illustrated anywhere, and as he gazed out to sea, he planned the first of his drawings. He hoped his pen could capture her soulful eyes, the only part of her that never changed.

Two whiskery snouts broke the surface and two pairs of eyes followed his retreating figure. "Every summer we will share our life on land with your father," she said to the pup nestled between her fins. "Each winter we return to our colony until the sun beckons us back to his cottage."

With a contented flick of her tail, she guided her son under the water and together they swam deep beneath the waves to join the rest of their kind.

Wendy Stackhouse

We Have a Bridge

Runner-Up Article 2018

We Have a Bridge. Ours, unlike the Oresund Bridge which connects Denmark to Sweden does not unite two countries. That spectacular Scandinavian bridge soars eight kilometres across the Oresund Strait from the Swedish Coast to the artificial island of Peberholm. From there a four kilometre tunnel runs under the sea to the Danish island of Amager. This combined road and rail bridge connects the Danish capital of Copenhagen to Sweden's city of Malmö. The bridge has become an integral part of the transport networks of Central and Western Europe.

Despite finding sixteen unexploded World War Two bombs on the seabed, workers completed the bridge ahead of time. When it opened in June 2000, almost 80,000 people ran across it from Denmark to Sweden to compete in an inaugural half-marathon.

Eleven years later the two countries joined again to produce the TV Series 'The Bridge'. This Nordic Noir series with the flawed detectives typical of these dark thrillers also starred the Oresund Bridge. The haunting music accompanying the opening shots of the sleek bridge spanning the strait, brought the Oresund Bridge into lounge rooms across the world.

We Have a Bridge. It does not share dramatic views across the harbour or Opera House, nor do the locals call it 'The Coathanger' because of its arched design. Sydney

Harbour Bridge alone lays claim to these attributes and more.

Our bridge began with less drama than that of the Sydney Harbour Bridge, which, in 1932 had its opening ceremony hijacked by a political stunt. In front of 300,000 onlookers, a member of a paramilitary group rode his horse towards the official ribbon and slashed it with a ceremonial sword. The startled Premier of New South Wales did not even have time to open his silver scissors.

Another rider who claimed his place in history that day was nine-year-old Lennie Gwyther. With the blessing of his father, young Lennie rode alone on his pony, Ginger Mick, 1,400 kilometres from Gippsland, Victoria, to witness the historical event. Later his hometown Leongatha erected a statue in his honour.

Eighty years ago the bridge's 49 metre clearance allowed most vessels to pass beneath it on their way out from the harbour to the Tasman Sea. With the increasing size of today's cruise ships, this has become more of a challenge. Cruise-ship passengers, drinks in hand, now gather on deck to cheer as the tip of the funnel slips beneath the steel girders with centimetres to spare.

We Have a Bridge. They did not paint ours 'International Orange', like the Golden Gate Bridge of San Francisco. At first the United States Navy wanted it painted in black and yellow stripes to enhance its visibility to shipping in the notorious fogs of the bay. Then the Army Air Corps put in a request for red and white candy cane stripes. The people of the 'City by the Bay' eventually picked its current unique shade, and are happy that their bridge escaped any resemblance to a giant wasp or overdecorated Christmas tree.

The bridge crosses the Pacific Ocean from San Francisco Bay on the south to Marin County in the north. Since its opening in 1937 both people and animals have travelled across the often fog-shrouded suspension bridge. Black-tailed deer once stopped traffic as they wandered through the lanes. Rescued from the slaughterhouse, a six-foot female ostrich en route to her new home kicked her way out of her trailer and bounded between the cars. However, the most frequent animal commuters are coyotes. They lope over in the dead of night from the north side to the city in search of the odd pet dog or cat to supplement their diet.

We Have a Bridge. So far no one has declared their everlasting love by attaching a padlock etched with their beloved's name onto the handrails of ours. This dubious honour belongs to the Pont des Arts Bridge across the River Seine in Paris.

The original bridge, built in the 19th century at the request of Napoleon Bonaparte, resembled a garden suspended over the river. Flowers decorated the railings, with benches each end for people to enjoy the view. After suffering aerial damage through two wars, they rebuilt it in 1981. The new bridge became a favourite with artists and photographers across the world for its romantic views across the Seine.

For years couples locked padlocks to the railings before tossing the keys into the river as a symbol of eternal devotion. This began to weigh the bridge down and in 2015 authorities removed 45 tons of these metal declarations of love to prevent the bridge from collapsing.

The Mayor of Paris auctioned millions of these unique padlocks for funds to help Parisian Refugees. They built a children's playground with the $400,000 raised by the sale. This gesture must gladden the heart of every Amelie who ever pledged herself to her Louis before throwing the key into the Seine.

We Have a Bridge. Hopefully, ours will never become a 'Dog Suicide Bridge', the nickname for the Overtoun Bridge in Scotland. This stone bridge spans the nearby River Clyde from Overtoun House, a 19th-century baronial mansion in West Dunbartonshire near Glasgow.

Over the past fifty years, 600 dogs jumped the high walls of this bridge to fall 15 metres into the river below. Fifty of these dogs died, but of those that survived, many tried to leap over the ancient stone bricks again and again. For 110 years before this, Overtoun Bridge remained a harmless stone structure. Then in the 1950s, the first dog leapt to his death over the parapet, followed in the same spot by many others.

All the dogs belonged to breeds known for their sense of smell, like Labradors, Collies, and Scottish Terriers. They only jumped on sunny days, which gave animal experts a clue to why these placid pooches ended their lives in such a tragic fashion.

When the experts examined the rough stonework of the 160-year-old bridge they discovered the nests of many rodents, including mink. Introduced from America into Scotland in the 1950s, the mink were farmed for their fur. When animal fur fell out of fashion, many of the mink escaped captivity.

Fine weather spread the rank musk odour from the urine of these animals, a lure no self-respecting hunting dog could ignore. Heedless of what lay beyond the high granite walls, one by one these unfortunate hounds bounded the ramparts to seek this compelling scent. Instead, they fell to their deaths on the rocks below.

Overtoun Bridge now has a sign posted each end warning dog-owners to keep a tight hold of their pets. Scotland also introduced a program to cull the mink as an introduced species.

We Have a Bridge. Unlike the Tower Bridge of London, our bridge lacks the bascules, which part to allow ships to pass beneath. Opened in 1894 by the future King Edward VII and his wife Princess Alexandra, Tower Bridge crosses the River Thames near the Tower of London.

The walkway running far above the bascules became the hangout for thieves and ladies of the night, forcing its closure from 1910 until 1982. Transparent panels installed in the walkway in 2014 now allow foolhardy souls to walk on glass and gaze at the River Thames 42 metres below.

Drama and theatrics have dogged this stately bridge. Several dare-devils flew a variety of planes through the span of the bridge over the years, including an Australian who performed the stunt in his sea-plane in 1919. The pilot of a Royal Air Force Hawker Hunter Jet became the first to fly a jet plane through the gap in 1968 as a protest against the government of the day. Once, a London bus driver hit the accelerator and sped over the one-metre gaping chasm when the bridge parted beneath his number 78 double-decker bus. A similar situation almost caused an international incident when the bridge opened just as President Bill Clinton's car passed. Panicked security guards remained behind while the President's car travelled on unaware. Bridge officials previously tried to contact the American Embassy to warn them of the opening time, but no one answered the phone.

Despite all its dramas, the Tower Bridge continues to be one of the best-known landmarks of the City of London.

We Have a Bridge. The Matagarup Bridge, the first cable sway bridge in Australia, is our bridge. Chosen by the local Whadjuk community, the name Matagarup means a place where the river is only 'leg deep'.

This pedestrian bridge crosses the Swan River from East Perth to the Perth Stadium on the Burswood Peninsula. Sports fans can park their cars, or travel by public transport to East Perth, then walk across the bridge to watch their favourite teams.

The week before the official opening on July 14th, 2018, three hundred of the bridge workers walked, ran, jumped and danced their way along its 400-metre span. This allowed a team from Curtin University to test it through special sensors. Later over 1200 people trotted backward and forwards to test its sway.

The tests proved more successful than those carried out on Central London's Millennium Bridge which closed two days after it opened. The weight of several thousand pedestrians on opening day caused it to swing back and forth like a pendulum.

Having survived every test, Matagarup Bridge allows footy fans to eat their meat pies without a hint of seasickness from a swaying walkway.

At night, colour-changing lights sprinkled throughout the two metal arcs above the bridge transform them into a pair of gigantic swans. With a majestic grace, they shimmer towards each other, mirrored in the river below that bears their name. Perth's beautiful new landmark is a welcome addition to the City of Lights.

And this is our bridge.

Wendy Stackhouse

Madeleine Tingey

Sand Writing

Winning Short Story 2004

I had loved going to the beach house when I was a child. Best of all was the view of the beach, and I considered it to be the most perfect place in the whole universe. When you curled up in the old settee on the front veranda, the tiny beach looked like an illustration torn from a picture book. Its perfect curve was curtained by drooping peppermint trees, but away from the shade a million fragments of shell sparkled like tiny jewels. Beside the waves the sand was so smooth it made you long to run across the track, grab a stick and start drawing. The desire to fill the whole beach with sand writing was irresistible to a nine-year-old.

After Mum died, my Dad, Bill, sold the family home and moved into the beach house. We still called it the beach house. Whenever I went there he said he had been renovating, but nothing ever seemed to change. The paint on the blistered weatherboards remained chipped, while the sun-bleached boards emphasised its shabby appearance. I thought he might have tended the little garden Mum had coaxed into existence, battling the ravages of the salt-laden winds. Instead, he built a big shed out the back and spent most of his days installed within it.

Dad had always been keen on working with wood. Now he trawled the beaches searching for pieces suitable for carving.

The huge winter tides yielded a prodigious bounty that was piled up around the outside of the shed, like ramparts surrounding a castle. His carvings of local bird life intrigued me. Each one was exquisitely perfect. I sat for hours watching him honing a piece of wood until it took on the shape of a bird. Broad-winged, long-legged gulls emerged, contrasting with slender terns caught in graceful flight, or poised to plunge beneath the waves. It was surprising that his big hands could be so talented. The scent of wood lingered as I drove back to the city, elusive as the drifting smell of gum blossom.

Of course, the coastline has changed over the years; brash new houses now rise above the dunes, each one bigger than its neighbour. There is a new house up the road from Dad, rearing from the sand like a monolith. It boasts acres of windows on all three levels and the developer's board spoke of views to die for.

I went and sat on our veranda. One thing they didn't possess was my favourite view of the little beach opposite. It was going to be another hot day and it wasn't long before the new neighbours trooped past. Dad had told me they came down from the city most weekends.

"Hello there," the woman called. "You must be Isabel. Your father has told me all about you."

Anna didn't look like a mum. She wore designer-style beach gear and chunky gold jewellery that was enhanced by an impressive tan. Her shoulder-length red hair was casually tangled. I didn't like her hard mouth or her restless, edgy manner. She looked unhappy. The older boy and younger girl had already run ahead and were plunging confidently into the blue water. The middle child lagged behind.

"Do come along, Sean. James and Megan are already in the water." Anna spoke in exasperation bordering on dislike. I looked at the boy. He had picked up a pebble and was holding it close to his face, staring as if mesmerised. He had straight, light-coloured hair and unusual, almost colourless eyes.

"Are you going swimming too, Sean?" I asked. He stared at me and his mother turned away dismissively.

"He doesn't talk much. We've learned to ignore his moods. Come on kid." She grabbed the boy's hand and wrenched the pebble from his grasp. Angrily she threw it. The boy watched as the pebble spiralled upwards before plummeting into the scrub. He watched silently. As they walked away I felt a faint unease stirring. Later, when I wandered down to the beach for a swim Sean was hunched against a rocky outcrop. He was sifting the powdery sand through his fingers, scooping it into his palm, and then squeezing his fists shut, trying to prevent it from trickling out. He was totally absorbed by the phenomenon. While he watched the sand, I watched him. Most of the time James and Megan played together as though their brother was invisible. He refused to join in their games so they ignored him. Megan was a resolute girl, bossy and assertive. "I can write hundreds of words," she told me one evening when I sat watching the sunset. "Probably thousands. Watch me." She grabbed a stick. The sand spread before her like the blank page of a book, demanding to be inscribed upon. I watched Megan write a large slightly wobbly M followed by each letter of her name. Her face was screwed up with the effort. She went on adding all the words she could think of, quite an impressive list. By the time she had finished the sun had almost disappeared in a spectacular blaze of crimson and a chill wind had sprung up. "Come on," said James. "We've got to go."''But you haven't written yet," the girl protested.

"You should see James write. He can join his letters up." This achievement clearly impressed her. James shrugged, acknowledging his superiority. It would have been difficult for any child to be in the middle of these two, I thought. Sean was standing staring at the empty horizon.

"What can you see?" I asked him, putting my hand on his arm. He pulled away. "Don't bother about him, he can't do anything," said James in disgust.

"He's three years older than me and he can't even read my books. And he has to go to a special school," added Megan.

A month passed before I returned to the beach house. The children didn't seem to be around. "School's back. They don't come so often," Dad explained. I imagined Megan, self-confident in her school uniform, learning more words she could practice at the beach. Then I pictured James, the high achiever, with his sights set on high school. But what about Sean? Where did he fit in? He was like a little ghost flitting in and out of people's lives. I could see him hovering at the edge of a classroom, staring at the fish tank. He would be inattentive to the lesson, his blank look frustrating the teachers.

My next visit was at Easter. I was glad to escape from the office, and was looking forward to long walks along the dunes. After a quick cup of tea with Dad I headed for the beach. I was intrigued to find lines of writing covering the sand. Megan's letters had now become bolder, while James was trying to execute intricate geometrical designs. I was fascinated by Megan's pictures, the rows of stick people and animals with four legs coming straight out of their round bodies. Dad had kept my childhood scribblings and I wondered if Anna treasured theirs. What mementoes would there be of Sean's childhood? That morning I had heard Anna screaming at him, but there had been no response. Did she punish him? He made me remember a pale girl at school who everyone was mean to. Later we discovered that her mother shut her in a cupboard because she couldn't stand the sight of her.

Easter fell late that year and Dad and I wondered whether the golden warmth would last or if sweeping rain would send the beach lovers scurrying indoors. By Monday, storm clouds were banking on the dark horizon. Seated on the verandah, I could hear children quarrelling on the beach. The next minute Anna came running down the track. She looked angry and there was a vicious expression on her face. She didn't speak even though she must have seen me. The wind whipped at her hair as she struggled with the hood of her jacket. The storm was going to be enormous. Above the sound of the rising wind I could hear the woman yelling at the children to come back, but her words were swallowed by the wind.

"Every time they leave she has to drag them off the beach, threatening all sorts of punishments if they don't come and pack and clean their rooms," Dad had told me. Now she was coming back, dragging Sean by the arm like a dog, while the other two ran ahead out of reach. "Does she hurt them?" I asked him.

"Yes. She hurts them. That's the problem," he replied. Later, as I peeled vegetables for our evening meal, I heard their four-wheel-drive roar away into the distance.

"Let's go for a walk along the beach before the storm hits?" I suggested.

Dad carefully placed the tiny bird he was whittling down on a shelf and grabbed his wet-weather gear.

The grasses whipped at my bare legs as we made their way down the track. The bay was bathed in a sullen light and the threatening sky pressed down like a bruise. "Better be quick. Once the rain starts it'll come down in sheets. Look at those waves!" he exclaimed.

I looked at the curling waves breaking angrily on the sand. They had a cutting edge, like cruel children teasing their playground victim.

"The children have been drawing," I said. "It will be washed away in a minute as if they were never here.'

I wandered over to the rocky ledge Sean so often lounged against while apparently busy doing nothing.

"Come over here, Dad. What do you make of this?" I shouted.

Someone had been writing in the pale sand beneath the rock ledge. Just one word was written there.

"S-e -a." I knelt on the damp coldness with the wind tearing at my scarf as I spelled out the letters. "What's that supposed to mean?"

Dad was peering at it closely. "What can you see after the 'a'?"

"It's an 'n' " I exclaimed excitedly. " It's his name. 'Sean'. He can write his name!"

"And not just that," my father was saying with the pride reserved for the achievements of a favourite child. "He can do it as well as his siblings! One day we can expect some interesting rivalry."

"He's going to be all right, isn't he?"

Just below the name a tiny bird had been executed with the few deft strokes of a stick, like a signature. It had been exquisitely formed.

"What does the picture mean?" I wondered. "It's beautiful."

"One morning Sean came to my workshop door, quiet as a whisper." As Dad spoke I could see the boy watching with those big eyes, too wary to enter. "He must have stood there for an hour before he ventured in. He stood at my elbow until the light faded and I had finished carving a tiny bird. As I placed it on the shelf, he held out his hand and gently touched it. If you could have seen the way he stroked the tail feathers, you would understand why I gave it to him. The bird was exactly like the one he's drawn in the sand. He's an artist, Isabel."

"Did he say anything to you?"

"He didn't need to. His expression said everything."

I put my arm through Dad's as we left the beach, buffeted by the mad wind. Already the first heavy drops of rain were splashing my face. I turned and looked back as a grey veil of mist-shrouded the coastline and clouds like damp puffballs merged with the pounding ocean. The waves had washed away the other children's writing, but Sean's remained safe in the lee of the rock.

Madeleine Tingey

English Class

Runner-Up Poem 2008

Bent over exercise books
laboriously copying each unfamiliar word
these six Moslem women.

Serious scholars from ancient times
from a different dimension
war victims, belonging nowhere.

Pens, unaccustomed utensils,
awkwardly form arcane shapes
fraught with misunderstanding.

The veil sets them apart
tenting their faces
silencing personality
demonising them in Western eyes.

One woman has finished
she glances up, reads hesitantly
'My home is Australia.'

Her veil slips revealing
raven hair loosely tied.
She smiles. Transformed

she could be my daughter.

Madeleine Tingey

Heading South

Commended Short Story 2013

As soon as we have packed away the tiny Christmas tree I know my mother will make her annual announcement. It happens as predictably as the hanging baskets on the balcony wilt and summer- hot fumes from gridlocked cars fill our kitchen. The tiny apartment is claustrophobic.

"I think it's time to head south," she declares. "What we need is a breath of fresh air."

Immediately images of turquoise water and silvery sand fill my mind.

We stay with my grandmother. Mum grew up in her sprawling, wooden house perched high above the inlet, listening to frogs croaking in the darkness and waking to full-throated birdsong. Now this windy coastline would be my place of adventure for a whole month.

Grandma is a little stooped but she is still almost as tall as mum. All three of us are tall and strong. When she hangs out the washing, moving with rhythmic regularity, bend straighten stretch, bend straighten stretch, I notice how powerful her arms and shoulders still are.

Grandma taught me to swim during the summer holiday I turned six, enduring the turmoil as I wallowed in the water, splashing and snorting, half pulling her under as I sank to the sandy seabed, my skinny body refusing to float.

"Your mother's a good swimmer," she says.

"But I was never a water baby like you, "Mum replies. "Remember that race you entered when we were at school? You had to swim out to Glass Rock and back round the bay."

I know this explanation is for me, and I have observed the rock; it is a fearsome two metre tall landmark at one end of the reef. Black and slippery it points finger-like to the sky.

"I've still got a medal somewhere to prove I did it," says Grandma, laughing.

At that moment a thought forms in my mind that wheels and spirals like a constellation. That is the turning point, when I know that I have to swim out to the reef. I remember my grandmother's warning.

"Never go beyond Glass Rock, it's an adversary even for strong swimmers. You must always be looking and listening. We need to respect the ocean and work out what it's telling us."

Of course I would be careful. I might be a townie but I'm not stupid. I look out across the dense coastal scrub to the thin blue line of the ocean. From the distance of the verandah the reef is nothing more than a few black marks against a blue horizon, a broken line of Chinese writing, only the occasional spume of white spray warning of its danger.

The next afternoon I slip out while the two women are arguing over what colour Grandma should paint the house. The weatherboards have been bleached to the colour of old bones by the sun and wind. Beyond the garden the threadlike track descends suddenly before disappearing through thick undergrowth. The bush spreads out in a grey-green quilt highlighted by splashes of yellow and white as if carelessly daubed from an artist's palette. Thorns, concealed by loose sand, aggravate the soles of my feet making me exclaim in irritation as I am forced to stop and pull them out. The vegetation with its sharp, twiggy shrubs conspires to warn me off. Inhospitable is a word that comes to mind.

As the track plunges towards the bay I lose sight of the welcoming blue glimpse of the ocean and find myself in an aromatic, humming, buzzing world. Whip-like branches snap at my legs and clouds of insects swarming round my face are small tortures to endure.

When at last I reach the beach the sky has clouded over, turning the sea grey, while a strong wind is whipping the water into a choppy blanket. Enclosed by two headlands and backed by the steep hillside it is an isolated place. I shiver. If I want to turn back, now is the time. But this is something I have to do.

I stop, remembering the boy I met at this spot a year ago. That day stands out because I had felt an immediate kinship with him; I called him the Fish Boy because he was such a brilliant swimmer.

"Do you live here?" I had asked, curious about the stranger.

"Not far away," the boy replied carelessly. His dark, curly hair whipped back in the brisk wind that threatened to snatch at his words. "Coming in?"

I had hesitated, uncertain about broaching the heavy swell and noticing the waves crashing against the reef. "Don't worry. You'll be safe with me. I promise you," the boy had reassured me.

Today I look around half expecting the Fish Boy to be there, wishing I had asked him his name and we could swim together again. The reality is less enticing. Clouds tumble like dark dragons on the horizon while a strange purplish light washes over the empty landscape, darkening the ocean. I watch uncertainly, as an angry sea surges against the reef. It looks a long way away. Then I stop thinking and plunge into the water, gasping as its coldness hits me, anaesthetising feeling. The waves are huge, towering walls of water approaching at an overwhelming speed. I feel like a mouse caught in a watery trap. With tremendous difficulty I start swimming towards the rocks; I struggle for about ten minutes, or is it twenty, time has no meaning out there, then look round; but it is incredibly rough and too much is happening to think of anything except surviving the next onslaught.

Now the alien sea looks really furious. Waves slap against my body stinging my skin. I have never felt more vulnerable. Before I can think further a bigger wave followed by an even more terrifying one crashes over me and my body is caught up and whirled frenziedly in a vortex. Powerless, I am totally commandeered by the ocean. My breath is trapped as helplessly I struggle against the tide.

For one brief moment the ocean spews me upwards and through slit eyes I catch sight of the shoreline as the huge swell rises and dips around me. It is then I think I see the Fish Boy standing at the edge of the water waving and shouting something to me, but his words are drowned by the wind. I know my friend is encouraging me to hold on; he is coming to rescue me. Minutes turn into wave crashing, sucking, tugging hours where survival is my only thought. I decide I will be dragged down towards the sea bed and am terrified. Then, when I know I can't hold out any longer, I sense strong arms beneath me and feel myself being dragged half- conscious to shore. I know the Fish Boy has saved me.

For a long while I collapse, half-conscious, coughing and choking up water. When at last I open my eyes a man in his thirties is bending over me, looking anxious. A brown kelpie sits patiently beside him.

"You're lucky I was down here and spotted you," he says. "Even from the cliff top I could see you were in trouble. You were crazy to swim on a day like this." He sounds angry.

"Did you see a boy, a bit older than me?" I struggle to get the words out.

"That was wishful thinking," he replies. "There was no one else. Be thankful I was around. Come on, my car's parked not too far away. I'll take you home."

Back at the house it is quiet. I sit down carefully in an old armchair on the verandah and close my eyes, exhausted. For once I don't want to look at the view. I am still shaking when I notice my grandmother sitting quietly in her favourite chair. She is looking at me.

"This is the kind of weather you don't want to swim in," she says.

There is a silence. I can hear my mother clattering dishes in the kitchen.

"I thought I saw a boy on the beach," I tell her. "An older boy with dark curly hair. Last year we swam together. He's the best swimmer. Do you know who he is?"

The quietness folds in on us and I think she has disregarded my question. Then she stands up and goes inside. When she returns she passes me a photograph. I look at it.

"Yes, that's him," I say excitedly. "Who is he?"

"That's my brother, David," she says quietly. "He drowned out near the reef not long after the photograph was taken. You were named after him."

Before I can say anything, my mother comes into the room, carrying the old brown teapot.

"Anyone for tea?" she inquires brightly, smiling at us. The spell is broken as reluctantly I gaze out once more towards the reef.

Madeleine Tingey

Contagion

Commended Short Story 2016

Mid-morning they drive out along the coast road to the ruins of the Quarantine Station. This scenic route follows the broken shoreline with its sweeping views back to the port. Several icons from early settlement days impress on memory; the bank, a hotel with an ornate white pediment and what looks like a store once used for imported merchandise. Susan feels they are leaving a refuge with a predictable pattern to daily life and entering the unknown.

Exactly what will happen she cannot imagine. Besides, if she says anything, Doug will give her the stare that means he seriously doubts her sanity. So instead she gazes out of the window at the threatening waves smashing against rocks and the low grey clouds wrapping everything in a grey cocoon. The landscape becomes steadily bleaker and more forbidding, the sparse vegetation beaten down by fierce winter storms, the pale grasses flattened.

The quarantine station, a forbidding rummage of buildings, had been built more than one hundred and fifty year ago at the far end of the windswept peninsula. It was strategically situated on the first piece of level ground the immigrant ships would have encountered, and provided a safe anchorage inside the harbour. Susan has read about this historic place in a brochure at the visitors centre. Now she can see for herself the stony outcrops and headlands where the men must have sourced rock from for the buildings. But surely the few bedraggled trees would not have supplied enough timber; they must have ordered wood from the mainland.

Doug swings the car off the road into the makeshift car-park and Susan thinks of how the medical officers believed that by enforcing strict quarantine the deadly diseases would not reach the general population. But how, she wonders, would that have made the benighted passengers feel about this terrifying place where they were put ashore? Many would have guessed at their dreadful destiny, felt their hearts sink as the ship approached the lonely outpost across turbulent waves.

"It was certainly a big place, hundreds of new arrivals must have passed through these walls, poor devils," comments Doug. Doug has always specialised in facts.

Although some would, without doubt, have found something to amuse them others would have had their resolve severely weakened at the dismal prospect. Would some have put their fate down to divine retribution or a wilful God?

On this bleak day there are no other visitors; the car park is empty. As soon as they climb out of the car into a sea of churned mud any warmth from the pale sun proves to be an illusion. A cold wind tugs at their jackets and whips Susan's short grey hair into tiny peaks. Doug is lugging the picnic basket across the lumpy ground.

"Come on," he shouts above the blustering of the wind. "Sit down in the shelter of this stone wall. It won't be so damp if we sit on the rug."

Leaning at an angle on the tussocky grass the picnic basket, with its cheerful gingham lining, looks incongruous. Susan had imagined picnics in tranquil settings, chairs placed in dappled sunshine, birds flitting in green branches. What a romantic she is, she thinks. No wonder that at times Doug becomes impatient with her. And how irrelevant her dreaming is has now been proved. She bites into a sandwich; even the bread tastes cold.

"These eggs are from that farm we stopped at yesterday. Eggs from the country definitely taste better," she comments, trying to sound cheerful.

"Eggs are eggs wherever you are," mutters Doug, pulling out his pocket knife and carefully selecting a fine blade to dissect his egg. The knife is his favourite possession when travelling; he never goes anywhere without it. The steel gleams dully in the overcast atmosphere.

"I'm going to look around," she announces, brushing crumbs from her trousers as she scrambles to her feet.

As Susan wanders from one collapsed building to another the chilly air makes her jaw ache. She strokes her face with one frozen hand, wishes she had worn gloves; her face hurts as if she is suffering a bad toothache. Pulling her jacket closer she stares at the cold sky stretched like a grey scarf across the bleakly sad surroundings, wishes they had never come here. About a dozen separate stone and timber-framed structures remain in various states of dereliction. Susan imagines rows of iron beds crammed in the confined spaces between the stone walls, thinks she can hear the cries of the patients.

It is then that she sees the inscriptions. At first they appear to be markings, the result of years of crumbling ruin, but then Susan perceives that they are names. Amelia, Sarah, Thomas, words that have been scratched by a sharp object, maybe the tine of a fork, and disappear on the bumpy bits of wall where there is nowhere to gain purchase.

Her eyes move slowly across the scraped marks as she reads the ghostly litany in a whisper as if they are runes, messages from another time that she is frightened of summoning to life. Ghosts. What superhuman effort the inmates must have made to ensure their confinement was recorded in this permanent testimony. Had they been survivors, she ponders, going on to live in their new country, marrying, having children, and working; or had they died at the station, the land they had yearned to reach so close but forever out of reach?

Doug is calling her, his words snatched by the wind.

"Over here, Susan. This part was the isolation ward harbouring those suspected of incubating disease, and back there is the shower block. There's information written up about each area; quite interesting facts. New arrivals were doused with a carbolic-acid solution. Imagine how that must have smelt." His words carry across the distance between them.

Hurrying over to where Doug stands, her skin crawling, Susan immediately smells the pungent odour of the fumigation bath house. She feels her stomach heave.

"What kind of diseases would they have suffered?" she asks, not wanting to know but feeling a compulsion to find out.

"Well, none of them would have been pleasant," Doug said caustically. "The authorities would have had to deal with epidemics of influenza. Spanish influenza killed millions across the world. There would have been fevers, often fatal, like scarlet fever. And diphtheria which would make your neck swell and closed airways."

"Want to look in here?" he asks, marching briskly down the labyrinth of broken walls and empty doorways, his boots ringing in the silence. A sign points to the mortuary.

"I'm so cold, Doug," she says, pleading in her distress. "Let's go.'

He grumbles about how she has dragged him out to this godforsaken place on some whim and is now no longer interested as she follows him to the car. In silence they drive back to the town. The car is warm, the radio played calming music; Susan feels that the quarantine station with its doomed buildings is a million miles away. Its tranquillity is spoilt by her knowledge of what happened there.

"I think we need a drink," says Doug. "And I could do with something to eat."

"But we've had lunch," Susan protests.

Doug ignores her.

Twenty minutes later Susan stands outside the hotel, one of the town's first buildings. She looks up at the sign depicting a splendid sailing ship, hears it creaking in the brisk wind. Had it been disease-riddled, rotting beneath its ebullience? Susan forces herself not to think of human cargos, the price people paid for emigrating and the likelihood of an enforced quarantine many would not survive. Below deck the hold would have been piled with trunks containing all their possessions. Was it down there, in the darkness, that the sickness festered? Beneath the picturesque sails, had the passengers journeyed on a plague ship?

They push through the glass doors and enter the old part of the building. A modern glass and concrete extension can be seen out the back. Hair streaming and eyes watering from the cold that has entered her bones, Susan stands for a moment savouring the welcoming quietness of mid-afternoon.

"Over here," Doug is calling. "This old part is cosy. The sort of place you like."

He directs her towards a table near a low-burning fire. While he goes to order drinks and sandwiches, Susan sank back into the comfortable armchair.

"Look at the lovely old fireplace, "she comments when he returns.

"Yes, the Ship Hotel is well over a century old. It would have been operating when the quarantine station was in use," says Doug, taking a long sip of his drink.

Susan puts her glass down. Suddenly she feels faint and the uneven whitewashed walls and low ceiling with its criss-crossing dark beams threaten to suffocate her.

"I think we should be getting back," she says quietly.

"But you haven't touched your drink. At least finish that."

Later, Susan stands at the guest house window looking out, imagining how the unfortunates must have gazed from their prison towards the town. Evening is falling; the ocean has become a pewter expanse of turbulence. On the misty horizon the walls of the ruined station rear gloomily, like an illustration in a history book. She shivers.

Doug has switched on the TV and is watching the news. If it wasn't for the spectre of the old buildings hovering in the distance it feels much like any other evening. Behind her the room is warm and inviting. Susan remains at the window, staring out across the water to where the quarantine station is now blanketed in darkness. It is as if the curtain had come down on a bizarre stage production.

What would it have been like to have been incarcerated there, she muses, day after endless day only to be plunged into a nightly blackness illuminated by guttering candles? Was that when the writing had been undertaken? She thinks of a woman desperately scratching as she crouched against the rough wall, implement grasped in trembling hand, relying on waning reserves of strength to complete her task. Perhaps she was struggling against a pestilence.

Susan presses her burning forehead against the cold glass. She discovers she is shaking, her stomach roiling, limbs aching. I must get to the bed she thinks. She crosses the room, body swaying and topples onto the quilt. The material feels cool against her cheek.

"Doug, would you mind going to the pharmacy and fetching me some medication. I'm sick." She utters the words with difficulty, as though somebody else is speaking.

He turns and looks at her, then gets up and advances slowly, staring with a horrified curiosity. For once his matter of fact commonsense appears to have deserted him. What is wrong? Susan has never known him like this. Even in her distress she understands the implications.

"Your eyes," he is saying. "They're yellow." Gently he pulls back the neckline of her blouse. "And there's an angry red rash, spreading up your neck, across your chest and shoulders."

His voice echoes from far away through a descending cloud of delirium.

He takes out his mobile and she listens to his voice through muzzy-headed pain.

"Is that the hospital? It is imperative that I talk to a doctor who specialises in infectious diseases. This patient's condition is urgent. There may be a need for isolation."

His voice is authoritarian, toneless. There is a pause. He is pacing the room as she strains to hear, unsure of how long consciousness will remain.

"I am not exaggerating. This sickness is beyond my comprehension. I can guarantee it is something you will not have witnessed before."

There is another pause. Then:

"No, I don't know how the disease was contracted. The evidence appears to be an impossibility."

Racked by pain and distress, exhausted, Susan listens helplessly to the conversation before lapsing into unconsciousness.

Madeleine Tingey

Rose van Son

Sensual Writing

Commended Article 2009

Writer, Elizabeth Jolley, once wrote of the "sound of a landscape", that to hear the familiar sound of a bus on a quiet day in Claremont as she was hanging washing on the line, suddenly transported her to a faraway place.

That place was the "narrow streets, of narrow terraced houses all with their front doors opening on whitened door-steps straight on to the street." In her mind's eye she had returned to a place that once held special meaning for her.

Many writers know the importance that the senses play in memorable writing. The language of the writer has flavour, texture, vision. It is the language of the senses used by writers to journey the streets of life; to be transported to somewhere else, somewhere deep in the memory bank, by a simple sound, as Elizabeth Jolley was.

The senses are so ingrained in language. They are the vehicle writers use to travel with the reader, to a place often long forgotten, much like the feeling we get when hearing an old song.

The writer's job is to observe. In this way, the writer is an enviable position, where senses become acute in day-to-day observation of places and people. The writer observes not only the obvious, concrete verbal language - what we see and hear - but also the non-sounds, the silences, the tensions between people and places, the smells and tastes that linger on the tip of the tongue and in the mind, long after the moment has gone.

In this way, the writer uses the senses as glue, flexible yet strong, to build and layer meaning, to write a fabric that stands firm but has the capacity to move with and across time.

The writer takes these different layers and levels of language; takes these sounds, textures, smells, no matter how simple, ties them together with words to paint a picture, that can transport the reader to a special place, a place the reader will want to visit time and again.

A writer is much like a painter in crafting the text; he or she colours the blank page with levels of meaning: metaphors, symbolism, irony. Just as a painter must be careful to paint a scene in a particular hue, to fill the painting with texture and colour, to allow the language of light to enter the work, to see the depth and drama on the canvas, creating an intensity of life within the framework, so, too, must the writer choose the right words with metaphorical flavours and textures. This writing will produce a masterpiece that emits the right balance of light, drama, vision: a text that is not over-written but flexible and includes gaps to challenge the senses of reader, and for the reader to fill in.

Like a painter, a writer needs language other than the obvious meanings of words to speak, to permeate the story. This dramatisation of a text, often by simple words, allows writing to live, to be seen, or be hidden, as the case may be, within the body of the text. The writer comes to the page, a blank canvas, and proceeds to fill it with all the senses.

Language is multifaceted and the writer must use these various pots of colour to paint layers of meaning into a story. If not for these layers, a reader simply faces empty words on a page.

For a writer, language is an edible feast. It is flavours and textures moulded by language and sent on a sensual journey.

Through layers, language is metaphorical, and the metaphorical language of the simple word is the most sensual taste of all.

This simplicity allows the reader to bring to the text their emotions associated with that taste. Because to taste the word on the page is to truly embrace it with the whole body, to mix the past with the present, to allow it to be juxtaposed with a sense of knowledge, depth, and respect. It is a kaleidoscopic mix that gives words life, and new meanings, that enables the writer and reader to journey together, as Elizabeth Jolley did, on the bus, to re-experience the past yet catapult this new experience into the future.

The use of the senses when writing makes words come alive. Only then can the reader take this live text, the writing, to treasured place, to read and re-read curled up on the sofa, or to copy favourite phrases into a journal, to review, to enjoy that lingering taste on the tongue. Only then can the reader take away those inspiring words as keepsake to revisit and enjoy time and time again.

Writers, too, are inspired by the language of other writers and often read their favourite authors before sitting down to write. It is this reading that gives them a starting point that jump-starts their senses, generates a flow of language and meanings, and gives a heady start to a day's work.

In *The George's Wife*, Elizabeth Jolley writes what could be regarded as secret notes to writers: a line or two here and there within a fictional text. She provides clues about writing when she writes that sometimes, "events cannot be transformed into fiction until they are sufficiently over." But she agrees there can be exceptions to this and there "can be a merging of the actual and imagined." And it is the "ability to hold on to the vision while being involved in the event which helps to bring about the making of a fiction writer or a poet."

Memory is a large part of our lives. The smell of roast lamb will transport many of us to the warmth of the kitchen of our childhood, to the Sunday roast of our youth. It is the ability to replicate or transport that feeling, that smell with its accompanying texture and/or drama of the past and use it metaphorically or literally in the present, that makes a good writer.

The sounds and flavours of language, the layers upon layers of meaning, and the gaps purposely left by the writer for the reader to enjoy and fill in, is writing that excites and challenges. Anything else is mediocre writing.

Rose van Son

Edward Thomas – a Story of Love and Words

Highly Commended Article 2015

Anglo-Welsh poet, essayist and literary critic, Phillip Edward Thomas, was born on the 3rd March, 1878; he died in the First World War at the Battle of Arras, France, on Easter Monday, 9th April, 1917. It was Thomas' determination and love of words that kept him focused on his writing during his lifetime.

Thomas's wife, Helen, the daughter of journalist, James Ashcroft Noble, did not completely recover from the trauma of losing her husband. She was so devastated after his death that their youngest daughter, Myfanwy, was sent to live with an aunt while her mother grieved for the man she had met as a teenager, had loved throughout his depression, his good days and his bad, and who, despite his changing moods, loved her. Their marriage had been tumultuous; his mind pre-occupied with carving a path for his writing; for supporting his family of three children through his beloved art. Thomas was determined to earn a living only from writing. In his later years, he was known to take long walks with his friend and mentor, American poet, Robert Frost, who had come to England in 1913 to kick-start his own writing. Together, Frost and Thomas inspired each other as only writers can. After Thomas' death, Frost wrote: *1914 was our year. I never had, I shall never have, such a year of friendship.*

For Helen, Thomas wrote the ultimate love poem, one of

sadness and humility, one of apology and wisdom, one of love. *And You, Helen*, was written at the Front, in the days before his death, as if he had a premonition that death was imminent, as if there was a need to make amends for the days when his depression had forced him to take long walks, over the moors, across stiles, often with Frost, but sometimes alone, to spare Helen the pain of his moods.

It was Frost, as mentor and confidant, who suggested Thomas write poetry rather than critique it; to look at his essays and see if he could find poetry in them. Until then, *In Pursuit of Spring* was one of Thomas' best-known works, a magical story of cycling through the countryside, from London to the Quantock Hills, documenting the environment's rich colours and plants. Frost encouraged Thomas to write poetry itself: its beauty, its nature, its transcendence. Certainly Thomas had so much to write about: his knowledge of and immersion in nature, his thoughts, his misgivings.

Novelist and essayist, Penelope Fitzgerald, writes of the friends' walks:

The meadows were full of windfalls from the old cider apple trees, and at every gate and stile they paused and talked of flowers, childhood, Shakespeare, women, England, the war, or looked at the far horizon, which some dip occasionally disclosed.

It was with and because of Frost that Edward Thomas grew as a poet. Like any two friends, the writers enjoyed each other's company; Thomas, sharing his love of nature and its callings: the hedgerows a favourite vista; and Frost, his mechanics of poetry, his homeland, his work. Together they immersed themselves in words and became part of the Dymock Gloucestershire poets: among them Rupert Brooke, Wilfrid

Wilson Gibson and John Drinkwater.

For Thomas, cadence was the most important element in writing: the sounds, the rhythms, how words fit together in ordinary and every-day language: the music in the words always there. But for Frost, poetry was an exploration, a discovery: he wrote to find out what he didn't already know. For Frost, the last few lines of the poem, was the telling, the all-encompassing find, as much a surprise to the writer as to the reader.

So it was that Edward Thomas, a man whose passions were nature and words, who had spent all his working life reviewing and critiquing others' works, wrote his first poems in late 1914, three years before his death, under the pseudonym, Edward Eastaway.

On the 19th July 1915, five months after Frost returned to America, Thomas enlisted in the infantry and was on his way to becoming a soldier. He told Helen of his enlistment by telegram from London where he had gone to find work. The news came as a terrible shock to Helen.

One of Thomas' famous poems is *Adlestrop*, published in 1917. It is a poem simply of a moment in time, when a train on which Thomas is a passenger makes an unscheduled stop at a station in the Cotswolds. The second stanza of the poem reads,

The steam-hissed. Someone cleared his throat.
No-one left and no-one came. What I saw
Was Adlestrop – only the name

In 1966, the station was abandoned but a plaque bearing the name *Adlestrop* and Thomas' poem was fixed to a bus shelter there.

And the moment fixed, too, when Thomas wrote his last

letter to Helen in the days before he died. *And You, Helen*, is a poem for his wife, in love, perhaps, or in apology:

And you, Helen, what should I give you?
So many things I would give you
Had I an infinite great store
Offered me and I stood before
To choose. I would give you youth,
All kinds of loveliness and truth,
A clear eye as good as mine,
Lands, waters, flowers, wine…

On a spring Easter Monday, 9th April, 1917, Helen Thomas lost the man she loved and the father of her three children, Merfyn, Bronwen and Myfanwy. Second Lieutenant, Phillip Edward Thomas, died in the First World War, whilst serving in the 244th Siege Battery Royal Garrison Artillery. He was just 39 years' old. In her grief, Helen went on to write her own books depicting their love: *As It Was*, and *World Without End.*

Helen writes of the last time she saw her husband as he packed for the war, organising his papers and manuscripts,

And I knew Edward's agony, and he knew mine, and all we could do was to speak sharply to each other.

On the morning of his departure, the sound of a train, shunting in the distance, a thick mist in the air and she standing at the gate, watching him go, Helen Thomas writes,

Coo-ee, he called; Coo-ee, I answered, keeping my voice strong to call again. Again through the muffled air came his Coo-ee.

And, again, her voice; then his voice, in return, like an echo,

Coo-ee! So faint now it might only be my own call flung back from the thick air and muffling snow. I put my hands up to my mouth to make a trumpet, but no sound came… and I ran through the mist and the snow to the top of the hill, and stood there a moment dumbly, with straining eyes and ears. There was nothing but the mist and the snow and the silence of death.

Thomas's *Six Poems* published under the pseudonym, Edward Eastaway, was his only poetry collection published in his lifetime. He was not to see his other poems in print; they were published posthumously, under his own name. But unlike *Adlestrop*, a train stop that is no longer there, the essence and beauty of his writing remains. Thomas's poetry, his love of nature, and the story of his love for Helen, is immortalised in his writing.

Rose van Son

Works Cited:

Fitzgerald, Penelope, Edward Thomas: Selected Letters, edited by R. George Thomas, Oxford, March 1996.

Hollis, Matthew, Now all Roads Lead to France, The Last Years of Edward Thomas, London: Faber & Faber Ltd., 2011.

Thomas, Helen, As it Was, London: Heinemann, 1926.

Thomas, Helen, World Without End, London: Heinemann, 1931.

Thomas, R. George, ed., The Poems of Edward Thomas, Oxford University Press, 1978.

Losing Sight

Winning Article 2018

My cousin, Liliana, writes that she is a candidate for glaucoma, that a recent *occhial test* found she has the gene for this blindness; that if left untreated, she could lose her sight, so her ability to read the beautiful books that she loves, those of culture and history, those of life, without which, she says, she could not survive, would be limited. She writes that our uncle and other family members, some of whom already have limited sight, carry the gene that causes this narrowing of sight. She writes of her fear.

I think of my mother and her words of misgivings,

Your grandfather, my mother says, *was blind when he died.*

I write back to Liliana, our emails crossing oceans, that I have already been tested for this debilitating disease after it was found that I, too, had a growing pressure behind the eyes and have an appointment soon for another test to follow its progression.

We are daughters of a brother and sister: a family of eight siblings. My mother has macular degeneration, another blinding and hereditary eye disease. But glaucoma is there in our genes, in the genes of uncles and aunts, of grandparents. This lack of sight concerns us; the fear creeping to the back of our throats and voiced in what we will miss. Reading is important to both of us: stories, literature, articles, poetry, history of people and places. We are passionate about reading, keen to know what is happening in the world and enjoy stories of diverse peoples. We question, ask where society is going; follow where it has been. For this passion to be removed by a sinister pressure behind the eyes is unthinkable.

I understand her dilemma and fear. I spend every available minute reading and writing my lines in the spaces of a purposeful life. Glaucoma would be an unwelcome guest, to say the least, and I fear this narrowing of vision, because it is with the eyes and the mind that I write – what guides the hand that guides the pen – to read and reread poetry, to hear the rhythm of the words. For poetry is as much about spaces and silences as it is words: the silence on the page heard as a drum beat in the ears when poetry is read aloud.

My mother sees faces as outlines. She pencils in noses and eyes, guesses who these people might be, and, although still able to shop, albeit not unaccompanied, she manages the sight she has left and still lives alone in her home of forty years.

I read that painter and art historian, Betty Churcher, a former director of the Art Gallery of Western Australia and National Gallery of Australia, was, in 2003, diagnosed with a melanoma on her optic nerve and was already blind in one eye when diagnosed with macular degeneration in later years. In an endeavour to record and remember the art she loved, Churcher, who died in 2015, published *Notebooks,* a series of journals containing sketches of her favourite works: drawings outlining the art she once shared with her audience and although she no longer saw the art as she once did: the colours, the clarity, she was keen to imprint the art she loved. The drawings became an 'enabler' to see in her mind's eye, the whole picture, as she remembered it, the light and dark, the texture, the flow in order to cope with her loss. Her sketches outline the bones of the old masters: her favourite artists' work, her mental processes annotated in margins, her vision fixed on the page.

I console my cousin. *Glaucoma can be treated*, I say, my eye specialist's words reassuring. *It can be held at bay*. But the words seem hollow. I know that to write poetry or prose, those phrases that feed the soul, I must read and reread, be inspired by the work of others, in a quiet inward gaze, travel others' journeys to find detail and irony, revel in the ever-changing colour of sky, the light of a new autumn as it creeps under the door; keep a journal of notes and favourite lines. I must discover the new in the old. I must hear the music of words on the page, see how they fit, this line with that line; must know what they mean, make connections and wait until they all come together, contained in verse.

But the fear of loss cannot be contained. 'Our fears are like dragons, guarding our deepest treasures,' writes poet, Rainer Maria Rilke. Our treasures, I realise, are those that can't be replaced: our senses, so critical to an artist, a lover of music or art; our sight, a personal imperative. For Rilke, the light and dark, the mystery of shadows, are critical to his writing. For me, as a poet, the light and dark, that *chiaroscuro,* turning, like regulating venetian blinds – allows me to *see* the possibilities. But to see one must first *look for things,* as Rilke says:

I wander in the thousand winds
that you are churning
and bring back everything I find.

The blind man needed you as a cup.
The servant concealed you
The beggar held you out as I passed.

You see, I am one who likes to look for things.

(Rilke, I, 55, p. 117)

I think of Ludwig van Beethoven, with his gradual loss of hearing: how devastating for him not to hear the magic of his music? But he could still see. He could write the notes on the page and hear the sounds in his head: the pitch, the highs and lows, the wonder. Beethoven's famous *Ninth Symphony* penned when he was totally deaf – leafing through harmony and tone in his mind. I imagine him trying to hold on to his hearing for as long as possible, jotting notes in the margins of his journals, the tempo of sound, much like Churcher, holding on to her vision on paper. To have had sound and lost it, must be devastating. I try, but cannot imagine not hearing what I love – the plaintiff cry of a raven at the end of a long summer; a magpie's warble in a thicket of paperbarks; the winter flame trees filled with colour and delighted lorikeets. I know the senses are connected – the seeing and the hearing, and that one without the other is incomplete. To hear the sound is to see the vision, the colours, and the textures, to welcome the light. To see and hear is also connected with touch, smell and taste: to imagine the flavour.

Henry David Thoreau writes in his famous nature essay, *Wild Apples, The History of the Apple Tree,* the 'flowers of the apple are perhaps the most beautiful of any tree's, so copious and so delicious to both sight and scent' (Thoreau's journals, p. 713). Here, Thoreau welcomes the beauty of the apple tree: its gloss, but also its aroma. Of course, the apple's memorable taste, is a given. For Thoreau, the 'body, the senses must conspire with the mind' (September 2, 1851). Certainly, the senses are critical to the poet, the artist or reader, but the most valuable sense must be sight; if one can see the beauty, then the rest can be imagined.

I think again of my cousin and remember her olive trees, potted, on her balcony: two trees captured in morning light, the fruit just starting to show, the trees not yet bent in a pregnant way. I imagine the taste: olives drizzled with oil on warm bread and I am instantly transported. Art does this. It takes us to places of memory.

My mother sees metaphorically; she imagines 'the other' to what she can see. She fears the glare of the dark. She fears a loss of sight: her father blind when he died, she tells me again. It is a mantra she repeats. A cataract operation some ten years ago left her with vision that was less than promised – not the miraculous operation normally touted, where she could throw her glasses away and dance gaily into a bright future but the blindness that comes from a failed operation. Everyday she works with the glare that left her afraid. The name of the disease is irrelevant to her, but the result is the same: loss of independence, the dark creeping in, shadowing what she knows. My mother works in filigree. She stands alone in the shade of a leafy fig tree in summer's heat; knows that in winter the leaves will peel off and there will be nothing but bare branches.

Eventually, however, we are all left alone to make our own journeys. My cousin's journey with her regular eye tests, her fears of losing the ability to read, to know other cultures, are her own: her acceptance, or not, of her condition. She is a relatively young woman, not yet mid-fifties and has many years to contemplate the road she may follow. My mother, of an older generation, copes as best she can. She has already accepted what she cannot change and has taken small steps to work with the growing darkness, making sure she is accompanied to places previously not visited. She wears dark glasses to keep out the glare – the consequence of her previous cataract operation – refusing a second operation in her 'good' eye for she no longer trusts the medical profession, finds a trolley at the supermarket to keep her upright and in check, driving it with confidence, at times to use as a battering ram.

Betty Churcher, too, drew battle lines. She etched her favourite art in her mind, drawing and redrawing in her sketch book, hoping, no doubt, that her mind would not fail her to recall her favourite art works: Rembrandt, Goya, Cézanne, Boyd, among them. Ironically, in so doing, she created a collectable visual journal with short essays and notes for her audience. Surely, a gift for her readers?

I write words on the page, know already my mind is not as sharp as it once was, keep my poetic lines short rather than long; know with the clarity of a poet, that life is a metaphor and sight is only one way of seeing; that so many people with sight do not take the time to see: the orange colours of the flowering flame tree in mid-winter outlined against a clear sky, its interaction with pesky rainbow lorikeets in colours of olive, mauve, mustard and red, and in mid-spring, the beauty of sky no longer visible through the leaf-green of flame trees almost fully dressed in summer's foliage.

In weak winter light I sit by the river's edge, my feet moulding with rocks and watch the frenzy of fishing: pelicans, cormorants and dolphins, a family of five, belong to this part of the river. They dive, take their fill, in the river's clear waters, the morning light in tune with their game, and I long for summer to come. Here, my cousin's fear seems far away, the distance filtered, my morning refreshed; my own brush with glaucoma almost forgotten. A specialist's report says I have nothing to fear for the moment. I try to remember the words of my poems, much like Betty Churcher tried to recall details of her art, and see, in my mind's eye, the last lines of some favourites but odd words are all I remember. But the play in my mind, pelicans, cormorants in the river and lorikeets in the flame trees, will stay and I know that the view in my mind's eye, that insight within, is one sight I will not lose.

References:

Churcher, B., 2011, *Notebooks*, The Miegunyah Press: Melbourne.
Rilke, R. M., *Rilke's Book of Hours, Love Poems to God,* Translated by A. Barrows and J. Macy, 2005, Penguin Group: New York.
Thoreau, H.D., (n.d), *Journal, The Works of Thoreau*, Library of America

Rose van Son

Old Kyneton Hospital 1865-2005

Highly Commended Poem 2020

I stand by your history, your
cast-iron facade, your lace-work,
veranda abreast of all you could say

boarded windows keep out the light
bluestone, iron awnings, chimneys
reject your salvation

a home for the sick, disease
rots behind timber doorways
plaster walls fill empty rooms

you are not what I imagine
you could be in this flush
country town, paddock

sown on the outskirts
a town grown above
expectations

once you were grand—
era filled with miners, men
came for the gold rush

some stayed for a short time
some took their passion
to the grave

a wire fence surrounds
my contemplation: no way in—
no point in trespassing

there is nothing here to see
wards remain idle, walls
void of still life, memories

owned by a few, ambience
heats a cold day's foreboding—
only ghosts walk these hallways

nurses' caps pinned to hairlines
hair pushed under, pulled back
hands work to keep you alive.

Rose van Son

Astra Warren

Frogs in the Loo

Commended Article 2000

I am often puzzled to read of concern over the Australia-wide dearth of frogs.

After several work stints as a governess on pastoral properties, I can definitely affirm that W.A.'s frog population is alive and flourishing - in the toilets and bathrooms of the mid-west'

On each occasion, I settled into my quarters as an alien invader. The frogs were already established and in confident possession of their territory. Clinging vertically to the bathroom walls, they looked like applique motifs or flock wallpaper. It was prudent to turn the soap over with a cautious finger; invariably a frog was clinging to its wet underside. One learned to zip up a toilet holdall after use, as its damp, dark recesses provided a froggy retreat.

The loo had to be flushed before use: the frogs' daytime preferred spot was under the inside rim of the pedestal. Denied light by a human posterior, they understandably became hysterically agitated. After dark, they emerged to squat, like a Greek chorus, round the rim, croaking encouragement while their mates performed water Olympics in the bowl and deep dives round the U-bend. As the light came on, croaks were silenced and unwinking eyes turned on the intruder before they fled, leaving behind droppings totally disproportionate to their size.

I had always liked frogs, or at worst could live in tolerant co-habitation. But I reached cracking point one night as I bent over the washbasin plughole to expel a mouthful of frothy toothpaste. Up popped a slimy head with a pair of button eyes in accusatory mode. My hasty recoil left me choking as I swallowed the toothpaste.

Counter measures were obviously called for. An organised offensive included barring the shower drain with flywire stuck down with blutak, and denying washbasin infiltration by keeping the plug in (slightly ajar to allow for the dripping tap). A reconnaissance established that their base camp was in the toilet cistern. Stun tactics were applied with a squirt of spray under the lid, then with an old soup ladle scoop them into a bucket to be relocated far out in the scrub. Done on a weekly basis, it kept the invasion at bay.

Their guerilla tactics included sitting on the door lintel and spitting fluid down on the unwary. At least, we hoped they were spitting. Any other bodily excretion would be too indelicate to mention.

And me? Well, if I had to get up during the night, there were 180,000 hectares out there.

I conceded victory to the frogs.

Astra Warren

Education: A Revolution Needed

Highly Commended Article 2006

After more than forty years at the coal face of teaching, I am convinced that education in Australia needs radical reform.

Still serving my profession by using my hard-won expertise to solve individual problems on a one-to-one tutoring basis, it is clear that present systems are failing a great many children, and failing to keep pace with the accelerating tide of progress.

Public and private schools are committed to buildings and systems originally designed to cope with the enormous influx of students which was a consequence of free education introduced in England in the 1800s.

Out of necessity and convenience, children were separated into age groups and confined in classrooms. This desperation structure has been retained while an increasingly top-heavy bureaucracy applies band-aid measures to prop up a system which is demonstrably inadequate and inefficient; it is in fact achieving less in successful outcomes than it did half a century ago. A Greek philosopher discovered this in the first century:

"Reorganizing is a wonderful method of creating the illusion of progress while producing confusion, inefficiency and demoralization."

We need a total rethink in education. Instead of reforming from the top downwards, let us reform upwards by starting at the grassroots, once more making the student the focus of attention.

Students are individuals, never more so than in contemporary society. We applaud the 'power of one', we support the sanctity and significance of each and every life. No longer are communities stigmatised under outdated labels like 'working class' and 'ghetto material'. Soldiers are no longer dismissed as faceless 'cannon fodder', but seen as suffering human beings.

Largely due to the media, people are aware of the power of protest, the possibility of individual opinion. Collective brainwashing is becoming a thing of the past; the public is informed and has access to diverse opinions. Women have thrown off the suffocating blanket of a traditional collective role and developed their individual potential. Yet we persist in lumping our youth together under that demeaning and execrable epithet, 'kids', and forcing them through anachronistic systems.

There was never a time when the younger generation has been so much in need of individual help and attention. The young are bombarded with subversive and seductive advertising. They live in an increasing number of dysfunctional families too busy to listen and nurture a developing psyche. In some schools, volunteer mentoring schemes relying on retirees is enormously effective, but touching only a fraction of the need. Overworked teachers, police and welfare agencies have neither time nor financial resources to make more than token attempts at a solution.

Yet the answer is in our hands.

All the once apparently immutable institutions like banking, medicine, big business, even religions, have already used it to upgrade their image.

The name of this game is computers.

Instead of deploring the waste of hours spent in front of the compelling screen, let us turn its mesmeric influence to educational advantage.

Distance Education, particularly in Queensland and Western Australia, has already capitalised on the potential of this powerful tool. Every station and remote community will soon have a terminal linked to a central system, giving personalized access. Through the modem, students can talk to the teacher; with a stylus, they write on the screen; teleconferencing is already common practice.

My own experience in outback areas has shown that students educated on this system learn faster with greater enjoyment, are relaxed, and develop independence of thought.

The concept of extending this system to an urban situation is exciting. Home learning could solve in one swoop all the problems which proliferate when students, like rats, are herded together.

Peer pressure and subjection to the dominant would disappear, allowing emergence of every personality. Drug distribution networks lose their recruits. The gang mentality would have no focus. Clever students would dare to reveal their talents, and we could restore pride in excellence·rather than conformity to the lowest common denominator. F.W. Sanderson, considered by many to be the most outstanding schoolmaster of all time, said in the 1880s:

"The greatest of tragedies is the slow decay of men and women caused ... by their unstretched faculties."

This is the Greek ideal of realization of personal potential. Speed of learning progress could be up to the individual; we might even consider cash incentives for units completed. Certainly we could afford it after the sale of outdated million-dollar school complexes with their enormous maintenance costs. Buildings could be converted to retirement use, much-needed hospitals, or community centres; uses which would benefit a larger proportion of society. Sports facilities would become recreational space for everyone, instead of lying deserted for one-third of the year.

Fatigue and wasted time in travelling, not to mention the twice-daily traffic frenzy, become past history, as they should be. We could think of better nutrition and banish soggy, plastic-wrapped sandwiches. Teachers are relieved of those lunch and recess duty penances. The acrimonious and unfair public versus private school argument could finally be buried.

Administrative empires would disappear, and emphasis return to where it belongs: the skill of the teacher, and onus on students for their own achievement. Recreational and competitive physical activity is aleady well catered for by independent groups whose sphere could be expanded.

This should not be dismissed as an idealistic, impossible Utopia. Technology has already achieved miracles impossible to visualize even half a century ago; internet, email, virtual reality. There are no doubt others beyond our present imagining.

We need a reformer with the breadth of vision and courage to move education out of its present morass into the bright future which should belong to all our children.

We threw away one great educational tool when we failed to capitalize on the potential of television. How much more powerful is the lure of the computer!

We need a reformer with the breadth of vision and courage to move education out of its present morass, so that it can make possible the bright future which should be the birthright of all our children.

Astra Warren

Taking the Lid off Teaching

Commended Article 2009

All teachers go mad in the end.

Not noisily, straight-jacket mad, but a gentle, imperceptible slide over the edge into a state of mental dysfunction. They become limbo souls, at a disjunct with the normal adult world of real people.

It is a well-known fact that an actor, preparing a role for stage or film, dons the character like a cloak and temporarily becomes that persona.

Likewise, a working life spent with adolescents, immersing oneself in their thoughts and attitudes in an effort to understand the developing psyche, leads inevitably to total atrophy of rational thought.

Imagine a dedicated teacher, daily performing before the world's most critical audience, trying to identify with the students, constantly self-questioning, "How do they think? What is it like to be them?" Those of you who have children know this is an unanswerable question, but at least your children grow out of this stage. A teacher is confronted every day of the year with a new wave of insoluble conundrums. The necessity of thinking like an immature adolescent guarantees severe social dislocation or at least mild schizophrenia.

There are, in addition, pitfalls engendered by being cooped up every working day, isolated from your adult peer group, in a room full of hostiles.

Teachers develop degrees of eccentricity to cope.

For instance, there are maternal types who want to mother every child, convinced in a woolly-minded sort of way that all problems can be solved by liberal applications of love and TLC. (They never recovered from flower power in their formative years,) and are a pushover for every sob-story invented by fertile minds.

Then there are the 'I'm-only-in-it-for-the money' types. They pretend indifference while taking to heart every setback, developing nervous dyspepsia and all manner of psycho-somatic ailments. They are sustained by endless cups of coffee and a roll of Quickeeze in the desk drawer.

We have men who bend over backwards trying to be all boys together, spending their breaks haring about the playing field, proving their ball skills superiority over hero-worshipping skinny juniors. (Familiarity usually becomes licence later in the classroom.)

There are the unorthodox who disappear with class into the furthest reaches of the school grounds making damper in order to teach a maths formula (you may well ask why), while the school secretary runs round in frantic circles trying to find them because Billy's mother is waiting to take him to the dentist.

There is the innovative type who decides to gear all lessons this week to the core theme of (say) chocolate and flogs the idea to extinction. The class, who on Monday entered into the spirit of things with great gusto, by Friday are wishing never to sight even a chocolate wrapper again.

They had divined early in the game that it was a weak disguise for the same routines, viz. how many chocolates will fit in this rectangular box, write an essay about chocolate, and, surprise! Let's do a chocolate-brown poster warning of the health hazards of too much chocolate.

There are discipline freaks. Someone wants a drink of water? Fine. We'll all have a drink of water, then no more until lunchtime. Such teachers paint dots on the concrete outside the classroom and line up the class, feet exactly on each dot. Good teachers are born, not made, and they are not necessarily academically able. There is another element, a flair, an animal instinct which ensures survival.

The acid test of courage is standing out there, alone, fighting a rising panic and hollow feeling in the stomach as you confront the focussed scrutiny of a new class of battle-hardened minds.

Those first moments are crucial, because if that initial penetrating appraisal does not immediately reveal your unswerving determination, selfless dedication and fair and honest character, you might as well go home because the situation will never be retrieved. These days it also helps to be able to spot the wavering eye that reveals that a mobile 'phone has not been switched off.

I once ran a parent talk about their jobs initiative.

One day, we welcomed a dentist, community respected, and an accomplished after-dinner speaker. We were anticipating a stimulating and educative experience. Educative it certainly was on many fronts.

Educative for the students who witnessed his disintegration, educative for him from the moment he floundered over whether it was "Hi girls" or "Good afternoon, students", realised he hadn't included the teacher and encountered thirty pairs of wide girlish eyes already ghoulishly scenting a debacle, and educative for the daughter who lost faith in her father. He had to be rescued after fifteen minutes with an excuse that fooled nobody about his busy schedule. He fled, refusing even a cup of tea, a broken, demoralised man.

The trouble is, everybody thinks himself an expert on education, simply by virtue of having gone to school. This applies particularly to the countless men whose lives (so they confess in a conspiratorial whisper) were ruined by a female teacher-tyrant. Faced with such a complainant, it is not tactful to ask what they did to merit such treatment.

And me? After forty years in teaching, of course I'm mad. Otherwise I wouldn't be writing this.

Astra Warren

Between Scylla and Charbydis

Runner-Up Short Story 2016

Rex and Inge Lindley married late in life after meeting at the University Rowing Club.

Rex, 41, was a lecturer in Ancient History at the University of Western Australia; Inge, 38, there on a two-year exchange from Stuttgart, was a specialist in Classical Architecture.

Both were fitness freaks and had exchanged nods of acknowledgment while on their early morning runs. Inge had become so enamoured of WA, its lifestyle and the sunshine that gilded her Teutonic blondeness, that she had enquired about the most expeditious way of obtaining permanent residence.

Rex was a life member and coach of the Rowing Club.

Inge turned up one morning for rowing training, whether by inclination or devious planning was open to conjecture.

It was inevitable that mutual interests, and for Rex, after years of·ascetic academia celibacy, a fascination with Inge's prodigally displayed healthy physique, drew them together in what became for both a satisfying relationship. After a holiday exploring mutual passions for sex and the history of French colonization in Mauritius, their relationship progressed to marriage.

Inge, believing she was into menopause, neglected birth control measures and fell unexpectedly pregnant. Early scans showed the stunned couple the presence of twins.

After a textbook pregnancy which Inge boastfully attributed to the rigorous discipline of her fitness regime, a relatively easy birth made them the parents of dissimilar twin girls. Determined not to let these new responsibilities curtail their activities, they set about organizing the two new lives with the same discipline that governed their academic lifestyle.

It was no surprise to their many friends that Rex and Inge (partly in revolt against their own prosaic names) turned to the watery classics for names: Scylla and Charybdis Lindley were duly registered and the christening feted with a champagne party at the Rowing Club on the banks of the lovely Swan River.

Early childhood friends of the twins soon perceived that, like the watery hazards after which they were named, it was prudent to steer·a cautious path between the two girls. Their names became abbreviated in Australian style. Syl was dark and brooding like her father's Welsh ancestry, and Carry convinced of her Germanic goddess qualities.

They were an unending maelstrom of disagreement. It was unwise to risk retribution by siding with either.

At school, being strong-minded individualists, each attracted a coterie of gullible followers who, at their leader's whim, could be incited into a boiling frenzy over any trivial incident. To avoid gang warfare, their expensive private school requested their removal. On the advice of a family friend, an eminent University psychologist, they were sent to separate educational establishments.

At tertiary, Syl, still dark and brooding, joined every deviant and rebellious protest movement life threw in her path. Carry ploughed a golden furrow, collecting awards and honours as tribute to her academic prowess.

Fate, or their common sibling origins, ordained that they set their nuptial sights on the same aspiring business tyro. He, ignorant of the portents, neglected to tie himself to the mast of indifference and impartiality. Excited by the novelty of parallel affairs with sisters, he became embroiled with both women, proudly boasting of his twin conquests. When they discovered his duplicity, they united against a common enemy and conspired to lure him to potential destruction with photographs on the Internet.

He left the fair city somewhat precipitately for a safe stockbroking refuge in the Eastern States.

After this setback, both forswore further male complications. Syl took solace in drink. Her brooding deepened into a drug habit, but with the remnants of her intelligence, she realized that dealing was more profitable. She kicked the addiction, lured by more powerful drugs – money and power – and in time acquired a string of dubious nightclubs, ruling her subordinates with the same ruthlessness that had controlled her gang at school.

Carry, meanwhile calling on the splendid Gothic tenacity and resilience inherited from her mother (who by now was Vice-Chancellor of the University), joined the police force. Equally ruthless with any opposition, she rose rapidly through the ranks. She had worked out that the emotive sight of uniforms bestowed power, and appeared at every photo opportunity splendidly kitted out, awesomely confident and usually accompanied by a posse of henchwomen. So, perfectly understanding each other's lust for power, they advanced in their own spheres without impinging on the other's territory.

Syl controlled the many-headed monsters of nightclubs and brothels: Carry, first female Assistant Commissioner, now navigated the deeper waters of public life and opinion.

Between them, they controlled a large proportion of the city.

This story should end with downfall, disgrace and tragedy,

a cathartic sense of justice done. But modern mythology does not work like that. The wages of sin is no longer death but financial rewards, temporal success and public acclaim.

Syl was made Business Woman of the Year. Flattering articles with images of Syl in designer dresses and escorted by upwardly mobile males, appeared in glossy magazines, highlighting her magic and glamour. Her biography was made into a carefully sanitized film, with music by a popular composer.

Carry meanwhile treasured her OBE, awarded for meritorious service, confident of adding an Order of Australia when she retired.

The many wrecked lives which littered their path to fame were never spoken of. Wealth and fame are efficient whitewashers of uncomfortable memories.

An ancient allegory is not lost; evil still has its genesis in simple beginnings.

Astra Warren

Died in the Wool

Highly Commended Short Story 2016

Edna raised her binoculars and watched the heron gliding down to its nest in a half-submerged paperbark. When the eggs hatched, she and Ken would be back in Perth, but after two months' camping and bird-watching in remote spots, there were several rolls of film in the bag – perhaps even a prize winner or two amongst them.

"I'll be off down to the roadhouse to fuel up," she started as Ken came up quietly.

"Then we can drive through tomorrow. I'm nearly out of smokes anyway. Is there anything you want?"

"Some fresh bread would be nice, if there is any. Oh, and cheese. The bit that's left is dried up. We'll have cheese sandwiches and the rest of the salad for lunch. Then I can start packing up."

"All right darl. See you soon."

She watched and waved as he eased the Land Cruiser over the sandy crest. Ken loved this area where he had spent most of his life shearing. He knew many secluded spots like this magic place on the edge of a freshwater lake, alive with birdlife in a semi-arid land.

It would be nice, though, to be back in her own kitchen. And see the grandchildren. They planned to surprise the twins with a belated birthday present – new pushbikes they would pick up in Geraldton on the way home.

At the roadhouse twenty kilometres away, two unshaven men were breakfasting on pies and cokes in the thin shade of struggling rivergums. Doug crammed the last of a third pie into his mouth.

"Now what, mastermind?" he sneered, spitting crumbs. He surveyed the deserted landscape and the patched-up building, already baking in the morning sun.

"Christ, what a dump. Might as well take our chances with the fuzz. But no. Let's go, you said. Get lost up north, you said. Off the bitumen – and up the creek, 'cept you'd be flamin' lucky to find a creek, much less a pub with some beer."

Wanted for a string of minor offences in Perth and running out of options, they had done a couple of bag snatches in widely separated car parks, which netted less than a hundred dollars, but a windfall in one bag was a petrol credit card.

Filling up Doug's old VB from an all-night station, with a yawning attendant too disinterested to check the scrawled signature closely, they drove through the night, stopping only when hunger and the empty petrol gauge compelled it.

"What about the old biddy in the shop? There's gotta be some money in the till."

"Nah. She didn't like the look of us anyway. And did yer see the size of that dog? Eat us both for breakfast."

He stood and viciously kicked his empty can at a tree. A 4WD had come coasting in from the road, trailing a light drift of red dust. It pulled up against the diesel bowser.

Through eyes slitted against the sun, Mike watched the elderly driver fill the tank, then pull a wallet out of his back pocket, opening it as he turned towards the shop.

Mike got only one flicker of the notes inside, but it was enough. A plum had dropped out of the skies.

"Here's our chance, matey," he breathed. "I'm going to the

bog. Bring the car around and wait for me between him and the Toyota."

They moved with the casual ease of long practice. Soon the man came blinking out into the sunlight, plastic bag in hand, letting the warped half-screen door slam behind him. Mike sauntered over from the toilet. Doug trickled the car forward so that the man had to hesitate, waiting for him to pass. As Doug swung the rear door open, Mike heaved the man by the collar and seat of the pants and fell on top of him in the rear seat. Doug slammed the door, casually took the car onto the road and gunned it away in typical yahoo style, chortling, "Bewdy, mate. Nobody noticed a thing."

Mike disentangled himself from the man lying stunned and winded face-down along the back seat. The wallet was sticking out of his unbuttoned back pocket. Mike wrenched at it, tearing the pocket. He flipped it open.

"Christ, look at this lot. Musta been going to buy a sheep station."

Their victim began to struggle and grabbed for the wallet.

"Now, now," said Mike, heavily humorous. "Behave yourself. No rough stuff."

Ken, reacting now, kicked out and reached for the opposite door, flailing with the plastic bag he was still clutching. It hit Doug on the back of the head. Doug bellowed.

"Smack 'im down or he'll have us off the flamin' road."

Mike reached the length of the back seat and hit the old bloke hard on the side of the head. Blood spurted from his ear as it struck the door handle.

Ken groaned, clutching his chest.

"Tablets," he gasped. "In the glove box. Go back."

"Tablets? What bloody tablets? You gotta be joking, mate. No way are we going back for any bloody tablets. Quit the tricks, you old bastard."

Doug was snarling, his head twisted round to look.

"Shove 'im out. Open the door and shove 'im out. We've got the money."

But even as the car lurched to a stop, the old man gave a shuddering sigh and his eyes rolled up in his head.

"Shit," said Mike. "I think he's croaked. Doug, he's carked it. We can't shove a stiff out. What do we do now ..." His voice rose in fright.

Doug wrenched savagely at the brake and got out.

"Make sure 'e's not faking. Then find a place to dump 'im. Bound to be plenty of places in this godforsaken lot."

He indicated the rock-strewn, shimmering landscape.

"Dingoes and crows, nobody'd know 'in a week."

They checked the body. Dead all right. Then the wallet: a thousand in hundreds and some smaller stuff. The plastic bag held a squashed loaf, cheese, a bar of chocolate and two packs of cigarettes. Doug grunted.

"Well, mate, you won't want that lot where you are now, so ta very much."

He went round to the driver's side and got in. Mike scrambled out.

"I'm not riding in the back with that."

He ran round and fell into the passenger seat as Doug bumped the car back into the ruts.

"Keep yer eye lifted for a spot and we'll soon be shut of 'im." Moving along just fast enough to keep ahead of their dust cloud, they scanned the country on both sides of the road. It was flat up to the horizon, open, dotted only with spindly scrub.

Suddenly on a bend was a faint track curving away into nowhere, with a rough sign, white painted on a jagged piece of tin: KARDAR SHED.

"This'll do."

Doug slewed the car onto the track, bumping over corrugations and washaways until they saw a windmill head over the scrub, then a corrugated roof, sheepyards and rusting machinery.

Dust eddied around as Doug circled the shed. He laughed. "Well, look. Even left the door open for us."

He eased the car into the high-roofed gloom of the shed and cut the engine. Silence surged in as the dust settled. There was only a flapping of tin and creaking of timbers in the heat.

"Made to measure, me little matey. Shelter, water, a bag of grub and nothing to pay. Now where'll we dump the old geezer."

His speculative gaze travelled over bales stacked up on the floor and fell on the hydraulic wool press. A half-filled bag was hooked up.

"There's a nice soft resting place for grandad." Mike flipped when he realized what Doug intended. "You can't ... somebody'll come and press ..."

"This's your trouble, Mikey boy. Same in the nick. Full of bright ideas, then guess who had to sort them out? No bloody guts, that's you."

He raised his fist.

"Get over there and pull some of that gunk out. I'll drop 'im in if you're too flamin' squeamish."

Mike scurried over and began pulling wool out of the bag. It fell to the floor in soft, white humps.

"Leave some in then. Want to give 'im a soft ride. He's got a long trip to wherever 'e's going."

He fetched the body, one arm under the knees, the other under the shoulders, its legs and arms flopping.

Stepping onto the presser's platform, he bent the head to the knees and dropped it in.

"There, see. All curled up cosy like. Now all we gotta do is tuck 'im in."

Helped by the intimidated Mike, he stuffed the wool back in. "Not enough. There's an arm sticking out."

Mike ran over to one of the heaps of wool lying in the bays, and brought some over.

"Ugh. Stinking stuff. Look at the shit hanging off. You'd have ter be a loony to work at a job like this."

Two mornings later, the shed again echoed to the sound of vehicles. A one-ton truck brought station hands to help load the semi-trailer which was lurching and swaying towards the shed along the track.

Old Sam was in a hurry and more irascible than usual.

"Still got three more bales of that fine wool off the lambs to press. So look sharp and start the engine, Col, before the boss gets here. He'll be ropeable anyway when he sees those car tracks. Tourists using the place like an effing motel. Remind me to take that shearers' sign down when we go back. No point in advertising. They don't need any invitation. Makes yer wonder what's going on, old Kenny disappearing into thin air and all."

He went over to the press.

"Jesus. Will yer look at this. Bludging water and a place ter camp is one thing, but when they start playing silly buggers with the equipment … Daggy skirtings jammed on top of the lambs wool. Pull it all out, boys, and let's start again."

Astra Warren

Perceptions

The Joys of Travel for the Young at Heart

Commended Article 2018

It is said to be impossible to put an old head on young shoulders. But travelling is one area where the reverse is not only true but indeed possible. We live in an age when those with old shoulders can joyfully follow the example of the younger generation and travel as they do, carefree, lightly burdened and free as the wind.

The young have the enviable ability, like the lilies of the field, to live in each day as though tomorrow may never come. With age and impending mortality, this takes on a more significant slant; the knowledge that tomorrow may indeed never come, sharpens the enjoyment of each experience:

"Nothing can bring back the hour
Of splendour in the grass, of the glory of the flower."

(William Wordsworth)

For women of my certain age, the joy of travelling is doubled. We grew up in a generation when no respectable female travelled without a male escort, who was a bag-carrier and protector. Brainwashed about being properly dressed, right down to gloves, stockings and ladylike hat, we have, however, cast off the shackles, relishing independence of thought and action. Tee shirt and jeans are comfortable and sensible; a backpack is actually beneficial for aging muscles. You can carry old clothes and throw them away when past wearing, with charity shops a treasure house for replacements. Image and appearance take second place to convenience and comfort.

The chore of sending postcards is also relegated to the past. I have joined the hordes of email devotees. The internet has to be the travellers greatest joy. Just when your family think they've heard the last of you for the duration, you can bombard them – every day if you are sadistically minded – with all the trivial details that on your return used to bore them to tears.

At this age you have the power of freedom; you can talk to anyone and people will talk to you. Men see you as a mother, and older women of any nationality acknowledge you as part of the sisterhood. Bemused officials become protective and helpful. Young emancipated chicks they can cope with but in most cultures, grandmothers like us should be sitting at home with a knitted rug over the knees. In Asian countries, I now qualify as 'lbu', (respected elder), and am offered a seat on public transport.

I was once used as temporary chaperone, invited to join a couple of girls fending off unwanted attentions. One smooth character, undeterred, offered to buy a beer 'for your mother'.

"She's not our mother, she's our grandmother," came the smart reply, uniting us in a conspiracy of hilarity.

Families are a delight, children the universal language. I always carry a packet of huggy koalas which I give away at any opportunity like a demented Australian Mother Christmas, but a degree of eccentricity seems to be expected and excusable in the elderly.

One young Chinese boy reciprocated by presenting me with a wooden amulet representing long life and happiness. I will never see him again, but we are friends for life. Young students feel that it is safe to approach you to practise their English and a smile crosses all language barriers.

That others have discovered the joys of travel- ing is evidenced by the remarkable increase in tours for seniors. Statistics show it as a growth industry for a generation who, had no chance to visit Alaska, Macchu Picchu, or go trekking in Nepal. Now we swap stories with our grandchildren. There are eighty-year-olds hot-air-ballooning or abseiling down cliffs, making up for lost time. I have had a beer with a Russian bureaucrat homesick in Samarkand, and sat on a Malaysian beach with a happy seventy-year-old Muslim woman. She had just divorced her second husband!

Taught by a xenophobic upbringing that all foreigners must be suspect, there is still time to unlearn those mistakes. Young travellers soon begin to understand that these are not aliens, just different human beings. People everywhere are just like us, fearful, loving, concerned for their families, and capable of great kindness. If by travel, the lessons of respect and tolerance are learned at an earlier age, there may be hope for the peace of the world. So let us all yield to wanderlust.

In the words of Tennyson:

"I am part of all that I have met;
Yet all experience is an arch wherethrough
Gleams that untravelled world, whose margin fades
For ever and ever when I move."

For the young at heart, travel creates its own joy, and keeps one young at heart.

Astra Warren

The Man Who Wanted to Disappear

Commended Short Story 2019

What the doctor said comes back in snatches. "Exhausted the possibilities of treatment … quality of life remaining …"

But the only thing that sticks is "six months".

I half-expected it, prepared myself in a way, but the reality is still harsh. I walked out in a daze. The receptionist, one quick glance summing me up, nice of her to make me coffee while I pulled myself together. I guess she's seen a few like that, walking like zombies while they get over the shock.

Went in an hour ago, now I'm out on the footpath, having heard the death sentence. Funny that, I'd always wondered how it must feel, the judge with his black cap; one dramatic moment, then what? The body still keeps on living. So stand up, walk across to the car park, watch out for the traffic. Do you keep on eating meals at the proper times, shower every morning, clean your teeth before going to bed? Or isn't there any point any longer?

Well, I'm soon going to find out.

Look at this old dear. Walking frame on wheels, coming down the ramp. Eighty if she's a day: glasses, hearing ids, false teeth as well, I shouldn't wonder. Dithering now at the crossing. Doesn't know she has to hit the button for the lights to stop the traffic.

"Thank you, young man."

Young man! I suppose to her I am, at least, thirty years younger. It's all relative, though I'll probably be gone long before she's ready. Six months. And she'll still be here, hanging on like grim death. So to speak.

Nice to know you've still got your sense of humour, Martin.

God, this car is hot, standing two hours in the sun.

Though perhaps not as hot as where I'll be in a few months.

I can see that I'm going to have a new perspective on everything I think and do. It's quite bizarre, really. Not many people know – how does it go? – the time and place of our death?

Pity that last lot of treatment didn't work. A lot of pain and trouble for nothing, but they kept my hopes up. Seventy per cent chance, they said. You always think you'll be one of the lucky ones. Hope springs eternal. Waste of time too, I suppose, though what would I have done with the time? That's another thing. What do I want to do with my six months? Travel? See the Taj Mahal, the Pyramids? Not much point when possibly I'll get a bird's eye view from the cloud I'll be sitting on. Wonder if you can float off where you like when you're a spirit?

Watch it, Martin, concentrate on the driving, you'd drifted off. Nearly got yourself wiped off under that bus. See! That's just what I'd been thinking about. The old chook at the crossing. Self-preservation. What would it matter? Quick. But likely not clean. Don't want to go as a road statistic. Besides, there's things I need to organize first.

Got home on automatic pilot, I think; don't remember the driving, and the phone was ringing as I put my key in the door, Jenny phoning from work.

"Dad? How did it go?" I mouthed some platitudes about further treatment. No sense in upsetting her in the middle of her busy day. I'll find a better time, quiet. I'm not ready to cope with sympathy yet.

"Have to go, love. I'm due at bowls practice in an hour and haven't had any lunch yet." You lying hound, Martin.

In the circs, weren't you thinking about giving it a miss today? Don't want to let them down, big Pennants match on Saturday. Though I'll soon be letting them down permanently, so it might be better to start now. Hang about; this thing is bigger than I thought, like ripples spreading across my universe. Cup of tea and a sandwich first, quietly think it through before we do anything rash. There's a different spin on everything now.

That's better. It was a good idea, stiffening the tea with a slurp of that good whisky Jenny and Ron bought me for Christmas, can afford a few indulgences now, oil the thought processes. Let's think of the negatives, easier that way. What don't I want to waste time on? Pity? Sympathy? Had enough of that when Edie was ill.

People came out of the woodwork, some we hadn't seen for months, indulging in gloom and doom, some of them practically dripping at the jaws over a tragedy to brighten their lives. What did Edie say? "I wish we hadn't told anybody. It's enough to have you and Jenny and her Ron. That's my world."

When you've watched people go, it's not such a big deal to leave everything behind. First ma, mind you, she was nearly ninety and in a home, her few possessions reduced to the drawers and cupboards in one room. Then in the next year Edie, nearly eight years ago now.

"Look after yourself, Martin," she said. "Don't mope too much. We had a good life together and it's to be grateful for. If I can, I'll be watching over you." Then with the old flashing grin, "Don't forget to change your socks every day, I'll still be counting them." That's what she did, counted the pairs on washing day to make sure I'd put on fresh ones. Six months is nothing; better get on with some decisions.

It's going to choke me if I dont tell anybody. Never been much good at hiding things.

Solution: go away, where you don't have to face people you know. This house, well, it's been comfortable, but not a home without Edie, and I'm into so many things since retiring, it's often no more than a convenient B and B.

All right, off to bowls while I get a handle on this. If I don't go, there's the trouble of making an excuse, and like I said, I'm no good at subterfuge.

Beautiful afternoon, the greens looking their best. I wonder, what's the weather like in Heaven? Here's that sod Maurice, still playing the superior public servant. He can't get over being retired and not the big cheese any longer. Irritates him when I call him Maurie, that's why I do it. I can manage without his sympathy, watching the wheels tick over inside his head.

I'm sure he's working out how to get on the committee and step into my captaincy. I know a few who'd drop off if he started throwing his weight around. And I do mean weight. Beer belly like a poisoned pup. Beats me how he can see to bowl when he bends over.

Tomorrow it'll be all clear in my mind what I want to do.

I enjoyed yesterday's practice, sharpens the pleasure when you realize it's going to end, then slept well, fresh air and more of that good whisky. What I'll do is invite myself round to Jenny's for a meal at the weekend; they're always on at me to go. Take the rest of the bottle and finish it with Ron. And a Baileys for Jenny, she likes that. By then, it'll all be worked out in my head.

Great meal Jenny put on. Just like her mum, plain but plenty of it and nicely laid out. My two grandkids, a pleasure to be with them, not like some of these spoiled brats. Know their manners and show respect. I'm leaving them both in good hands.

Jenny and Ron took it quite well. Mind you, Jenny's no slouch, has to be bright to keep that job, and I think she had some idea what was coming.

I told them, I want to be by the sea. That's where we scattered Edie, open and free. I'd always feel she was waiting for me. Tell everybody I'm going on a long journey, a round-the-world ticket. Sort of true and I'd be smiling inside.

The house is yours, I told them, I'm making a deed of gift. Sell it or rent it. You'll be doing it anyway in six months. We'll go through it together. Tell me what you want to keep and the rest goes to auction. Put it about that I'm moving into a retirement village when I get back from the trip. Meanwhile, I'll rent a serviced apartment down the coast, not too far from a hospital, got a few nice spots in mind. Close enough for you to visit, but not too often mind, once a week perhaps.

They could see I'd worked it all out. Arrange a doctor transfer with all my records. Then just disappear.

When my resignation went in to the club, it caused a real bubble. I'd forgotten about the mandatory farewell evening, but I wouldn't have missed it for worlds. The President, like "we wish we were coming with you on your trip" [not if you knew where I'm really going] and "don't do anything I wouldn't do." [*chance would be a fine thing, with your hatchet-faced jailer watching your every move. She even rations the middies you down. Many's the time I've carried one into the Gents so you can have an extra swallow.*].

"And in concluding, we had a whip-round and to speed you

on your way [*if only you knew what you were saying*] it gives me great pleasure to present you with a luggage voucher so you can travel in style." My stunned look must have been about right, they gave me a terrific round of applause.

I'm thinking, does it impress St Peter when you say, be careful with my Louis Vuitton? And afterwards, there was all the chat. "Where you having your stopovers, Martin?"

"Oh – er – it's not finalised yet. Travel agent's working on it [*God as a travel agent? That's novel*] But hope to see some old friends on the way." That was enough to start her off. She's a been-everywhere-done-it-all type. Europe in three weeks, that sort. Dragging the old man along to carry the cases. "Venice. You don't want to miss that. And Rome. Lovely. Don't mind what they say about Italians, I got on with 'em all right. Didn't we, Ted?" Her old man nodding glassily. Lost the habit of speech, has poor old Ted, been on automatic response for years.

Then June, what's her name? and Jack, fittest pair in the club. "Course, if it were us, we'd go round Australia again."

Considering Australia's so flat, they've been down more gorges and up more hills than you ever knew existed. Must have tripled the travelling distance. In shorts, they're a comic pair, him with stringy legs and muscles like broad beans in a pod, and June so fat she waddles.

And Maurie. Did a world trip ten years ago and never got over the shock. I knew he'd offer to show me his videos. Came to shake hands to show how relieved he was to get rid of me.

"Well done, Martin. You'll be a hard act to follow, but I'll do my best to walk tall and tread in your footsteps [*What is he talking about? Makes it sound like High Noon*]. I might be able to help you with some sound advice about your travels. [*Here it comes. Inside info from the Foreign Department*]. We've got some excellent videos I'd like to show you [*I bet*], prepare you for foreign parts. [*Now for the bribe*] My lady wife's an outstanding cook [*can see that by your paunch*] and we'll send you on your way well fed."

Alleluia! There'd be places on those videos that don't even exist any longer. And this is only for a round the world trip, non-event as it may be. What would it have been like, if they'd known I was tripping to my death?

Mind you, it would have stopped the been-there-done-that brigade in their tracks. A first to you, Martin.

And that was the Sports Club. Thank God I don't have to spend the rest of my life with them. I need the time to repent of the nasty thoughts I've had about some of them. There were a few more farewells, mostly drinking evenings and a lot of the don't do anything I wouldn't remarks.

I've always noticed that those most given to this are the sort who wouldn't know how to misbehave even if you drew pictures for them. See you when you get back [*or when you get where I'm going*]. Numerous requests for postcards if I go somewhere interesting. But since the interesting places I intend to visit are all in my own thoughts, they have Buckley's of hearing about them.

Quiet dinner last night with Jen and Ron. They gave me a bottle of that whisky I've got so fond of. No tears, just "See you next weekend, Dad." Slept restlessly, the pain troubling me a little, it's time to disappear while I can.

Whoever put a seat under this old peppermint tree was a genius, I reckon. Now that I can't walk so far, in the last month I've made it my own, perfect place to watch the sun go down over the sea. Metal plate in the seat back in memory of Annie Barstow. Don't now who you were, Annie, but your seat's in the right spot. Be funny if I meet up with you on the other side, saying like, I was watching you sitting on my seat, Martin. Sometimes feel as though I've got one foot on the other side, must be all the dope I'm full of. Silver Chain nurse wheels me across for an hour each evening, but she's saying, almost time to go and be looked after, Martin. Well, I'm not fighting it. It's all organized, even wrote my funeral notice and order of the cremation service. Jenny and Ron understand what I want.

Ryder, Martin John. Passed away peacefully at
Brentridge Regional Hospital. Husband of Edith, (deceased)
father of Jenny, Father-in-law of Ron, grandfather of Ben and Julie.
It was a great trip

Astra Warren

Treasure

Commended Poem 2020

No pirate chief was evermore delighted by his swag,
No buccaneer more boastful of the contents of his bag
Than Amelie, her eyes alight, her cheeks as pink as peach.
Her seaside bucket heavy with the treasures of the beach:
A tiny starfish cast ashore,
Its coral arms asprawl,
Some seaweed wet and plumply brown,
Just rescued from a pool:
A limpet and some cockle shells,
A clutch of winkles too:
A piece of driftwood curved and smooth,
Some polished glass of blue:
Such swag which may to other folk
Seem neither rich nor rare,
To Amelie, they are her jewels, rich beyond compare.

Astra Warren

Janet Woods

The Homecoming

Winning Short Story 1998

She'd been five when she'd left this place.

Beneath her, the red earth was warm and uneasy against the soles of her shoes. She slipped them off, curling her toes into the dust.

Her mother's feet had sent up little puffs of red dust as they'd pounded after the truck. Her eyes had bulged and her breath had been harsh with the effort of keeping up.

Eventually, she been able to run no more and had fallen to her knees, her head bowed against her chest. As the truck gathered speed he'd got smaller and smaller, until she'd become little more than a dot in the vast landscape.

There had been the white mother in a flowered frock. From her, she'd learned of the God of love. From the white teachers in black robes, she'd learned that love was a word of less importance to God than discipline and gratefulness.

Cleanliness was next to godliness on the scale of things. Godliness was earned by diligence and the application of a rod.

She'd grappled with the notions of clothes being ironed, or spending hours learning to stitch evenly along a hem of an apron. And could never understand that a garment designed to collect dirt had to be kept scrupulously clean.

As she'd grown older, the hems had become less important, the books more. Inside them, she found the answer she'd been seeking.

God was a legal system, his laws interpreted to suit the situation. There could be victims, but no real oppressors under God's system. He controlled the universe through man – and they controlled him.

Her mother's body was like warm silk and smelled of the mud and reeds that grew at the edge of the water-hole. She'd giggled when her mother had splashed water over her small body and had shaken the water from her hair, squealing with delight as the iridescent drops caught the sun. She'd caught a fish with her hands that day, herding it into a circle of stones she'd made, then closing the gap so it couldn't escape. Her mother wrapped it in a leaf so it wouldn't spoil on the long walk back to camp.

The truck had been there when they got back that day.

"Be grateful you have a good brain we can work with."

It had been hard to remember all the things she was expected to be grateful for. High on the list were the good sisters who taught her lessons, followed by the white mother who trained her in cleanliness, and how to sew, cook and iron.

Then there was the nourishing food she found on her plate each day when other, less fortunate people starved to death. The sampler on the dining room wall was a paradox: "God helps those who help themselves. God loves those who help others."

She remembered it on her graduation from university. The white mother had watched her accept the law degree with a look of self-congratulation and pride upon her face, her place in heaven assured.

She began to help others too, those who helped themselves. No victims, no oppressors. God's law meted out justice and punished without favour.

But there was something inside her struggling to be released – something that called uneasily to her.

One day, when the voice became too strong to ignore, she looked in the mirror and saw the sad eyes of her ancestors gazing back at her.

Now her journey was nearly over. Spreading her arms wide, she shouted: "I've come home."

Her words echoed around the purple hills bordering the spinifex plain. A few crows rose in the air, wheeling lazily before they settled back down amongst the dry yellow grasses. Sweat trickled down her back as the sound died away to nothing.

The sense of aloneness was acute after the city. The sky was too blue and vast to comprehend, the silence unnerving. She stood, breathing in hot, dusty air and swatting the flies that tried to invade her eyes, nose and mouth.

All around her was life and death. There was a lizard sunning itself on a rock , a teeming termite tower, a spider web glowing iridescent in the sun, a butterfly beating its wings in panic as a spider approached it.

A hawk circled above, then hurtled on silent wings towards the earth.

A tiny, alarmed squeak reached her ears, then nothing.

She shuddered, and moved back to the safety of the car when a metre of brown snake slithered across the track.

She should never have left the road.

Her mother's name was Ruby Namijara, she'd discovered.

The hands of the man had been strong as he'd dragged her from her mother's side. The little fish she'd caught so gleefully had fallen into the dust and was churned underfoot by the man in the white collar. He'd been a fat man, his eyes burning with God's righteousness.

The journey had been long. The children had huddled together for warmth, too frightened to cry. Sleep brought forgetfulness.

Awakening brought a changed landscape. Gone were the wide spaces, the dust storms, the old man's dream-time tales. Gone were the simple everyday tasks and the security of knowing your place. Dream-time became a dream replaced by a different dream.

Several decades had passed since she'd left this place they called the Pilbara. The journey back had been long and twisting.

Mining companies had built towns for their workers and were raping the land for iron ore. A railway line curved like a ribbed snake through the country she'd been born in. The trains brought the ore to the ports where the carriers sailed away with it to foreign countries.

There, the red heart of the land was crushed and moulded, then brought back changed beyond all recognition into neat silver slices.

Despite all this, there was a timelessness about the place. It would be here in centuries to come, when the human race was an endangered species, and the steel, mountains of rust. The rain would still gush through the dry river beds in the wet season, and that which the earth didn't swallow would fill the scars, turning them into lakes before rushing onwards to the sea.

Though she couldn't see the shore, she knew the tide was out. Her nostrils were filled with the warm and slightly acid aroma of mangrove mud.

The mangroves thrust their roots deep into the brine-saturated mud.

They'd caught crabs when the tide was out, placing them in baskets woven by the women. The sea had crept back silently over the mud, slowly at first, making seductive little sucking noises. A swift, hissing inrush of water followed, trying to catch them unawares as they skipped, laughing over the twisted mangrove roots.

The town of Roebourne was built mostly of local stone.

The post office, the courthouse with its flag flying gaily at the mast, the jailhouse where the drunks were penned like animals – all were hewn from the earth, and set block upon block to celebrate this early administrative centre.

Around the outskirts of the town were newer dwellings, weather-board houses painted pale pink or green with tin roofs and small verandahs. The house stumps were rooted in red earth, to which even the grass clung tenaciously.

The settlers roots had dug deep.

A bend revealed the hotel. There was a woman slumped against the wall outside, a bottle in her hand as she baked on the hot pavement, and oblivious to the music and laughter coming from inside. Two children crouched patiently by her side, their eyes old.

Further out of town the camp, radiating watchfulness. Several emaciated dogs rushed to threaten her, their hides lumpy with bush ticks.

They were in the place where her mother was born. She lay warm between the two dogs, half-listening to her mother's song of how the moon crept out of its hiding place in the earth. The sky was dark, the creek a gentle murmur in her ears. She was sleepy. Just behind the trees, the moon glow softly lightened the sky. Cicadas began to call to one another. One of the dogs lifted its head and growled when a dingo howled in the distance. Suddenly, a star shot in a blazing arc across the sky. She smiled as she snuggled into the dogs' warm bodies and listened to her mother sing.

She had known that her mother was still alive. But not like this.

It was hard to believe the old women in a pink, stained dress was her mother. Her eyes stared unseeingly towards the hills, and she made a low keening noise in her throat as she rocked back and forth. Her skin was thin, brown bark sagging over a frame of bones.

Neither of them knew the other in the void created for them.

"Ruby, she hit 'im 'ead on a rock an ain't never bin same since," her uncle said. "She die soon. White fella, 'im want to take 'er away to 'ospital. We wouldn't let 'im."

Her uncle was white-bearded and big-bellied – his woman and six grandchildren all lived in the tiny house amongst the dogs, flies and cockroaches.

"Where are their parents?"

"My son, he did a bloke in, 'im in jail long time. 'is woman, she gone walkabout."

She'd had a younger brother, long gone.

"Poor fella, petrol took 'im." Her uncle tapped his head. "Ruby took it real hard."

Her uncle was a man of few words. The silence between them stretched into the evening.

The children stared at her through earth-brown eyes, their faces shy and solemn – somehow guarded.

So achingly like her own grandchildren, only different – less knowing of their place in the future, wiser of their place in the past. They made her feel uncomfortable.

They made her a bed on the floor next to her mother's.

A rope tied to the bedpost was looped around Ruby's wrist. "To stop 'er goin' walkabout in night."

Something as soft as silk touched her tears. Her mother was sitting on the edge of her bed, her eyes full of secrets as she gently stroked her face.

She knew what her mother asked of her. What she'd been taught, fought a losing battle with her intuition.

Rising to her feet, she loosened the binding and silently followed her out of the house.

She left the car on the highway, and they walked for a long time.

Instinct guided their feet through the darkness to the creek.

Above them, the stars were cradled in the mystery of the sky – around them the earth exhaled the fragrance of honey.

They lay upon the warm red earth, joined in spirit as her mother told her of the time of her birth.

Here, her aunts and grandmother had drawn her from her mother's womb. The creek had washed the birthing from their bodies, and carried away the signs so the place would remain a secret amongst the women.

Their hands touched, then entwined.

Beside them, the creek flowed onwards in a never-ending journey as they talked their women's business.

When they fell silent the reeds began to whisper in the breeze, like voices from the past.

"My sisters," Ruby whispered, her smile young again.

It was the only gift she could give her daughter – the time of belonging they'd once shared.

As the moon climbed out of the earth, Ruby began to sing to them in a sweet, high voice.

She began to sing too, calling them to her mother's place to celebrate her homecoming.

Janet Woods

Hanging Around

Winning Short Story 2001

"Why don't you go and haunt somebody else." One swipe from Judy's broom propelled the dust through the door. The bell tinkled when she closed it.

She gazed around the tea room with satisfaction. It was all hers, the wood-panelled walls, the tables set with embroidered tablecloths, the shelves filled with homemade jams and preserves - and the damned ghost.

The tourist season was over now, except for the occasional car or tourist coach, which ventured off the main roads during the week. Now she'd have time to redecorate.

The house had been neglected over the years, passing through the hands of several owners. She'd got it cheap. Too cheap. The real estate salesman hadn't told her it was haunted. Not that it would have made any difference to Judy. She'd loved the place on sight, the view over the sweeping bay and the quiet seaside town. The whole place spelled peace to her.

Judy was small. Her eyes were blue and enormous in a finely boned face, her skin the colour of lightly toasted almonds. A dark fall of hair scythed around her jawline. She wasn't easily scared.

A ghost isn't going to get the better of me, she'd thought, when the apparition had appeared. He took the seat across the table from her, shouting "Boo!" then fell off the chair laughing.

If he hadn't been see-through, she would have thought him a normal man. She managed a sour look, but she'd nearly thrown the salt pot at him.

"Cool chick," he said, sounding impressed.

At least the ghost didn't rattle chains, carry his head under his arm or do anything remotely goulish. Even so, the cat had climbed the curtains and sat on the pelmet, where she swore at the ghost in a decidedly unfriendly manner.

Judy gazed curiously at the apparition. He didn't look very scary, and was dressed in narrow trousers, a bum freezer jacket and pointed shoes. His hair was slicked back with cream and he was rather handsome, with dark eyes and a sardonic lift to his lip.

"Listen to this," he said and sang a rock and roll number. "What d'you think of it?"'

"It's a bit dated," she said.

"Yeah, well … I suppose it would sound that way now. It would top the charts if it was promoted properly."

That had been yesterday. Today, he was strumming on a guitar. His face seemed familiar to Judy. She considered the increase in business if she could get him to do a gig.

"You don't happen to be the ghost of Elvis by any chance, do you?"

"Nah." His chuckle set the lace curtains fluttering. "Elvis haunts Carnegie Hall; the tourists chased him out of Gracelands." He held out a hand. "I'm Gary Frost."

"Ah yes … the pop star who disappeared on a trip into the bush. I've read about you. And I'm Judy. It's nice to meet you." Her hand came away sticky from the encounter as if it was draped in spider web. She rubbed her palms together. "At least, I think it is."

"Why aren't you scared?" he said. "Everyone else who bought this place was."

"Why should I be? You're dead. Uh … why are you …"

"I never thought you'd ask." Hands behind his head, he reclined and hovered. "My chick, Candy, told everyone I'd disappeared on that trip."

"That was long before I was born."

"I know. I met your grandparents at a convention a couple of months ago. They told me you'd bought the place with the inheritance they left you. Nice old geezers. They sent their love and said they'd arrange for someone special to come into your life soon."

"How were they?" she said eagerly.

His laugh was slightly mocking. "Not bad, all things considered. Your gran's arthritis has gone and gramps has lost the craving to smoke, so his temper's improved. He would have lived longer if he hadn't quit. It was the stress that killed him."

Judy smiled. "They didn't make it to heaven then?"

"Most of us hang around for a bit first. Your grandad was waiting for your gran. Now she's there she can't make up her mind between a luxury flat in Eden or a house in Paradise. Your gramps fancies a warmer climate but gran said she's past all that sort of thing, and so should he be."

"Gran always was a ditherer." Judy ignored the other. "Why are you hanging around here?"

"I'm waiting for Candy to come back to the house."

"Why should she come back?"

"She comes on every anniversary. I can sense her, but she hasn't been inside yet. Now it's a tea room I reckon she won't be able to resist it. She'll be wondering if anyone's disturbed the wall."

"The wall?" Judy said, dread curling through her.

"Which wall?"

"The one behind you. She and the drummer drugged my coffee, then took me down to the cellar and panelled over the door. A pity you put all those shelves over it, hmmm?"

Judy's hair stood on end. "You mean there's a cellar, and your remains are in it?"

He gave a bit of a cackle. "The thought gives you the willies, huh?"

"Just a bit."

She experienced dread when another thought occurred to her. "When's the anniversary?"

"Tomorrow. Don't be scared if a bit of bumping goes on tonight. Some disturbances are noisy, and there might be a re-enactment going on."

Judy couldn't sleep. She tossed and turned as the silent night was alternated by long periods of banging and scraping. Snatches of singing drifted up to her, the tinkling of a piano. Towards dawn, there was a mighty crash and the whole house shook.

"Okay, I've had enough," she yelled, and pulling on her dressing gown and slippers, side-stepped around the weaving cat to make it safely down the stairs. "Gary, what the hell are you up to?"

"Promise you won't get your knickers in a twist," he said against her ear.

When the light went on, she sucked in a ragged breath. The tea room wall had been pulled down, exposing a solidly constructed cellar door.

"Oh, my God," she groaned, looking at the dust over everything and the jars of preserves on the floor. "I know why she murdered you now. Where can I display them to sell?"

"Don't worry. You can put some on each table and I'll sell them for you." The cellar door creaked open and Gary smiled at her. "Wanna come down and have a look?"

Judy was torn between macabre curiosity and reluctance.

"I'm not sure."

"Aw come on," Gary said. "I'm quite clean now, and you know you're dying to."

She couldn't help but smile. "Wait until I get dressed then."

"I'll spirit you up a cup of tea, shall I?"'

The cellar was furnished as a studio, the walls sound-proofed by paper mache egg cartons. To one side was an upright piano. Music sheets littered the table, which also held a reel to reel recorder and a couple of guitars.

What remained of Gary was seated in an easy chair. Headphones dangled over his skull. His empty eye sockets gazed at an exercise book in his lap. "My last will and testament," he whispered reverently. "I left everything to charity."

Tears sprang to her eyes. "Oh Gary, you poor thing," she sobbed.

"You're a soft-hearted little bird. You'll make sure my remains are dealt with properly, won't you?"

The only customers for the day was a coach party of pensioners whose bus had lost its way.

Gary walked amongst the tables playing his guitar and selling preserves. Although they didn't see or hear him, the pensioners left with their stomachs chock full of Devonshire cream tea and their bags loaded with jam.

Judy had hardly cleared up after the coach party when a man came in. He was gorgeous. His eyes were bluer than blue, his smile a dream, his hair as dark as night. "I'm Detective Constable Bond. You said on the phone that you had information about a crime, but the matter wasn't urgent."

"Nice, isn't he?" Gary said.

"Gorgeous," Judy breathed.

The steady blue eyes flicked over her, missing nothing. A smile flirted at his mouth. "What's the problem?"

She pointed to the cellar. "Down there is the problem."

Nice bum, she thought, as his long legs carried him across the room.

"Christ," he said when he came back up. He flipped open his notebook. "You don't know who he is by any chance?"

"Gary Frost, the famous pop singer. He was supposed to have disappeared on a bush trip, but really his chick … umm … girlfriend and the drummer drugged him, then locked him in the cellar and left him to die."

"How do you know all this?"

"Gary told me."

"Hmmm," was all the policeman said, looking deliciously puzzled.

"Moron," Gary muttered. He walked around the detective, stretched his mouth into a grimace with his fingers and poked out his tongue. "Brrrrrrr."

"Be quiet."

"Fancy the dude, do yer?"

"Butt out."

The detective looked surprised.

"Not you," she hastened to assure him. "I'm talking to Gary."

His eyebrow raised.

"The ghost," she said lamely.

"Ah, of course … the ghost." His smile was bemused. "Don't touch anything, Mrs …"

"Miss, actually."

He double-checked by casing her fingers for rings. Judy liked a man who was thorough.

"'I'll get on to forensics. It might be best if you move out until they're through."

"He can't go yet," Gary hissed. "Candy is on her way. Make with the chick eyes stuff."

Desperately, Judy fluttered her eyelashes at him. "You can always phone them from here. Would you like some tea and scones?"

"I really need to report this, Miss … er …"

"Judy."

"Judy, about this ghost … "

" You don't believe me, do you?"

"Quite frankly, no."

"Are you married, Mr … uh …?"

"James."

She choked back a laugh and he grinned. "My mother is a fan."

"Gary, do something spooky to convince him," she ordered.

"What about an Elvis impersonation?" He took up a stance, strummed his guitar and swivelled his pe1vis in a quite spirited manner.

The detective gave her an odd look. "Better get your things together, Jude, I'll take you to a hotel."

"You don't have a girlfriend, do you?"

"Not yet. Are you propositioning me?"

"I think I might be."

Sticking his finger in a socket, Gary's hair stood on end and he began to pulsate with neon lights.

James looked impressed. "All right, you've got my attention."

"You must wait. Any minute now Gary's murderer is coming through the door," she said.

The doorbell pinged, but the only person who came through was a grey-haired woman.

"Geez!" Gary said in a disappointed voice. "Candy's become

a wrinkly old hag."

Candy's eyes darted towards the cellar door and her face blanched. "Oh, my God! You've found him." She moved across to the open door and peered down the stairs.

"He's still there." Behind the pebble glass spectacles, her eyes strained to see into the gloom. "Hell, he's grown thin."

"You'd be thin if you hadn't eaten anything for fifty years," Gary snarled and lifted his guitar.

"Don't!" Judy yelled, but she needn't have worried. The guitar had no substance and it passed right through her.

James stepped forward and took Candy by the arm. "I believe you might be able to help me with my enquiries into the death of Gary Frost."

"See you later, alligator," Gary said threateningly to her.

"The death sentence has been done away with. You can visit her in prison," James said sternly to him.

Judy caught James's eye and grinned triumphantly. He gave an unbelieving and decidedly shaky laugh.

"There's been a resurgence of Gary Frost stuff since his remains were discovered," James said six months later. "His songs are top of the charts."

"I've been offered a small fortune for this house by a fan, and a clairvoyant has exorcised the ghost. I'm not selling, but I'll miss Gary."

In the cellar, an old transistor radio began to hum, then a voice belted out, 'Oh Yeah! It was lurve. Lurve at first glance. and I didn't have a ghost of a chance."

James laughed. "Sounds to me as if he's still hanging around."

Janet Woods

Bird of Prey

Runner-Up Short Story 2010

Catherine's hands are frail, the bones of her fingers lean towards her thumbs, kept from collapsing by the stretched, silken strands of her skin. Her nails are long but unlovely, square and ridged before they are shaped. The curved slivers peel away from the fingertips under the steely slash of the manicure scissors and lie in her lap like miniature scimitars.

She always took pride in her hands. Today she wants the nails red. Not a pale watered-down blood red or the sweet, crushed raspberry of the berry tarts she used to make, but a flaming, flaunting letterbox red.

'Today is my birthday, I received a parcel from grandma,' she says to Evie in a whispery little girl voice.

Catherine always tells Evie when she's having a birthday, and Evie is ready for it. She takes a pile of cards from her bag – the ones she brings every week.

The old woman is excited. 'Oh … this one is from Marlene and Tim … they send me one every year. So kind … look, they've sent a photo of the baby. Such a sweet child,' and her frown comes. 'Odd, how he never seems to grow any older.'

Evie smiles to herself. While her mother is distracted she turns her attention to the parcel. It has come from overseas and was mailed in one of those sturdy padded bags. Another's name and address is on it; a blue airmail sticker and custom form attached. The card reads: To my dearest Katie. Have a lovely birthday and I will see you at Christmas when you visit Much love from Grandma.

Glittery things spill from it, some hair slides with glass diamonds and a disk of an all-female pop group with spiked hair, miniature breasts, and cute toothy smiles that chipmunk voices drill through. They look to be about thirteen, an unlucky number for some.

A red cropped tee shirt with a yellow sequined sun on the front is tossed on to a chair. Pink ballet shoes pose in the second position, ribbon ties dangling, and a small beaded purse is in a corner where Catherine threw it in a fit of pique. It's unzipped, and the purse yawns open in a snarl of even, black, plastic teeth.

'Nothing fits,' the old woman frets, her face petulant. 'And grandma sent me play money … the stupid woman.'

Somewhere, a child is crying over a missing birthday gift. 'I'll ask the post office to send them back,' Evie tells her.

Autumn has brought with it a swirling dance of metallic leaves from the trees, Bronze … copper … brass and gold. Catherine's hair is pewter mixed with sterling silver and has a newly washed sheen. Once it was as red as her nails – hair that deserved to flow free in the wind instead of being disguised as a length of rope.

She waves her hands about to dry her nails when Evie finishes her manicure, inspects them.

On the bedside table is a picture of the family standing on a cliff top. Evie is seated securely on broad shoulders, her feet tuck back for safety. They have their arms outstretched, pretending to fly,

'If we let go we could fly off the cliff and ride the wind like birds,' he'd said that day. He'd flown with Evie attached to a glider, leaving Catherine shredded by the turbulence he'd created.

Catherine had brought him down to earth – then to a layer beneath it.

She is wearing her rings today. Evie bought them to replace her mother's good ones, in case they were stolen. They flash as she flutters her fingers, like a young woman captured by the future offered in the acceptance of an engagement ring. Catherine found herself purchased body and soul for a small gold token, and prayed for sons when her daughter became a rival.

'Your father always said red nail varnish was tarty.'

'Did he?' Evie begins to pick up the contents of the parcel, placing them neatly back into the bag. There's a British twenty-pound note on the table. She places that in the purse and closes the zip into a grimace, wishing her mother didn't steal, no doubt It isn't the first time Catherine has wandered the streets and stolen other people's mail.

'She does it to draw attention to herself,' a nurse had told Evie. 'She's very demanding.'

'Your father bought me this ring … it's my birthday.'

'So you said.' Evie takes out a lipstick and paints the wrinkled mouth to match the nails. He'd left many years ago when she was thirteen, and the apple of his eye. Girls were so very innocent and lovely at that age. Did she but know it, he hadn't gone far away.

'How was he?' Evie asks, humouring her and surprising me. She's not really interested in the answer, since she's used to her mother's fabrications and no longer believes them.

She begins to arrange the flowers she'd brought, pink and white carnations from the deli handily sandwiched between the fertility clinic and maternity hospital further up the hill.

The flowers smell like funerals … everything smells like funerals in here since they opened an undertaker's establishment next to the hospice. Black limousines come and go with sedate regularity. The cemetery is a mere mile away down the hill.

'It's getting to be like a production line,' one of the nurses had once said to another with a laugh. 'You start off as a bloody good orgasm at the top and end up as a fart of fertilizer at the bottom.'

Catherine, who's been staring at the photograph, suddenly says, 'Your father regrets it, you know. He said so. The baby …'

'What baby?' Each word is a stab so vicious that momentarily Evie's face adopts a feral look. Catherine shrinks back into her pillows.

A nurse goes by, noticing nothing, her smile fleeting. Her face droops back into grey lines after she passes, thinking of retirement, of being able to drink tea when she feels like it. No rose-coloured glasses on her, when all around is a reminder of what twenty years will bring. What was once a noble profession has become a nuisance of leaking bodies, aching back and blistered feet. It's hard to smile when she has a mortgage.

Catherine leans forward, her courage returned, her expression one of malice. The lipstick is already melding into the network of creases that radiate outwards, and her mouth resembles the puckered kiss of a venomous snake as she shows her fangs and hisses out, tongue flickering. 'It was for the best.' She makes a grab for the scissors but Evie gets there first, placing them safely into her bag.

Wasted hands fold one over the other; nails displayed like enamelled daggers. Catherine's smile becomes sly. 'You led him on, turned him against me. You got more than you bargained for, didn't you? I buried him in the cellar, you know. He deserved it.'

They've had this conversation before, and Evie's not listening.

Janet Woods

Twelve months in an English village

Runner-Up Poem 2011

1. I went there in the summer.

Waves of wheat, waves of water
Undulate and curl over the child,
A naked creature unashamed in hat
Sunshade and smoothed zinc balm.
She attracts a crust of sand grains, like
Sunday's rhubarb crumble and cream.
Wasps in stripes drink cola and
Sharpen stingers in sugar.
Crabs swell inside their carapaces.
Boats slice the sea and cast sails wide
To capture the fuel in the wind
And follow the ferries to France.

2. It feels like autumn now

Soggy, the forest floor disturbs
Aromas of decay and mushrooms
Above, fall wears drifts of metallic colours,
Brass, copper, gold, and bronze
Hazelnuts slide from shells and spiral
Blackberries plump drip and prick.
Days shrink into contemplation as
Earth meditates to slow each heartbeat
Like squirrels we scurry to store.
Apples lie in the attic, nuts nudge
Shoulders in jars, plums stew in syrup
And mice nibble in the grain.

3. So this is what winter is like?

The mist swallows the thatch
An apple tree tangled and gnarled
Splays naked limbs against a wall
Splashed with gaudy lichen,
Orange and red berries kiss pearls
Of mistletoe. Holly stabs the air
Lies in wait for the draughts to stir and
Scratches fingernails against shutters
To mark the haunting hours.
The captive is offered no comfort by the firelight.
The remains of the hibernation rarely stirs
But the slap of the sea on shore is a frenzy.

4. A spring thing happens!

The pines have an over-abundance of sap.
Streams of slow, seeping amber captures a gnat
And congeals. It claims a maiden's finger
Or presses a golden toffee against her breast.
Beneath the bridge the water scurries,
And froths. Such a carry-on of drakes
Parading their territory like battleships.
Lady ducks are imprisoned by egg clutches.
Speckled troutlings dart in dappled light
Buds unfold into lambent country dancers,
A fiesta against a sky drenched in lapis lazuli
To celebrate a fruitful copulation.

Janet Woods

The Bronze Quill Winners

Below is a list of the winners of the competition since its inception.

Year	Category	Winner
1981	Poetry	J. Taylor
1982	Article Writing	Wynne Whittaker & Jean Lang
1983	Short Story	Jacqueline Stewart
1984	Poetry	V. Prince
1985	Article Writing	Tess Berry
1986	Short Story	June Smith
1987	Poetry	D. Elliot
1988	Article Writing	Mary Hicks
1989	Short Story	Pat Fletcher
1990	Poetry	Griselda Hitchcock
1991	Article Writing	Constance Herbert
1992	Short Story	Dianne Wolfer
1993	Poetry	Claire Grose
1994	Article Writing	Pat Watson
1995	Short Story	Beryl Richards
1996	Poetry	Jan Alcorn
1997	Article Writing	Beryl Richardson
1998	Short Story	Janet Woods

1999	Poetry	Margaret Scrymgeour
2000	Article Writing	Pamela Clarke
2001	Short Story	Janet Woods
2002	Poetry	Jennifer Langley-Kemp
2003	Article Writing	Margaret van Putten
2004	Short Story	Madeleine Tingey
2005	Poetry	Geraldine Day
2006	Article Writing	Pat Curtis
2007	Short Story	Helen Iles
2008	Poetry	Gloria Foreman
2009	Article Writing	Raelene Hall
2010	Short Story	Helen Iles
2011	Poetry	Frances Richardson
2012	Article Writing	Dorothy Henderson
2013	Short Story	Frances Richardson
2014	Poetry	Fran Graham
2015	Article Writing	Maria Bonar
2016	Short Story	Wendy Stackhouse
2017	Poetry	Fran Graham
2018	Article Writing	Rose van Son
2019	Short Story	Elizabeth Pappas
2020	Poetry	Asha Rajan

About The Society of Women Writers WA

The Society of Women Writers was first established in Australia in Sydney in September 1925 to bring together women writers and journalists in New South Wales. Their aims were to be a social body; to promote knowledge of literature; to encourage women writers, and to strengthen the ties of interest between Australian and visiting writers (www.womenwritersnsw.org/history/).

Until the 1970s, the Society was based in Sydney, using a postal critiquing system to keep in touch. During this decade, branches were established in other Australian states and the first Federal Constitution was adopted in 1978 with an agreement that Federal responsibility be transferred from state to state every two years. Twenty years later, the decision was made to decentralise, with each state forming its own Society.

The WA branch initially operated only through correspondence groups until the first President, Ethel Webb, was appointed in 1981, and members began to meet regularly. The Society of Women Writers WA was incorporated as an autonomous body on 25 February 2000.

Contact Details

The Society of Women Writers WA Inc
PO Box 434
Northbridge
Western Australia 6865
Tel: 0415 840 031
Email: swwofwa@gmail.com
Web: www.swwofwa.com.au